W9-BYW-442

8-22-06

Hampshire County
Public Library

1000113971

YOUR
IMMORTAL
REALITY

Also by Gary R. Renard

The Disappearance of the Universe: Straight Talk about Illusions, Past Lives, Religion, Sex, Politics, and the Miracles of Forgiveness

Enlightenment Cards: Thoughts from *The Disappearance of the Universe* (a 72-card deck)

༺ঌ৩ঌ৩ৎ

Hay House Titles of Related Interest

Angel Visions: True Stories of People Who Have Seen Angels, and How You Can See Angels, Too!, by Doreen Virtue, Ph.D.

Ask and It Is Given: Learning to Manifest Your Desires, by Esther and Jerry Hicks (The Teachings of Abraham)

Experiencing the Soul: Before Birth, During Life, After Death, by Eliot Jay Rosen

Inspiration: Your Ultimate Calling, by Dr. Wayne W. Dyer

Miracle Cards, by Marianne Williamson

The New Golden Rules: An Essential Guide for Spiritual Bliss, by Dharma Singh Khalsa, M.D.

Power vs. Force: The Hidden Determinants of Human Behavior, by David R. Hawkins, M.D., Ph.D.

Touching the Divine: How to Make Your Daily Life a Conversation with God, edited and interpreted by Gay Hendricks and James Twyman (book-with-CD)

What Happens When We Die: A Groundbreaking Study into the Nature of Life and Death, by Sam Parnia, M.D., Ph.D.

༺ঌ৩ঌ৩ৎ

All of the above are available at your local bookstore, or may be ordered by visiting:

Hay House USA: **www.hayhouse.com**®
Hay House Australia: **www.hayhouse.com.au**
Hay House UK: **www.hayhouse.co.uk**
Hay House South Africa: **orders@psdprom.co.za**
Hay House India: **www.hayhouseindia.co.in**

YOUR IMMORTAL REALITY

How to Break the Cycle of Birth and Death

GARY R. RENARD

HAY HOUSE, INC.
Carlsbad, California
London • Sydney • Johannesburg
Vancouver • Hong Kong • New Delhi

Copyright © 2006 by Gary R. Renard

Published and distributed in the United States by: Hay House, Inc.: www.hayhouse.
com • *Published and distributed in Australia by:* Hay House Australia Pty. Ltd.:
www.hayhouse.com.au • *Published and distributed in the United Kingdom by:* Hay
House UK, Ltd.: www.hayhouse.co.uk • *Published and distributed in the Republic
of South Africa by:* Hay House SA (Pty), Ltd.: orders@psdprom.co.za • *Distributed
in Canada by:* Raincoast: www.raincoast.com • *Published in India by:* Hay House
Publications (India) Pvt. Ltd.: www.hayhouseindia.co.in • *Distributed in India by:*
Media Star: booksdivision@mediastar.co.in

Editorial supervision: Jill Kramer • *Design:* Tricia Breidenthal

All rights reserved. No part of this book may be reproduced by any mechanical,
photographic, or electronic process, or in the form of a phonographic recording; nor
may it be stored in a retrieval system, transmitted, or otherwise be copied for public
or private use—other than for "fair use" as brief quotations embodied in articles
and reviews—without prior written permission of the publisher. The intent of the
author is only to offer information of a general nature to help you in your quest
for emotional and spiritual well-being. In the event you use any of the information
in this book for yourself, which is your constitutional right, the author and the
publisher assume no responsibility for your actions.

Library of Congress Cataloging-in-Publication Data

Renard, Gary R.
  Your immortal reality : how to break the cycle of birth and death / Gary R.
Renard.
     p. cm.
  Includes bibliographical references and index.
  ISBN-13: 978-1-4019-0697-9 (hardcover)
  ISBN-10: 1-4019-0697-4 (hardcover)
  ISBN-13: 978-1-4019-0698-6 (tradepaper)
  ISBN-10: 1-4019-0698-2 (tradepaper)
  1. Spiritual life. 2. Course in miracles. 3. Ascended masters. 4. Gospel of
Thomas (Coptic Gospel) I. Title.
  BP605.C68R48 2006
  299'.93--dc22   2006004027

    Hardcover: **ISBN 13:** 978-1-4019-0697-9 • **ISBN 10:** 1-4019-0697-4
    Tradepaper: **ISBN 13:** 978-1-4019-0698-6 • **ISBN 10:** 1-4019-0698-2

                09 08 07 06   4 3 2 1
                     1st printing, August 2006

            Printed in the United States of America

CONTENTS

This book is lovingly and respectfully dedicated
to all those who love *A Course in Miracles,*
or who are just about to discover it for themselves

Who is the "you" who are living in this world?
Spirit is immortal, and immortality is a constant state.[1]

— *A Course in Miracles*

INTRODUCTION

For those of you who have not yet read my first book, *The Disap-pearance of the Universe,* you will surely burn in hell. Just kidding. However, a reading of that book, which was originally published in 2003, will make *Your Immortal Reality* even more meaningful to you, since it's a continuation of that initial work. If there's a differ-ence between the two, it's that this book is more freewheeling, less linear, and jumps from subject to subject even more. This is a way to help generalize the ideas to every aspect of the reader's life, while maintaining an uncompromising focus on a radical but entirely consistent spiritual discipline that produces immediate and practi-cal results if utilized, and eventually leads to enlightenment and the end of reincarnation. Because the end of reincarnation is the end of the body, it should be emphasized from the beginning that what you really are—that is, your immortal reality—has absolutely nothing whatsoever to do with the body or the brain.

As the human race is exposed to new ideas, it becomes more and more apparent that the teachings given by the masters in this book are, and will continue to be, demonstrated by science to be true, and the old ideas will be shown to be outdated. With the breakthroughs in modern psychology, as well as quantum physics, we are learning that there is no such thing as separation, even on the level of the world, except as an idea in the mind. The overthrow of the old ideas does not come without tremendous resistance, for as we approach the hidden cornerstones of the mind, our seemingly separate, individual identities are threatened. This is death to the collective ego, and it will not go quietly.

During the last three years, it's been my privilege to personally meet thousands of students of spirituality and metaphysics. I've gained the insight that people are ready for much more than most teachers or the media are willing to give them. I've gained respect for people's willingness to not only receive new ideas, but to question old ones, not the least of which are the ways in which great spiritual masters such as Jesus and Buddha have been presented to us by organized religions.

In that spirit, the following text relates true events that occurred from December of 2003 through September of 2005. Except for my narration, they are presented within the framework of a dialogue that has three participants: **Gary** (that's me), and **Arten** and **Pursah**, two ascended masters who appeared to me in the flesh. My narration is not labeled unless it interrupts the dialogue, in which case it is simply labeled "NOTE." The many italicized words you will see indicate an emphasis on the part of the speakers.

It is not absolutely essential to believe that the appearances of the ascended masters took place in order to derive benefits from the information in these chapters. However, I can vouch for the extreme unlikeliness of this writing being done by an uneducated layman such as myself without inspiration from these teachers. At any rate, I leave it up to you, the reader, to think whatever you choose about the book's origins.

I've made every effort to do this book right, but I'm not perfect, so this book isn't perfect either. However, if there are any errors of fact in these pages, you can be certain that they are my mistakes and were not made by my visitors. Also, the reporting of these discussions, as I mentioned previously, is not always linear. Sometimes things that were said earlier are included later in the book, and sometimes things that were said later are presented earlier.

This is not your typical spiritual book. I believe that my teachers appear to me as people because they want the conversations we have to be human. That's the only way we would ever have the style of discussions that we do. We end up talking like people actually talk. That may or may not be to your liking. Some people want to have their spirituality sugarcoated. But the world is not sugarcoated, and we must be led out of the illusion of time and space from where we think we are. I've come to realize that my teachers' style is a method they use for a good reason, and that my job is simply to be myself and play my part.

References to *A Course in Miracles,* including each chapter's introductory quotation, are noted and listed in an Index in the back. Limitless gratitude goes to the Voice of the *Course,* whose true Identity is discussed herein.

I also want to thank my publishing consultant, D. Patrick Miller. Patrick has worked for more than two decades as a journalist, reviewer, editor, and publisher in the field of alternative spirituality. He was the first to recognize the significance of the messages I deliver, and is more directly responsible for my success than any other person. He has earned not only my thankfulness, but my respect. I also want to thank my literary agent (and a fine novelist), Laurie Fox. With Laurie on my team, I couldn't lose.

There are far too many people whom I should thank for helping me over the last few years. I hope they will forgive me for not listing them. My writing and my speaking are my ministry, and there are many people who have made important contributions to it. I will never forget you. But I do want to publicly thank Reid Tracy, the president and CEO of Hay House, for bringing me on board and making it possible for this message to reach a worldwide audience. And finally, my gratitude goes to Jill Kramer, the editorial director at Hay House, for having the discernment to do her expert job and keep my teachers' words intact at the same time.

This book contains many quotations from *A Course in Miracles,* which are noted in order to assist you, the reader, in studying the *Course* later if you choose to do so. The author and publisher would like to express our gratitude to the members of the Foundation for Inner Peace in Mill Valley, California, and the Foundation for *A Course in Miracles* in Temecula, California, for their decades of important work that have resulted in making *A Course in Miracles* available to the world. Ordering information for the *Course* is printed in the back of this book.

Finally, although I am not affiliated with them, I would like to take this opportunity to extend my sincere thanks to Gloria and Kenneth Wapnick, Ph.D., founders of the Foundation for *A Course in Miracles* in Temecula, California, upon whose work much of this book is based. I was guided very early on by Arten and Pursah to also become a student of the Wapnicks' teachings, and this book cannot help but reflect all of my learning experiences.

— **Gary Renard,**
somewhere between Maine and Hawaii

PROLOGUE

In the 1880s there was a rich rancher who lived in Texas. He was not a particularly spiritual dude, but he was very good at manifesting abundance, making some of his neighbors suspect that the two things weren't necessarily connected. He did claim to be a Christian, but his actions in the world made this claim a doubtful one.

One day, a poor farmer who had no food sneaked on to the rich rancher's land and stole one of his chickens so that his family could eat. He was caught by one of the ranch hands and brought to the rancher. There were a lot of things the rancher could have said, but all he said was, "Hang 'im! It'll teach 'im a lesson."

A couple of years later, a man from Mexico was trespassing on the rancher's land. He was very poor, and hoping to find a new life. What he found was the rancher's men, who took him to their boss. After looking the trespasser over, all the rancher said was, "Hang 'im! It'll teach 'im a lesson."

There were many episodes like this in the rich rancher's life, in which he never stopped to put himself in other people's shoes but simply reacted in anger and judged and condemned them, usually ending with the phrase, "Hang 'im! It'll teach 'im a lesson."

Then one night the rancher's body died, and he saw himself going up toward the pearly gates of Heaven. The rancher was hoping that no one would recognize him and maybe he could just walk in. But right before he got to the gate, St. Peter stepped in front of him and said, "Wait a minute. Jesus wants to talk to you."

Now the rancher was very worried. He remembered some of the things he had done in his life, and here he was, about to be judged by Jesus himself! Suddenly, the rancher was shaking in his boots. Jesus appeared, walked slowly up to the rancher, looked him right in the eyes, and then said to St. Peter, "Forgive 'im. It'll teach 'im a lesson."

ARTEN AND PURSAH!

> . . . a good translator, although he must alter
> the form of what he translates, never changes the
> meaning. In fact, his whole purpose is to change
> the form so that the original meaning is retained.[2]

In the two years since I had last seen Arten and Pursah, my life
had been turned upside down, and I didn't know that it was just
the beginning. I wasn't sure if my ascended-master friends, who
appeared to me from out of nowhere as very real-looking bodies,
would ever return. In fact, the last question I asked them was, "Will
I ever see you again?" To which Arten replied, "That's up to you
and the Holy Spirit, dear brother. You should talk to Him about it,
as you should everything else."

I did talk to the Holy Spirit, and listened. I used the method of
true prayer, which was actually a form of meditation and joining
with God, which Arten and Pursah had taught me. A fringe benefit
of this was inspiration, a way of receiving Guidance through the
mind as to what I should do or what decisions I should make.

The last time Arten and Pursah left, I heard their voices combined into one, as the Voice of the Holy Spirit. This reminded me
of an earlier experience I had of hearing the voice of Jesus, whom
my teachers usually referred to simply as "J." In pondering the
difference between J's voice and that of others, I couldn't help but
think about Brian Wilson of the Beach Boys. As a musician and
admirer of Wilson's, I knew that he had never heard his own music
in stereo, because he was deaf in one ear. So he only heard part of

it. When I heard J's voice, it was as if I were hearing in stereo for the first time. Every voice I had heard before that had something missing, but J's voice was full, whole, and complete. Just as Wilson would surely be amazed to hear the full range of the sound of his own great music, I was amazed to hear the full range of the sound of J's voice, knowing that it was really my own voice—the Voice that speaks for God.

This was also what the combined Voice of Arten and Pursah sounded like, and it had stayed with me. Now I could hear it much more clearly, and the Guidance I received did not fail me. It didn't always fit my pictures, but it always seemed to work in some way that was best for everyone, not just me. Indeed, this was a hallmark of the Holy Spirit's Guidance. He could see everything, where I could only see a small part. So the Holy Spirit's Guidance was good for one and all. This was sometimes annoying. I wanted what was good for *me,* and I wanted it now! Yet I had to admit that in retrospect, my ideas would have failed, and the Holy Spirit's ideas would have worked. Plus, the Holy Spirit already knew everything that was going to happen, and I didn't. So whose judgment was likely to be the most dependable? I was determined to listen, and I was usually successful.

NOTE: The Holy Spirit, being One and whole, is not male or female, which is a concept of separation and the resulting opposites that reflect seperation instead of oneness. The correct word to describe the Holy Spirit would be *It.* However, for artistic purposes, Arten and Pursah used *He,* and so will I. It should be understood that this is metaphor, and not meant to be taken literally or seriously. If some prefer to call the Holy Spirit a *She,* then as far as I'm concerned, they are more than welcome to do so, but that is no more accurate than using the word *He.*

At the end of 2001, when Arten and Pursah had left, I had no intention of ever speaking in public. My plan was to put out the book and let it take care of itself. Pursah had asked (rhetorically, because she already knew everything) early in our discussions, "You don't like to speak to a crowd of people, do you?" My response was, "I'd rather stick broken pieces of glass up my butt."

That attitude had begun to slowly change when I went for the first time to the annual *A Course in Miracles* Conference in Bethel, Maine, in October of 2001, shortly after the 9/11 tragedy. In the 1990s, I had almost become a recluse, living in rural Maine without much social contact. One exception to this was a *Course in Miracles* study group I started going to in 1993, about six months after Arten and Pursah's first visit. It was a small, comfortable group that I would attend for 11 years, making some good friends but not challenging myself in terms of interacting with people.

I first heard of the annual Bethel Conference in 1993 and decided to go, but I didn't. I also meant to go every year after that from 1994 through 2000, but I never went. In 2001, the ninth year in a row of promising myself I would go, I finally did. It's a good thing. It was the final time they would ever have the Conference. Of course there's no such thing as an accident. The fact that I knew that my book *The Disappearance of the Universe* was almost done (Arten and Pursah had promised me one more visit by the end of the year) combined with the 9/11 tragedy had started to light a fire under me. I'm not a high-energy person, and it's always good for me to have extra motivation.

I found the people at Bethel, who were mostly from the New England and New York areas, to be the most loving people I had ever encountered, and it made me want to meet with more spiritual students. However, speaking in public was still not on my radar. While at the Conference, I also met one of the earliest teachers of *A Course in Miracles,* Jon Mundy. Jon would play a role in changing my mind about public speaking. While Jon was in the makeshift bookstore selling some of his products, he became the first person I would go up to and say that two ascended masters were appearing to me and I was writing a book about it. His reaction was not enthusiastic, but it was not judgmental either.

After December 21, which was my Ascended Master friends' final visit, I took the next three months to finish typing and proof-reading the manuscript. My teachers had told me what to do with the book. This was the only information they gave me that, per their instructions, was not included in *Disappearance.* Their plan didn't match mine. My idea would have been to take the book to a big New York publisher, have it sell a million copies in six months, and move to Hawaii. They said no and gave me their blueprint. I was very naïve, and didn't have a clue about the realities of publish-ing or the politics of the divided, though mostly loving, family that is referred to as the "Course Community" that would await me.

The first pleasant surprise that would come about as a result of following the guidance of my visitors was the amazingly easy time I had getting approved by the Foundation for *A Course in Miracles* to use the hundreds of quotations from the *Course* that my teachers had spoken in the book. It had been many years since a book was allowed to use so much of the *Course,* and I had heard stories of people waiting for a year for an answer and then being declined!

I had gone to Roscoe, New York, a couple of times to attend workshops by Ken Wapnick, the friend of *Course* scribe Helen Schucman, who was now the premier teacher of the *Course,* and who also controlled its copyright. I met with Ken in between ses-sions, approaching him as guided with an attitude of respect and cooperation. He responded with kindness and a good sense of humor. Later, in April of 2002, I sent Ken the manuscript in order for him to go over and approve the quotations from the *Course.* The Foundation sent me a letter of permission to use all of the quotes just one month later.

NOTE: Not long after, a maverick judge, who displayed lit-tle public respect for *A Course in Miracles,* would invalidate the *Course's* copyright over the seldom used and dubious issue of "prior distribution."

The next pleasant surprise that would come about as a result of following the guidance of my visitors was the amazingly easy time I had getting the book published. I was a completely unknown author with no credentials and a strange story about two beings appearing to me on my living-room couch. I didn't know that I didn't have a sucker's chance in hell of finding a "mainstream" publisher, but I did know I had been told to send the manuscript to D. Patrick Miller, the sole proprietor, and only employee, of Fearless Books in Berkeley, California. Patrick had never published a book by anybody else, only his own. When he read my manuscript, he said, "I think you've got something here," and decided to make an exception. By October we had a deal. The official publication date was May 1, 2003, although advance copies of the book were being read by our first 100 online customers in March. Those first readers had bought the book based on some excerpts Patrick had placed on his Website.

In fact, there were three books that had been many years in the making that were all published at the same time: *Beyond Belief: The Secret Gospel of Thomas,* by Elaine Pagels; *The Da Vinci Code,* by Dan Brown; and *The Disappearance of the Universe,* which some readers immediately began referring to as "D.U." It amazed me how certain ideas churned around in the unconscious and then would rise up to the surface of public consciousness when the time was just right. These three books explored many of the same themes. The difference with D.U. was that it contained not only the teachings of *A Course in Miracles,* which the other books didn't, but also a major clarification of those teachings. This was a gift to both long-time students of the *Course* as well as beginners who would be introduced to the *Course* through D.U., although most beginners probably couldn't appreciate how much time was being saved for them by reading it.

I remember less than a year later hearing Doug Hough, a teacher at the Association for Research and Enlightenment (The Edgar Cayce Group in Virginia Beach), tell his students that reading D.U. would save them 20 years when it came to studying the *Course.* I realized that was not only true, but that it was clear that such an accomplishment could not have been done by me alone. This helped prevent me from letting things go to my head. If I wasn't responsible for most of the content of the book, then there was no reason for me to feel special about it.

In October of 2002, once I had a publisher, I sent an e-mail to Jon Mundy and told him more details about the book. He didn't answer me. Annoyed, I forgave him after a little while. Although I didn't always forgive things immediately, I always forgave them eventually. It was that quality of perseverance that would enable me to continue to practice the *Course* during what was to come.

After the book was published, in the spring of 2003, I got a phone call. It was Jon Mundy. He told me that he was reading the book, and his reaction was, "Wow!" He also said that he was coming to Portland, Maine, to do a workshop at the Unity Church, and he thought it would be a good idea for me to come. He said I didn't have to speak, but he'd introduce me to the crowd and tell them about the book. I went, and when Jon introduced me, I quickly stood up and shyly said, "Hi," and then sat down just as quickly. That was my first speaking engagement.

We went to dinner later, and Jon said, "You're going to get out there and speak about this, right?" I said no, I didn't think I could. Jon said, "That's all right, Gary, but if you don't, then people will never know for sure what your experience was. Some of them won't be certain if it's all true or if you made some of it up." That got me thinking. Then, as we continued talking, Jon invited me to come to New York City in the fall and present a workshop that he would sponsor. I could hardly believe it when I heard myself say yes. As soon as I left that night, I started trying to think of a way to get out of it.

I still had no real intention of talking in front of people and made no effort to do so. I was also procrastinating about telling Jon that I didn't want to come to Manhattan. I then decided to handle my problem of procrastination, if I got around to it.

Then, that summer I got a call from a woman in Massachusetts named Vicki Poppe. She told me that she was coming up to Maine to do a prayer circle on Peaks Island, off the coast of Portland. She asked me to come. That sounded pretty cool to me, as Maine is nice in the summer, and I had never gone out on the ferry before. Vicki brought about ten people with her. Then when we were on the island, she suddenly said, "Hey, Gary, why don't you tell us about your experiences with Arten and Pursah?" I had been letting the Holy Spirit in, and I was pretty relaxed on that hot, sunny afternoon. I went ahead and told the people in the circle what it was like to be visited by my teachers. Afterward, on the way back to the ferry, Vicki came up to me and said, "You know, Gary, you just told your story to ten people. If you can tell your story to ten people, you can tell your story to a hundred people. What's the difference? It's all an illusion."

> "If you can tell your story to ten people, you can tell your story to a hundred people. What's the difference? It's all an illusion."

Vicki knew that I was supposed to go to New York in November, and she said, "I'll tell you what. You can come and do a workshop at my house. If you don't like it, then you don't have to do it again. But at least try it once!" I gave in and said yes. I thought, *How many people are going to come to her house?*

Vicki has a house on Adams Street in Quincy, Massachusetts, across the street from the home of President John Quincy Adams. The book was being read, and I was amazed by how many people came that first weekend of September. But what really surprised me were the people themselves. They were so open, so loving, and so supportive that I was almost overwhelmed. I figured, *If this is what's it's going to be like, then how can I lose? With these spiritual-type people, even if I suck, they're supposed to forgive me!*

Although I actually did a pretty good job for my first workshop, I was so nervous before I went on that I said, "I don't want to do this anymore." But something interesting happened about 20 minutes after I started. I had the group do the form of meditation that my teachers had taught me, which is also a form of prayer and joining with God. After doing so, I felt as if I were connected with something higher than myself. After that point in the presentation, it was as if I wasn't the one doing the workshop anymore. It was more like I was watching myself as the Holy Spirit sent the messages through me. I thought, *Hey, maybe I should let the Holy Spirit take over sooner!* The next time I spoke, I did exactly that. Two months later I was in New York City, the place where I thought I'd be the most nervous, speaking for about the fourth time in public, and feeling less nervous in front of a crowd than I ever had.

The book was gaining momentum, selling more copies every month than the month before. It wasn't huge yet, but it was getting noticed, and more speaking offers came in. I didn't know how far I wanted to take this. Did I just want to speak a few times, or did I want to get serious about doing it more and even start traveling long distances? I hadn't flown anywhere. I had only driven to a few places in New England and once to New York. I was at a crossroads.

Then, on December 20, 2003, I found myself at Vicki Poppe's house once again, this time for a Christmas party. I had gone there with Karen, my wife of 21 years. We spent the night, and then on the next day, December 21, prepared to drive home to Maine. I said to Vicki, "You know, I have a feeling something's going to happen." She said, "I feel it, too, and I have an idea what it is." There was no need to say anything else.

Late that night I was sitting in the living room of the same apartment in Auburn, Maine, where Arten and Pursah had paid their last three visits, having moved there from the house in Poland Spring where their appearances had begun 11 years earlier to the day. Suddenly, I felt a presence in the room. I had to turn to my left because the couch was pointed in the same direction that my chair was, toward the TV set. I looked over and became ecstatic at the sight of my two old friends, sitting there on the same couch they had sat on for almost all of their visits. I exclaimed, "Arten and Pursah!" and then ran over and hugged both of them. I wouldn't realize until later that it was the first time I had ever touched Arten, the man, although I had touched Pursah, the woman, once before.

They looked the same as ever, my beautiful Pursah and that guy. I thought it was interesting that I didn't actually see them appear, because I recalled that this was also the case during the very first visit they had made 11 years earlier. I sat down with wobbly knees from the excitement of seeing them. Pursah then began to speak.

PURSAH: Hey, dear brother. How's it going? Has anything interesting happened since the last time we saw you? Just kidding. You know we're always aware of everything that you're doing.

ARTEN: Yes. For example, you were just reading about that guy in Germany who killed somebody and then ate him. It's a big story there. He's accused of cannibalism, and now they're putting him on trial.

GARY: Yeah. There's no such thing as a free lunch.

PURSAH: I'm glad to see your smart-ass tendencies haven't been completely cured. You may need them by the time we're finished with you.

GARY: Oh yeah? What'd you have in mind?

ARTEN: All in good time, Gary.

GARY: Wait! Let me put on the recorder. It's so great to see you guys! I can hardly believe it. I had a feeling about it, though, being our anniversary and all.

NOTE: December 21 is the feast day for St. Thomas, and Pursah had identified herself as being Thomas, a man, in that incarnation 2,000 years ago. Arten had identified himself as being St. Thaddaeus at that time.

PURSAH: We know. So let's get right down to business, just like before. We've come back to tap people on the shoulder, so to speak. Although for some it may seem like getting tapped on the shoulder with a sledgehammer. There's an important reason for that. We want to help keep people focused. It's by applying advanced, or quantum, forgiveness, which we'll explain, that you can most quickly experience your immortal reality. We are here to instruct you on how to break the cycle of birth and death, once and for all.

GARY: Is that all? I was hoping I could learn how to measure my consciousness.

ARTEN: You're being facetious. But what you just said is one of the reasons we're here. People are being distracted by things that may seem fascinating to them but are really only there to take their attention away from what's important, and instead put it on things that will keep them stuck here.

PURSAH: We'll get into that more. But to start, let's point out that most spiritual students spend almost all of their time in the phase of *gathering information*. This is encouraged by the belief that the more spiritual information they put in their heads, the more enlightened they'll be. So they jump around from one thing to another, reading dozens of books on different spiritual subjects. During our first series of visits with you, we referred to it as the "spiritual buffet line."

Now there's nothing wrong with learning information. Indeed, it gives people a necessary background. The problem is that people make a false idol out of gathering information, and it doesn't lead anywhere. It's a trick, a carrot and a stick. That's why what's really important isn't what you know, but what you do with what you know. What really matters in terms of quickening your spiritual development is the phase of *application.*

At some point, the serious spiritual student and teacher will have to take everything he or she has learned and actually apply it to every person, situation, or event that comes up in front of their face on any given day. That applies to everything. And usually it's not a mystery. Whatever is happening in your life, that's the lesson that the Holy Spirit wants you to apply the teachings to, and the Holy Spirit's great instrument of salvation is forgiveness. But as you know, this isn't the old-fashioned kind of forgiveness. This is not your parents' spirituality. This is a whole new ball game, a new paradigm.

It's only through disciplined application that the practitioner can enter the glorious phase of *experience.* And I guarantee you, dear brother, that experience is the only thing that will ever make you happy. Words will never do it; intellectual concepts, theology, philosophical speculation—forget it. *A Course in Miracles,* which as you know, is J, our English symbol for Y'shua, speaking the word of God, says that words are but symbols of symbols, twice removed from reality.[3] And when you think about it, how is a symbol of a symbol ever going to make you happy? No. The only thing that will make you happy is the experience of what you really are. What will truly satisfy you is *not* a symbol of reality, but an *experience* of reality.

At one point in that same *Course,* J is talking about all the difficult questions people have, and he makes the remarkable statement, ". . . there is no answer; only an experience. Seek only this, and do not let theology delay you."[4]

That experience comes as a result of allowing your mind to be trained by the Holy Spirit to think and see others as He does. But it takes a good system, like Buddhism or *A Course in Miracles,* to be hastened on the road to accomplishment. Left to its own devices, the mind cannot be healed. As J also says in his *Course,* "An untrained mind can accomplish nothing."[5] That's quite a statement, because it's saying that 99.9 percent of all the people on the earth are accomplishing nothing. Until the mind is trained, you're just spinning your wheels.

GARY: Yeah. I've realized more and more how important the Workbook of the *Course* is in that regard, and I think I've also realized that no matter what comes up, it's all for the same purpose, which is forgiveness. I'm not saying I always do it right away. I don't. But I always do it eventually. And the sooner I do it, the less I suffer. Take speaking in public, for example, which I never thought I'd do. I was really nervous about it, but by letting the Holy Spirit help me, I started to realize that I wasn't nervous for the reason I thought. It's like the *Course* says: "I am never upset for the reason I think."[6]

ARTEN: That's right, hotshot. Everybody's afraid of something in this world, and as difficult as it may be for people to believe, because it's unconscious to them, all fears that people have can be directly traced at the level of the unconscious mind to the fear of God that is a result of your seeming separation from Him and the unconscious guilt that resulted from it.

GARY: Hey! Does this mean we're gonna do another book? Because if we are, there are people who might not understand what you just said.

ARTEN: Well, why don't you give us a little review, then? Tell us the teachings in a nutshell so both the uninitiated and the experienced practitioner will have a better idea what we're talking about. You can do it. Things are going pretty good for your speaking, as well as for *The Disappearance of the Universe,* so far, right?

GARY: Yes, everything's under control. Mistakes have been made, but others have been blamed. Just kidding. But I don't know if I should go any further with this speaking thing. I mean, I did what I wanted to do. I went right out there, even in Manhattan, and said that this is my experience. The book is just the way it happened. People can believe it or not, but if they don't, at least it won't be because I didn't tell them.

PURSAH: I'm afraid your forgiveness lessons are just beginning. What if I told you that starting at the end of February, you'll start flying over 100,000 miles a year to teach spirituality?

GARY: I'd say you're kidding, right?

ARTEN: That's what will be the most helpful, brother. Including yourself, you could count on two fingers the number of people who are out there on the road accurately teaching this message. But don't think that's what it's really about. At the same time you're traveling and speaking, we want you to do your *real* job, which is forgiveness. Not the old-fashioned kind, but the new kind.

PURSAH: Are you willing to undergo drastic changes in your personal lifestyle, knowing that no matter how things look, it's really just a trick to convince you you're a body, and then forgive it?

GARY: Ah, no.

ARTEN: Well, we know better. So get your affairs in order, buddy. You've got quite a ride coming up. Now how about that review we talked about?

GARY: What about those who already know this stuff? Won't it seem repetitious?

PURSAH: Don't forget something we told you the first time around. Repetition isn't just all right, it's mandatory. You can't hear right-minded ideas too much. It takes time for them to sink into the deep canyons of your unconscious mind. We've already said that it's not how much spiritual information you put into the mind that determines how enlightened you are, and that's true. However, at the same time, the background provided by knowing the metaphysics of a teaching like *A Course in Miracles* can help you to make the *decision* to apply what you know, which is the most important part of the application. Once you understand the truth, then remembering it when the stuff hits the fan is the hard part. If and when you get into the habit of remembering the truth in difficult situations, it becomes almost second nature for you to apply it. When that time comes, you'll be progressing light years toward the experience we've been speaking about. As the *Course* puts it, "It is this experience toward which the *Course* is directed."[7]

GARY: All right. Can I tell you a joke first? I like to tell jokes in my workshops.

ARTEN: You went to Manhattan last month. Tell us that New York joke you like.

GARY: No problem. This Buddhist is walking in Central Park. He walks up to a hot-dog vendor and says, "Make me one with everything." The vendor gives the Buddhist a hot dog, and after the Buddhist pays for it, he asks for his change. But the hot-dog vendor says, "Change comes from within."

PURSAH: Yes, you get a nice laugh with that one. We like that you have a good sense of humor in your presentations. It's important to remember to laugh. Remember what J says in the Text: "Into eternity, where all is one, there crept a tiny, mad idea, at which the Son of God remembered not to laugh."[8]

GARY: And of course that tiny mad idea is the thought that we could have an individual identity and be separate from God. So, as for that review you asked for, the *Course* is a three-books-in-one spiritual document that includes a Text, which gives the entire theory; then there's a Workbook for Students, which is a one-year program that often takes people longer than one year to do and which trains the student to apply the *Course* to everyday life; plus there's a Manual for Teachers, which reinforces the whole thing. The *Course* was given by J over a period of seven years to a research psychiatrist in New York City named Helen Schucman. She would write down in her shorthand notebook what J said and then say it to her colleague, Bill Thetford, who typed it out.

When you guys appeared to me, you gave me, through your teachings, a different vision of J 2,000 years ago, whose real name was Y'shua, a Jewish rabbi who never intended to start a religion. Since then I've had some memories of my own. I found that when you talked to me about some of my past lifetimes, it would trigger more memories of those lifetimes in the following weeks and months. For example, you told me that a thousand years ago I was a friend and student of the enlightened American Indian teacher known as the Great Sun. That brought up feelings, memories, and visions of that lifetime as an Indian in Cahokia. [*Note:* The Cahokia site is located in Collinsville, Illinois, and represents the most sophisticated prehistoric Native American society north of Mexico.] I even remembered that I should put the emphasis on the third syllable when I say Cahokia, instead of on the second, which is the way white people say it.

ARTEN: That's right. We had pronounced it the modern way, because we're speaking to you in English, but you just pronounced it the way an Indian from a thousand years ago would say it.

GARY: And when you told me who I was 2,000 years ago with J, that also triggered more memories of that lifetime.

PURSAH: How'd it make you feel to find out you were Saint Thomas at the time of J, and I'm you?

GARY: I know you know the answer to that, and you're just asking rhetorical questions. You know everything. And I still can't believe you're here! But when I found out who I was at the time of J, it felt really great for about two days. I mean, it was really cool. But then after a while, you get up and you realize you have the same old crap right in front of your face. The forgiveness lessons are right there, and it doesn't matter who you were in another lifetime. You always have to choose to forgive whatever's happening right now.

PURSAH: Very good, dear brother. Everyone's been enormously famous and seemingly important in some lifetimes, and all have been the dregs of the earth in others. That's duality. What matters is doing your forgiveness work right now. That's the way out. But it's not the old-fashioned kind of forgiveness at all. Would you care to explain why?

GARY: I'll do my best. First of all, as a rabbi and a mystic, J understood well the teachings of ancient Jewish mysticism. Among those would be the idea that Heaven is closeness to God, and hell is distance from God. But J, being an uncompromising kind of a guy, didn't stop there. For him, Heaven wouldn't just be closeness to God, it would be Oneness with God. In fact, it would be *perfect*

Oneness with God. And hell wouldn't just be distance from God; it would be anything that is *separate* from God. That narrows it down to two distinct choices, and only one of them is real, because perfect Oneness cannot have a counterpart, or else it wouldn't be perfect.

So to J, God is changeless, perfect, and eternal. And God is synonymous with spirit, because nothing He makes would be any different from Him, or else it wouldn't be perfect. And besides, if God could make anything that wasn't perfect, then He Himself wouldn't be perfect either, would He? And spirit doesn't have to evolve, or else it wouldn't be perfect.

Heaven wouldn't just be closeness to God, it would be Oneness with God. In fact, it would be perfect Oneness with God.

Of course, God is not a He or a She, and I'm using biblical language like the *Course.* I could call God an It, but that wouldn't exactly turn anybody on either. So right off the bat we notice a couple of things about our friend J. First, he's uncompromising. Second, no matter how complicated things may *appear* to be, there are always only two things to choose from, and only one of them is real. The other choice would be an illusion, which was taught by the Hindus and Buddhists long before J, but he elevated the alternative to a flawless version of a God who really is Perfect Love, rather than a God who is conflicted and imperfect.

Next, you have to remember that J was from the Middle East. He would have had more of an Eastern slant than a Western one. So he certainly was familiar with the teachings of Buddhism. He would know about the Buddhist concept of ego. He would understand and experience that there is only *one* ego *appearing* as many, in what the Hindus call the world of multiplicity and the Buddhists call impermanence. So there's only one of us that thinks that it's here, and I'm it. There isn't really anybody else. There's nobody out there. It only looks that way. It's a trick. The conscious part of the mind looks out and sees all kinds of separation, different bodies and forms, but that's an illusion. And the unconscious part of the mind, almost all of which is hidden, just the way most of an iceberg is hidden underneath the surface of the water, knows that there's really only one of us.

Time and space and differences turn out to all be untrue, despite appearances. The reason everything is connected is because there's only one illusion, just like there's only one God. But God has nothing to do with the illusion. That was a false assumption on the part of people. People then made up a God in their image, who was like what they believed themselves to be. But God made us originally in His image: perfect, innocent, and One. The oneness that exists in the illusion is an imitation oneness, because the ego attempts to mimic God.

Today, quantum physicists are confirming that time and space are just illusions, also. Past, present, and future all occur simultaneously. We are actually nonlocal beings having a local experience. It may look like you're over there and I'm over here, but it's a lie. Space is just a separation idea, as is time. We divided up time and space to make it look like different intervals of time and different places, when it's really all made up and everything's the same, even though it looks different, because it's all an illusion that's based on the thought of separation. Except the physicists don't know that part yet. They just know that our experience is an illusion compared to the way things really are when you look closer! They don't have the whole picture yet, just part of it. Science and spirituality haven't completely met yet, but they're getting there.

For example, they know that if I look at a star that's 20 billion light years away, I cause it to change instantaneously at the subatomic level. How is that possible? It's because the star isn't really 20 billion light years away; it's really in my mind. Or more accurately, it's a projection of my mind. I made it up, and it's coming from me, not at me, like most people think. And it's not even matter until I look at it or touch it. It's energy, which is really thought, which is why energy can't be destroyed. And matter is just a different form of energy, returning to energy and then recycling.

PURSAH: And how did J, 2,000 years ago, use all of that Buddhist and Jewish mystical knowledge, which matched the findings of today's physicists?

GARY: Well, he figured out something that people still don't understand, even today with all these advances in knowledge, including psychology, and it's this: If there's really only one of us here, and if the unconscious part of the mind knows that, then what are we doing when we go around judging and condemning other people? All we're really doing is sending a message directly into our own unconscious mind that *we* are worthy of being judged and condemned. Whatever we think about others is really like sending a message about ourselves to our self. So J decided that if there's really only one of us who thinks it's here, and if the unconscious mind knows that, then he was going to go through life seeing everyone as being what they really are, which is perfect spirit, instead of seeing them as bodies, which is really just a false idea of separation. He would see everyone as being Christ, pure and innocent. He would think of them as being what they really are: immortal, invulnerable, and something that cannot even be touched by this world.

Thus, the key to enlightenment lies in a secret that very few people have ever known, but which J knew well. The way you will experience and feel about yourself is not determined by how other people look at and think about you. The way that you will experience and feel about yourself is actually determined by how *you* look at and think about *them*. Ultimately, this determines your identity. You will identify yourself either as a body or as perfect spirit, as either divided or whole, depending on how you see others. And once you understand that, I would think you'd want to get pretty damn careful how you think about other people!

PURSAH: You honor us as teachers. And of course you know who *our* teacher was. Please continue.

GARY: What . . . ? Do you want me to do all the talking?

PURSAH: We'll have plenty to say, including contributing to this review.

GARY: I should hope so. By the way, I've been thinking, because of the way our talks went before, I had a lot of personal stuff in the last book. I don't mind talking about my personal forgiveness lessons, but a couple of the people I mentioned weren't too thrilled by the fact that I portrayed myself in my narration as forgiving them. There are two sides to every story. That's duality, right? Yet all I can do is present my experience. Can you give me any advice on how to talk about personal stuff?

PURSAH: Don't worry, Gary. Because of the direction your life is taking right now, we're going to be discussing your professional forgiveness lessons more than your personal ones. It will all work out. Trust us. Would you like to continue with our review?

GARY: You asked for it, but I must say, you look more beautiful than ever. Tell me something, just between you and me. Would it be incest to make love to your future self?

PURSAH: No, but it would be weird. Please proceed.

GARY: Okay, I can take a hint for now. To continue, every time J forgave, he was actually rejoining with himself.

ARTEN: Do you get the larger meaning of that?

GARY: I get it. He was actually going from an experience of separation to wholeness. And the word *holy* actually comes from the word *whole*. As he said in the Gospel of Thomas, "I am the one who comes from what is whole, I was given from the things of my Father. Therefore, I say to you that if one is whole one will be filled with light, but if one is divided, then one will be filled with darkness." So you can't have it both ways. You can't be a little bit whole. Your allegiance must be undivided, or else *you're* divided. No matter how complicated things seem to get, there are always really just two choices. One is for wholeness, or holiness, which is one and perfect. That's why the old prayer said, "The Lord our God is One." The other choice is for anything that isn't perfect Oneness, which is division. There's no getting away from that. So J completely forgave the world. His love and forgiveness were total and all-encompassing. He knew that if you partially forgive the world, then you will be partially forgiven, which is to remain divided. But if you completely forgive the world, then you will be completely forgiven.

Thus, the great teaching of J and the Holy Spirit is for forgiveness, but in a quantum sense, rather than the old-fashioned, Newtonian, subject-and-object kind of forgiveness. The old-fashioned kind of forgiveness is saying, "All right, I'm forgiving you, because I'm better than you are, and you really did it, and you're really guilty, but I'm going to let you off the hook, except you're still going to hell." All that does is keep the strange separation beliefs that we really have about ourselves recycling in our own unconscious mind. It's not really forgiveness. J, on the other hand, knew about a deep, unconscious guilt that's in everybody's mind over the original, seeming separation from God; and that there's a different kind of forgiveness that's the fastest way to undo it, which is the equivalent of undoing the ego.

ARTEN: We'll have to explain that a little more at some point, perhaps with a quick version of the miscreation story, in order to point out where that guilt came from. After all, you can't break the cycle of birth and death and stop appearing to reincarnate as long as that unconscious guilt remains in the mind.

GARY: Sure, but do me a favor. Tell me more about the idea of all this being a dream. In the few appearances I've done, I've gotten a lot of questions about that. And I still can't believe that you're here!

PURSAH: None of us are here, Gary, as you know. So let's talk about the dream. Say you're a parent, and you have a four-year-old daughter who's in bed at night, and she's dreaming. You peek in on her to see how she is, and you can tell that she's dreaming; she's tossing and turning a little, and you can see she's uncomfortable. For her, the dream has become her reality. She reacts to the figures in the dream as though they're real. Now, *you can't see the dream.* Why? Because it's not really there, and your four-year-old has never really left her bed. She's still safe at home, but she can't see it. It's out of her awareness, and the dream has become her reality.

You want to wake her up so she won't be afraid anymore. So what do you do? Do you go over and shake the hell out of her? No, because that would scare her even more. So you wake her up quietly and gently. Perhaps you whisper things to her like, "Hey, it's only a dream. You don't have to worry. What you're seeing is not true. And all the problems, all the worries, all the fears and the pains you feel are really just kind of silly, because there's no need for them, and they're taking place inside of a dream that doesn't really exist. They're the product of the same silly ideas that produced the dream in the first place. And if you can hear my voice right now, you're already starting to wake up."

That's because the truth can be heard in the dream. Remember, *the truth is not in the dream,* but it *can* be heard in the dream. Your four-year-old hears you and starts to relax. She wakens slowly and gently. Her dream becomes happier. And then when she finally wakes up, she sees that she never really left the bed. She was actually home all the while. Home was still there, but it was out of her awareness. As awareness returns, she wakes up, and the fact that she is safe at home becomes her reality. You knew she was there all the time. There was no need to see her dream or to react to it. And where is the dream when she wakes up from it?

GARY: Nowhere. It disappears because it was never really there anyway. It may have looked real and felt real, but it wasn't really there. The images we see in our dreams at night are projections. We're seeing them with one part of our mind, and they're actually being projected by another part of our mind, but that part is hidden.

PURSAH: Very nice. As you said, it's a trick. And here's the fun part. When the four-year-old wakes up from the dream, it's just another dream. And when you woke up this morning in your bed, it was just another form of dreaming. It's a function of levels, which don't exist in the reality of pure spirit. In fact, you could say that the reason this dream feels more convincing than your nocturnal dreams is to convince you of its reality. And convincing it is, but it's not really there. And the people who you think are out there aren't really there either. Yet for you, the dream has become your reality, and where you really are is out of your awareness. As *A Course in Miracles* puts it, "All your time is spent in dreaming. Your sleeping and your waking dreams have different forms, and that's all. Their content is the same."[9]

The Holy Spirit is whispering the same kinds of things to you right now in this dream that you would whisper to a four-year-old in bed at night. He's saying things like, "Hey, it's only a dream. You don't have to worry. What you're seeing isn't true. And all the problems, all the worries, all the fears and pains you feel are really just kind of silly, because there's no need for them, plus they're taking place inside of a dream that doesn't really exist. They're the product of the same silly ideas that produced the dream in the first place. And if you can hear my Voice right now, you're already starting to wake up, because the truth can be heard in the dream."

The truth is not in the dream, but it *can* be heard in the dream. And when you start to know the truth, which will be communicated to you by the Holy Spirit in many different ways, you start to relax. You awaken slowly and gently through a cocoon process called forgiveness. Just as the caterpillar goes through a cocoon process to be prepared for a higher and less restricted form of life, you become prepared for a higher form of life by changing your perception of the world. As a result of this, your dream becomes happier. But that happiness is not dependent on what appears to happen in the dream. It's an inner peace that can be there for you *regardless* of what appears to be happening in the dream. And then, when you finally wake up, you see that you never really left home, which is your perfect oneness with God. You were actually home all the while. Home was still here, but it was out of your awareness.

As J put it in the Gospel of Thomas, "The Kingdom of the Father is spread out upon the earth, and people do not see it." As awareness returns, you wake up to the reality of the Kingdom, and you have the knowledge that you are always safe at home.

GARY: But if all that's true, then it means that God doesn't even know I'm here!

ARTEN: You're completely missing the point. The point is you're *not* here, and God knows where you *really* are. And instead of diving in and making an unreal dream real, God has a better idea. He wants you to wake up and be with Him. Eventually you wake up to Heaven, where God knew you always were. There was no need for God to see your dream or to react to it.

As *A Course in Miracles* says, "You are at home in God, dreaming of exile but perfectly capable of awakening to reality."[10] And tell me, Gary, where is a dream of time and space when you wake up from it?

GARY: Nowhere. It disappears, because like any dream, it's a mirage that vanishes, a spell that is dispelled. And now reality becomes my reality.

ARTEN: Yes, so when you awaken from the dream of time and space, there *is* no more time and space, which means that you don't have to hang around for a million years waiting for everyone to wake up. There *is* nobody else to wake up. There was nobody out there but you, the one ego, appearing as many. And the ones you *thought* were out there are already with you in Heaven, not as bodies, but as what they really are, which is spirit. Nobody can be left out in oneness, and nothing can be lacking in wholeness. So everyone you ever loved or cared about, including animals, are there in your awareness. Once again, not as anything that was ever separate, but as something that can never

When you awaken from the dream of time and space, there *is* no more time and space.

be separate. Nothing can be missing in perfection. It's all perfectly one, and it's constant, which is an attribute that doesn't exist in the universe of time and space. However, it *can* be experienced by you, even though you may appear to be in a body.

GARY: I've had that experience.

PURSAH: We know, and we can talk more about it later, because it *is* the answer to all questions. Despite your demeanor, we know that you can never fully believe in the ego again. And once you have that experience, then it becomes easier to build your house upon the rock instead of on the sand. The sand represents the shifting sands of time and space, where nothing can really be depended on except the fact that it's going to change, because this is a world of time and change. So the only thing you know for sure is that it *won't* be the same one minute from now. But the rock is permanent; it's something that can be depended on.

GARY: Yeah. Once you experience reality, even if it's brief, then everything in this world is just kind of like chicken crap compared to what's available.

ARTEN: Yes, and you're doing well remembering to make the right choice between the two. You're not perfect, but you're doing good, and we're pleased.

GARY: Thanks. Hey! Can I use some of this stuff in my workshops?

ARTEN: You use the first book in your workshops, don't you?

GARY: I'll take that as a yes. So, what seems to go on here in the world may look and feel real, but it isn't. The images I see in my dreams at night are projections. I'm seeing them with one part of my mind, and they're actually being projected by another part of my mind, but that part is hidden.

And during the day all I'm seeing with the body's eyes is a projection from my own unconscious mind of something that I secretly believe to be true about myself. Just like Freud said that everyone in your dreams is really you, it turns out that everyone in our life is also a symbol of us. J knew that, and being a pretty smart guy he realized that all people do by judging and condemning others is keep their own false ego identity in place as a result, but if they forgive, in the true sense of the word, then they undo the false ego identity and return to spirit.

ARTEN: Yes, and it's interesting that Freud didn't actually use the word *ego.* He used the word *ich,* which means "I," and which indicates a personal identity. You could combine that with the all-encompassing Buddhist term *ego,* and what you have is one being that incorrectly thinks it has an identity that is separate from its Source.

PURSAH: And I'm glad you're talking about undoing the ego. It's definitely *not* enough to just tell people the world isn't real. That won't get them anywhere. It's true that knowing that the world is an illusion is a necessary part of the picture. But it's only true forgiveness, which we'll talk a lot more about eventually, that undoes the ego. Without it, little progress is made. It's all about how you think. If you think the person you're seeing is a body, then you're a body. If you think the person you're seeing is spirit, then you're spirit. That's how it will be translated by your own unconscious mind. There's no getting away from that. The way you think of the other person determines how you will ultimately feel about yourself. We'll do a little more of the review with you later.

GARY: It's funny how a spiritual document like the *Course* can use Christian terminology but incorporate so many Buddhists ideas into it. Maybe that's why some Christians are reluctant to embrace it.

ARTEN: Yes. Conservative Christians don't recognize the *Course*.

GARY: That's okay. They also don't recognize each other at Hooters.

PURSAH: Cute. And just so people will recognize us, we want to make it clear that we *only* appear to you and will *never* appear to anyone else or give channeled information to anyone else.

GARY: I'm not complaining, but why?

PURSAH: It's simple. Helen Schucman took seven years to scribe *A Course in Miracles*. Before that, almost all channelers were trance channelers. Whether it was the psychic Edgar Cayce; or Jane Roberts, who channeled Seth, people who received information from a higher source did not hear it themselves, but needed a device to be able to get out of the way and let the information come through them. As *A Course in Miracles* itself says, "Only very few can hear God's Voice at all . . ."[11] But then, after the *Course* came out, and people heard that this woman was simply hearing the Voice of Jesus, who was the manifestation of the Holy Spirit, then all of a sudden *everyone* was hearing the Voice of J or the Holy Spirit, even though you had the *Course* saying that they couldn't! The reason is obvious. If people could hear the Holy Spirit's Voice, then they didn't really have to understand the *Course* or do the forgiveness work it asked of them, did they? They didn't have to look at the ego or their unconscious guilt, or do anything about it. Rather than accepting the challenge to come up to a whole new level that J was offering them, through the same kind of forgiveness work he had done, they could simply make up their own *Course* to their own liking. So right away you had people acting as teachers of the *Course* who couldn't possibly have taken the time to learn it and do the work, and before you knew it, you had people reporting that J was saying things to them that actually contradicted things he said in *A Course in Miracles*.

We don't want people doing the same thing with our words. So here's a disclaimer. If anyone ever says Arten or Pursah are appearing to them or speaking to them and giving them information, now or in the future, then they're mistaken. It's not us. We will never do that. That way, no one can ever contradict our words in our names or compromise what we're saying. We'll leave the flawed reporting of J's and the Holy Spirit's teachings to those who claim to be inspired by the *Course* without ever really having learned it.

GARY: That's a pretty provocative statement, and some may take it to be a little harsh. After all, they can't get your loving attitude without seeing you.

PURSAH: Sorry, Gary, but *someone* has to point out these things. It takes many years of practice to make significant progress, but a lot of people want to skip to the end without utilizing the means, which is forgiveness. They want to be a master without being a student. That's why we're pleased that you present yourself as just a student who shares your experiences and passes the teachings along.

If you try to be more than that, then strange things happen. For example, there are a couple of so-called *Course* teachers who have set themselves up as cult leaders. Sometimes it's obvious that this is what's going on, and sometimes it's more subtle. In any case, if a teacher or their assistants try to get you to surrender any personal property to them or make large donations, something is rotten in Denmark. Ditto if they want you to live at their location.

It's clear that the *Course* is not meant to be used as an escape from society, but as a tool to forgive society. Invariably, cult leaders will present a façade of being infallible. Rather than empowering you to do your own forgiveness work, which is clearly the intention of the *Course,* they'll try to make you think that it's being in their presence and following them that leads to enlightenment. In fact, you'll get to experience one of them in person within a few months. Don't react to him. Forgive instead, and know that he's a fine example of what happens when you don't feel the need to learn and practice the *Course* and decide to use people instead, all the time masquerading as a master.

NOTE: The kind of teachers Pursah is referring to above would *not* include those affiliated with Pathways of Light® in Kiel, Wisconsin, run by Reverends Robert and Mary Stoelting, which is a fine teaching organization.

GARY: None of that is new in the world, but why do these cult leaders have to say they're teaching the *Course?* Why don't they just use the Bible or something?

PURSAH: Sometimes they do use the Bible, and other things, and mix them with the *Course,* which you also shouldn't do, unless you're being absolutely true to the message of the *Course* and are using the other things either for contrast or as supporting tools.

GARY: Is it possible to both teach and practice the *Course?*

ARTEN: Possible? Yes. Difficult? Absolutely. The only way to do it is to always remember what everything is for, which is forgiveness. You, dear brother, don't always remember that right away, but you do eventually. Your forgiveness isn't perfect, but it is persistent. And as long as you do it, you'll make good progress. The time you delay forgiveness simply contributes to your own suffering!

GARY: So the kind of forgiveness you're talking about should also be applied to the cult leaders you were just discussing.

ARTEN: Yes, and as we said, you'll have a chance to forgive one of them in person, just as you'll have many new experiences to forgive in the next couple of years.

GARY: Great. Just what I need . . . more forgiveness opportunities.

ARTEN: Remember, that's what will get you home the fastest.

GARY: What about meditation?

PURSAH: The best form of meditation is the kind we taught you before, at the end of the chapter called "True Prayer and Abundance." That kind of meditation actually reflects the original form of prayer, which was silent and really about joining with God. By putting God first, and acknowledging Him as your one true Source, it not only helps to undo the separation in your mind, but can also result in the aftereffect of inspiration. I'm glad you still do that meditation five minutes in the morning and five minutes at night. That's really all you need. There *is* no better way to be inspired. You simply get lost in God's love, feel gratitude toward Him, and imagine yourself as being perfectly one with Him.

Remember something, though: There is no substitute for practicing forgiveness, and that's the spiritual "life in the fast lane" that our brother J was teaching by both word and example 2,000 years ago.

GARY: What about being in the now?

ARTEN: Where the practice of "be here now" will get you is here. Sure, it will relax you, but it won't get you home. One aspect of that kind of a system is to watch your judgments. But watching your judgments is not forgiving them. And the now that is experienced is *not* the eternal always of Heaven, which can only be consistently experienced when the ego has been completely undone by the Holy Spirit. That requires that you do your part to forgive, and the Holy Spirit takes care of the part of the job you can't see, deep within your unconscious mind. Then as you go along, you'll have experiences that tell you you're on the right track. Sometimes it will simply be a feeling of deep inner peace. That's a lot more important than you realize. If peace is the condition of the Kingdom, then your mind must be returned to a condition of peace before it can reenter the Kingdom. Otherwise it wouldn't fit in. It would be like trying to fit a square block into a round hole. The "peace of God which passeth understanding" is a prerequisite to going home. Once again, it's not achieved on a permanent basis until all unconscious guilt has been removed from the mind by the Holy Spirit. And remember what we said about teaching; there's nothing wrong with repetition. In fact, it's essential.

GARY: You already said that.

ARTEN: Funny. Yet you've no doubt had the experience of reading a paragraph in the *Course* that you know you've read before, but it's like you're seeing it for the first time. This also happens when people reread *The Disappearance of the Universe*. They know they've seen the words before, but they're getting it on a completely different level. The words haven't changed, but they have. The ego has been undone a little bit more, and now they're seeing the words from a different place. Repetition is important not just in learning these ideas, but in practicing forgiveness.

Sometimes it may look like you're forgiving the same thing over and over again. You forgive the people you work with. Then you go back the next day, and they're still there. But even if it looks like you're forgiving the same thing, that's an illusion, too. What's really happening is that more unconscious guilt is coming to the surface of your mind, and it's a chance for you to release and be rid of it by continuing to forgive.

PURSAH: We're going to take our leave shortly, but we'll be back in two months. When we return, we'll talk about power. Real power. What it is and how to use it. That will eventually lead to a deeper practice of forgiveness, which will show you how to end reincarnation by using the very things that come up in front of your face in the world where you appear to live and work.

GARY: I don't work here. I'm a consultant.

ARTEN: You still want to break the cycle of birth and death, don't you?

GARY: Sure, but you told me last time that I'm coming back for one more lifetime, so what's the deal? If I'm going to learn how to end reincarnation, then why do I have to come back again?

ARTEN: Don't ever forget, Gary: The Holy Spirit can see everything, and you can only see part of it. The *Course* teaches that the Holy Spirit "recognized all that time holds, and gave it to all minds that each one might determine, from a point where time was ended, when it is released to revelation and eternity."[12]

Did you ever stop to think that your coming back one more time might be a big help to others? You really only have one big forgiveness lesson to learn in that lifetime. By practicing forgiveness on the little things, as well as that one big thing, you'll serve as an example to others. As Pursah, you'll also be a tremendous help to me. Usually your final lifetime is not just a great lifetime for you personally, it's one where you perform a tremendous service for others, maybe publicly, but often not. It all fits together, like the hologram that it is. In order for all minds to determine when they're released, each must do their part to bring about the "interlocking chain of forgiveness which, when completed, is the Atonement."[13]

So play your part, brother, and be grateful. You have fascinating times ahead of you. So do many others. Remember we said that there are more people today than ever on this planet who either are enlightened or will be this time around. You're helping people to get that way by sharing the teachings. Some of them won't have to come back again, partly because of you! There's no better vocation than to share the truth with others and forgive as you go along.

PURSAH: Two months from now you're going to be hitting the road for the first time, flying all over the country and spreading the message. You'll be a little nervous and tentative at first, but that will pass if you use it for forgiveness. That's what it's for. Practice and you'll be fine. We'll be back with more just after you return from your first cross-country trip.

GARY: Wow! That's exciting. I haven't been to that many places, you know.

ARTEN: Just remember that it's all a dream, and just how happy a dream it is will depend on your forgiveness.

Arten and Pursah then disappeared instantaneously, but I felt a deep satisfaction that my friends were in my life again. I had become a little overwhelmed by all that had happened in the previous year, and it felt good to have some coaching. I had no idea at the time of the deep extent to which I would be challenged by both them and my life in the next two years.

⁂

2

REAL POWER

> The power of decision is your one
> remaining freedom as a prisoner of this
> world. You can decide to see it right.[1]

During the next two months, I often thought about what Pursah had said about experience. The previous year had not lacked forgiveness lessons as related to the publication of the book. The unseemly viciousness of a small minority of supposedly spiritual students on the Internet had come as a great surprise to me. Some of them maligned the book without ever having read it because they had some kind of a political ax to grind. I wouldn't have believed such people even existed within the so-called *A Course in Miracles* community. Having been initiated into this community, I quickly started to think of it as a family that needed to practice the very *Course* it claimed to believe in.

Fortunately for me, through my travels, I was about to get to meet the real *Course* community in person, and understand that unlike what I was sometimes seeing on the Internet, the over-whelming majority of these people were really interested in making the kind of amazing spiritual progress the *Course* was offering them. At the same time, there was an online discussion group about *The Disappearance of the Universe* (which, as mentioned previously, the members immediately started referring to as "D.U.") that was start-ing to grow. After a rough start because of some visitors who wanted to try to attack the book and me, the forum was turning into one of the most loving and supportive groups on the Internet.

I did the best I could to practice forgiveness, knowing that the habit of application would result in spiritual experience.

Success didn't always fit my pictures. Even with the book starting to do very well, there always seemed to be obstacles to overcome. This included attacks, which were sometimes subtle and sometimes outrageous. When things didn't appear to be going my way, I did the best I could to practice forgiveness, knowing that the habit of application would result in spiritual experience, whether in the form of inner peace or in the kind of unpredictable mystical experiences I had grown accustomed to. The *Course* taught me that I couldn't really be attacked on the level of my mind, although it could certainly *appear* that someone was attacking me. Still, at times the practice was very difficult, and I would delay my decision to choose the Holy Spirit as my teacher instead of the ego. This made me wonder why I couldn't *always* live the *Course* directive I was so fond of, which says, "Love holds no grievances."[2] Why was it possible to forgive some people and so difficult to forgive others?

I knew that the *Course* also taught, "As you see him you will see yourself."[3] Whatever way I looked at and thought about another person would surely create how I experienced myself and ultimately determine my own identity as either spirit or a body. I wanted to know why it was sometimes so hard to make the right choice.

Arten and Pursah said I was going to be traveling a lot. It was increasingly obvious that writing and speaking, and my forgiveness of what I had to do in connection with them, was going to be my work. Only six months before, I had never spoken in public. But now, after just a handful of talks and workshops, I was about to hit the road and engage regularly in a new vocation.

I couldn't help but think back to October of 1992, two months before my friends had first appeared to me. Things weren't going well for me financially, and I strongly considered going back to playing my guitar, which I had done for 20 years, in order to bring in some money. I took my Les Paul Custom out of the closet, stood in my living room with it on my shoulder, and started to practice. Both of my hands and arms were occupied playing the instrument. Suddenly, and to my astonishment, I felt another hand pushing the end of the neck of the guitar slowly but steadily toward the ground, and me along with it. It was as if an invisible entity was stopping me from playing, interfering in a firm but gentle way, and giving me a message I couldn't escape: *No, this isn't what you're supposed to do anymore.* I got the message. I didn't know yet exactly what I *was* supposed to do, but after this experience, I had a feeling it would show up. Two months later I saw Arten and Pursah for the first time, and eventually found out that I was being given a chance to dedicate the rest of my life to nothing less than a way to return home to God.

On my very first trip to California, at the end of February, I went to see Mel Gibson's just-released movie, *The Passion of the Christ.* I was taken aback by the suffering, brooding depiction of J and the horrific violence of the film. I looked forward to talking with my ascended visitors about it. I didn't have to wait long. Two months after their previous appearance, while sitting in my living room, Arten and Pursah were there with me once again. As always, their appearance was instantaneous, as if I were watching a television channel and then flicked the remote control, causing the picture to change instantly. My friend's entries and exits were very similar. It was as if they were changing frequencies or even dimensions, although I certainly didn't want to limit them.

ARTEN: You have a lot on your mind, hotshot. Where would you like to begin?

GARY: As I'm sure you know, I went to see Mel Gibson's movie, *The Passion of the Christ.* I'd like to talk a little bit about it.

ARTEN: Maybe a little, brother, but I think today would be best served by discussing other things.

GARY: Really? You usually talk about what I want to talk about!

PURSAH: There's a subject we want to cover later that can best incorporate Mel's take on the Crucifixion, but you *did* notice the little trick we played on you regarding the movie, didn't you?

NOTE: Pursah had told me during the first series of visits that if I wanted to see Christianity in a nutshell, all I had to do was go back to the old scripture (they never called it the Old Testament) and read The Book of Isaiah, Chapter 53, verses 5 through 10. Their statement was published a year before *Passion* was released. That part of the Bible talks about a lamb being led to the slaughter, and says: "By his wounds we are healed." It's the old idea that somehow you can atone for other people's sins through the sacrifice of an innocent. The problem is that it was written 700 years before J, and had nothing to do with him. It was about another prophet. Later, people would try to make a prophecy out of it and apply it to J, but it wasn't about him at all. They then took this belief, although it had nothing to do with what J was teaching, and superimposed it onto him, assuming that like them, he believed in a thought system of sin, guilt, fear, suffering, sacrifice, and death.

The "trick" Pursah is referring to is that they told me to read that section, Isaiah, Chapter 53, verses 5 through 10, knowing that the statement would be published before the movie came out. Then when I went to see *The Passion of the Christ,* the very first thing that Mel Gibson put up on the screen was a quotation. It was from The Book of Isaiah, Chapter 53, verses 5 through 10! What follows is a sample of those verses from the Bible, from which Mel also used an excerpt. It displays a thought system that was already in the unconscious mind, and was being expressed through the writer:

> But he was wounded for our transgressions, he was
>   bruised for our iniquities;
> Upon him was the chastisement that made us whole, and
>   by his wounds we are healed.
> All we like sheep have gone astray; we have turned every
>   one to his own way;
> And the Lord has laid on him the iniquity of us all.

He was oppressed, and he was afflicted, yet he opened
    not his mouth;
Like a lamb that is led to the slaughter, and like a sheep
    that before its shearers is dumb,
So he opened not his mouth.

And they made his grave with the wicked and with a rich
    man in his death,
Although he had done no violence, and there was no
    deceit in his mouth,
Yet it was the will of the Lord to wound him; he has put
    him to grief;
When he makes himself an offering for sin. . . .

Many centuries later, Saul of Tarsus, better known as the Apostle
Paul, who was in deep guilt over his killing of numerous Christians,
had a conflicted (part-ego) experience on the road to Damascus
that caused him to take up what he thought was the cause of Jesus.
Being a Jewish man who believed in the old scripture, it was not
surprising or difficult for Paul to incorporate the beliefs from the
above verses into his developing theology about J. This led to a
religion that lost most of J's true message and substituted it with a
thought system of their own.

My experience with *Passion* wasn't the first time my teachers had told me something while being aware that I would later
see or hear it at the movies, which they knew was my favorite
hobby. They had pulled a similar thing on me by saying, "People
are like ghosts, except on a seemingly different level. They think
their bodies are alive, but they're not. They just see what they
want to see."

A couple of years later, I saw the excellent film, *The Sixth Sense*,
written and directed by M. Night Shyamalan. When the boy in the
movie decided that it was time to tell the psychologist his secret,
two of the lines he said about the ghosts he was seeing were: "They
think they're alive. They just see what they want to see." I almost
came up out of my chair when I heard those lines during this somewhat scary and very fascinating film, knowing that my friends had

gotten me. But I also knew that they were doing more than just playing a joke. They had managed to bring the point home to me even more.

ARTEN: Yes, we were watching you at the beginning of the movie to see your reaction.

GARY: You mean the quotation at the beginning, "By his wounds we are healed." I guess if we're healed by them, then that would explain why Mel showed so *many* of them.

ARTEN: That's the ego thought system, brother. We'll talk more about that and the movie later. There's a section in *A Course in Miracles* called "The Hero of the Dream." When we get into that, we'll also discuss *Passion* and how the world's beliefs are so heavily rooted in the body.

PURSAH: And speaking of bodies, you know that "love-holds-no-grievances idea" you've pondered so much can be thought of as the antidote to the body. As that lesson in the *Course* says: "To hold a grievance is to forget who you are. To hold a grievance is to see yourself as a body."[4] You've been having a tough time with certain forgiveness lessons lately.

GARY: You know it. Why is it that some people seem so easy to forgive, and some so hard?

PURSAH: You've got to remember that the unconscious mind knows everything. It knows every relationship you've ever had, in any lifetime. You should also consider that the lifetimes you appear to go through are like a dance in which you play the role of victim in one lifetime and victimizer in the next. So a murderer in this lifetime gets murdered in the next one, sometimes by the same person whom they killed in the other lifetime. That's true with actions as well as occupations. A minister in this lifetime may be a prostitute in the next, and vice versa. In fact, the prostitute J saved from being stoned to death, who was *not* Mary Magdalene, had helped J in a lifetime previous to that. You're always switching roles. You may be a police officer in one of your dream lifetimes and then a criminal in the next.

GARY: Or worse, a politician.

PURSAH: Politicians have issues. Be kind to them. Then you're being kind to yourself.

GARY: I'm trying. Hell, I even succeed a lot. I used to get irritated when a certain politician, I'll let you guess which one, came on the TV screen. I'd react and get upset at how I perceived he was screwing up the country and the world. Then one day he came on the screen and I started to react to him, and I remembered the truth and started to forgive him. Like you taught me, that's the hardest part . . . remembering the truth when the stuff hits the fan. So I started to forgive him and then I thought, *You know, he doesn't even know I'm watching!* So who's the one who's suffering here? He's probably having a good time. He doesn't know it's an illusion. He thinks he's really the President!

PURSAH: Yes, forgiveness is always a gift you're giving to yourself, not the person you think you're forgiving. You're the one who receives the benefits, in both practical and metaphysical terms. True, you're acting as a reminder of the truth to the other person. All thought has effects on some level, and it's good for the other person, too. Not that the other person is really there. I'm talking about a seemingly split-off aspect of your own mind.

GARY: Yeah, I think that's really cool. I'm actually rejoining with myself at the level of the mind when I forgive. I'm becoming whole again. Plus, if I forgive, I don't suffer. And if I forgive after just 1 minute instead of 30 minutes, then that's 29 minutes of my life that I didn't spend suffering.

ARTEN: Yes. Do you remember how your father-in-law used to get so upset when Bill Clinton came on the TV?

GARY: I sure do. He used to actually get red sometimes. He'd even have to change the channel once in a while or leave the room. He suffered for eight years, and then he died. And I can almost guarantee you that Bill Clinton was having a good time.

Getting back to our "reincarnation instant breakfast" here, you seemed to be hinting that the reason I have a harder time forgiving some people more than others is because I've known the person who's hard to forgive in another lifetime, and I've got something going on with him or her that I'm not consciously aware of right now. And I understand what you're saying about how it *looks* like we're reincarnating, but we're really not; it's really just one big gigantic freakin' mind trip. We don't really go anywhere. It's like the *Course* says . . . we're reviewing mentally what has gone by.[5]

We're watching our own projection, which is actually coming from our own unconscious mind. It's like when I go to the movies. I want to forget that it's not real. I want it to be real, and my attention is diverted to the screen. Maybe I'll start reacting to the screen as I get into the story, but there's nothing happening there. The screen is just an effect, and the images I'm seeing are actually coming from someplace else. If I tried to fix the screen in order to change what's on it, it wouldn't do any good. But there's a projector. It's hidden in the back. I'm not supposed to think about that. Yet that's the cause. That's where what I'm seeing is really coming from.

> **We're watching our own projection, which is actually coming from our own unconscious mind.**

If I want to have real power, then I'd be a lot better off dealing with the cause rather than the effect. If I can change what's in the projector, namely the film, then that would change everything. But in life, or what passes for life, most people spend their entire lives trying to fix what's on the screen, which is just the effect, instead of changing the projector and what's in it, which is the mind and whatever thought system it adheres to.

The thoughts come first. I remember reading about doctors doing a study of depressed people and their thoughts. The doctors assumed the patients were having all these bad thoughts because they were depressed. But what they found out was pretty startling. It turned out that the patients were depressed *because* they had been having all these bad thoughts!

ARTEN: Very good. You know, you're almost coherent at times.

GARY: That's the nicest thing you've ever said to me.

ARTEN: Don't tell anyone.

PURSAH: By the way, you'll use that cause-and-effect movie analogy in your workshops. Your public teachings, along with your first book, will force other *Course* teachers to get more accurate about what the *Course* is teaching. Right now there are a lot of them who play fast and loose with the *Course*'s message. If you point out to them that what they're teaching isn't the same as what the *Course* is saying, then they'll call you a "*Course* fundamentalist"! Apparently a *Course* fundamentalist is anyone who thinks you should go by what the *Course* actually teaches. You'll go a long way toward ending all that silliness. Your message is so clear that other teachers won't be able to get away from it, and they'll have to adapt or else look like they don't know the *Course* very well.

I've got another compliment for you, also. I believe that in the last couple of years you've become a genuinely spiritual man.

GARY: That's right, baby.

PURSAH: So we can see how silly it is to deal with the effect and how important it is to deal with the cause, which is the mind. That's where the real power is. Before we do a little bit more of our review, we want to make sure you understand that all of your difficult relationships were set up ahead of time and that you wanted them.

GARY: Yeah, so someone comes along whom I did wrong in a previous life, which I've forgotten, and they give me a hard time, or worse, and I just think it's their fault. The truth is that in a previous lifetime I gave them a hard time, or worse, and they're just in the payback phase. Usually neither one of us knows why we're having such a hard time getting along with the other person. But the whole thing was really set up ahead of time in an ego-ridden script of time and space, where we take turns being the victim and the victimizer. Would you say that's accurate?

PURSAH: As true as a dream can be. The reason some of your forgiveness lessons are so hard is because your unconscious mind remembers the bad relationship you had with the other person in a previous lifetime, so you've been set up to have tremendous unconscious resistance to forgiving them in this lifetime. Plus, there's the resistance to giving up your personal identity that is always there, because the ego senses that if you practice forgiveness, then this is its end. *Everyone* has these past-life relationships, and the memories are unconscious. That's why it's so much harder to forgive your special hate relationships than your special love relationships.

GARY: It's easy to forgive your special love relationships—your family, friends, and lovers—just because you love them. On the other hand, your special hate relationships, the people you don't like, well, you're *never* gonna forgive those bastards because they don't deserve it. But you think the people you love deserve only good. So even if a member of your family killed somebody, you'd be right there in the courtroom, rooting for them to get off. Yet *real* love and forgiveness wouldn't exclude anyone. They apply to everyone. They're not special, but universal. The wholeness of them is what makes them real.

PURSAH: Yes. Now, part of what makes the unreal seem possible is that you make some bodies more special than others, and it's a trick so you'll find some of those bodies guilty in your mind and project your own unconscious guilt onto them, which is the reason you made them up in the first place. *But,* what if you really understood that those bodies aren't so special, if anything, just by the sheer number of them that you and those close to you have occupied?

GARY: How many bodies have I occupied?

ARTEN: Thousands of them.

GARY: You mentioned something about thousands of lifetimes during your last visit of the first series, but that seems like an awful lot.

ARTEN: Really? Would you like to see them?

GARY: What do you mean?

ARTEN: Hold on to your seat, brother. You're in for a mindblower.

GARY: Uh-oh. I don't know if I like the sound of that.

NOTE: What happened next made me gasp. Arten and Pursah began rapidly changing into different bodies before my eyes. Pursah became a black man, and Arten became an elderly woman. They stayed that way for two or three seconds so I could see them and then changed again. This time Pursah was a teenage girl, perhaps 16 or 17, and Arten was a boy of the same general age, reflecting the duality of male and female. All of these bodies looked perfectly real, just like Arten and Pursah's other bodies.

Suddenly they started to change even faster. Within a minute, there were two streams of bodies flowing in front of me, showing countless incarnations of different forms and dressed from different time periods. I then remembered that Arten had asked me, "Would you like to see them?" That's when it hit home. All of these bodies were me! They were showing me all of my different incarnations, thousands of them.

The rapid parade of bodies was hypnotizing. I felt almost drawn into the stream of forms, as though I could join with Arten and Pursah and change bodies myself. Then I realized that I had already been changing bodies as long as there had been time, which was why I appeared to be here now in the first place. Suddenly the idea of being "Gary" felt much less significant. If I appeared to incarnate as all of these bodies, then how special was the one I appeared to be in now? Arten and Pursah kept changing. There seemed to be a swirling energy throughout the room that peaked at the area of the couch where they were sitting. As the bodies went by, one would occasionally appear that didn't really look human, although they were definitely humanoid. I intuited that these were perhaps alien life-forms, but they were going by so quickly I couldn't get a very clear look, only a brief glimpse. Most of the bodies were a variety of men and women (and others not recognizable) of varying shapes, sizes, and colors: young and old, babies and the elderly, well dressed and practically naked. For what seemed like an hour, it kept flowing—this rapid, holographic show of apparently real bodily images—and then it all stopped instantly, with Arten and Pursah appearing once again in the same places where they started.

GARY: Hey, wait! Go back one!

NOTE: Pursah then became a perfect mirror image of my body as it appears now, but Arten disappeared.

GARY: Where's Arten?
PURSAH APPEARING AS GARY: Nice try, but it's not time yet for you to see who Arten is in this lifetime. We'll talk about that subject later on.

GARY: All right, all right. Can you go back one more?

NOTE: Now Pursah changed again and appeared as a man approximately 30 years old, and another man appeared where Arten had been sitting. Because of memories I had after Arten and Pursah's final visit of the first series, I realized that I was looking at Thomas and Thaddaeus, who were later called saints. The most impressive feature of the two, aside from their very kind demeanor, was the fact that they looked much shorter than the people of today. I was not given much time to gaze at them, as Arten and Pursah returned very quickly to the form of the bodies they occupied in their final lifetimes, which occurred in our future. A part of understanding this would be that time is holographic: past, present, and future all occur simultaneously, and, according to the *Course,* it's really already over. But we have to complete our lessons to make that real in our experience.

PURSAH: There. So now you've seen yourself as you appeared in the past as Thomas, as you look in the present, and as me in the future. You've also seen Thaddaeus as he appeared in the past, and as Arten in the future. I think it would be appropriate to let you relax for a minute.

NOTE: After sitting there for another minute or so with my mouth open in stunned contemplation, trying to absorb the astounding visual trip of the previous hour, I started to focus a little, and Pursah began speaking again.

PURSAH: The bodies you occupy in your various dream incarnations are symbols of duality. Thus, you have just as many lifetimes where you are rich as you are poor, good as you are evil, good-looking as you are unattractive to the eye, famous as you are obscure, healthy as you are sick; and every polarity, duality, and opposite you could possibly think of. None of them are true. It's all a trick. You are your own counterpart. Ultimately, the bodies that are not your own incarnations are also you. Like your own bodies, they reflect the oppposites of duality because they symbolize the condition of separation from God. Yet there can be no separation from God. Only God exists, and all else is false. The *Course* is completely uncompromising on that, for those who care to see it.

ARTEN: Remember what I told you before about the idea of separation from God. Because your idea is not of God, He does *not* respond to it. To respond to it would be to give it reality. If God Himself were to acknowledge anything *except* the idea of perfect oneness, then there would no longer *be* perfect oneness. There would no longer be a perfect state of Heaven for you to return *to*. As you will see, you never really left anyway. You're still there, but you have entered into a nightmare state of illusion.

> **Only the perfect, nondualistic oneness of God is real, and nothing else is real.**

GARY: Is that why Bill Thetford referred to the *Course* as the Christian Vedanta?

ARTEN: Yes! Bill understood what the *Course* was saying. Only the perfect, nondualistic oneness of God is real, and nothing else is real, which is exactly what that ancient Hindu text, the Vedanta, was saying, although of course, people then took it and misinterpreted it in much the same way they're doing today with the *Course*.

It's imperative that you stick to the message. Don't compromise on it. *A Course in Miracles* is purely nondualistic. We don't want the same thing to happen to the message of the *Course* that happened to J's message 2,000 years ago. That's one of the main reasons we're back: to help keep people focused, including you. We want you to tell it straight, and if someone criticizes you or your message, then after you forgive them, tell them that they are in error. You have the right to *not* remain silent.

GARY: What about that *Course* Workbook lesson, if I defend myself I am attacked?[6]

PURSAH: Remember that the teachings of the *Course* are *always* applied at the level of the mind, and *never* at the level of form or the physical. That's why it's a course in cause and not effect.[7] In your mind, you use right-minded ideas. Then sometimes after you forgive, you may feel you are being guided in some way by the Holy Spirit as to what you should do or not do. It doesn't have to happen that often. You don't have to be bombarded with inspired ideas. Just *one* inspired idea can make a huge difference in your life. That's inspiration, which comes as an aftereffect of forgiveness in much the same way as it comes as an aftereffect of true prayer.

GARY: These bodies you showed me, which were all me . . . what about the ones that looked like aliens? What's that all about?

PURSAH: You'll be told all you need to know, brother. Sometimes an incarnation doesn't take place as a human being, even though those who are human spend *most,* but not all, of their lifetimes as humans. It has to do with the way the universe is set up. What's important is that you realize what your lifetime is *for,* which is to use it to get home.

GARY: It's not gonna be easy for me to describe what I just saw.

ARTEN: Don't worry about it, just do it. Anyway, I could repeat a piece of advice we gave to you before. Don't spend a lot of time trying to describe us, and that would include the way we looked as Thomas and Thaddaeus. The purpose here is not to dwell on bodies. What we do is use bodies to teach you of the unreality of *all* bodies, and to stress that ultimately no body is more important or more real than any other body. That's what the Holy Spirit does. He uses the illusion to lead you out of the illusion. True forgiveness is an illusion, too, but it gets you home. Without it, you'd be stuck here in unhappy dreamland forever.

GARY: It's not always unhappy.

ARTEN: Just another trick, brother. I'm not saying it isn't good *sometimes.* But even then, without wholeness, it feels like there's something missing. What's missing is your perfect oneness with God. The universe of time and space is meant to cover over the one and only problem, which is the seeming separation from God, and especially the one and only solution, which is to go home through forgiveness. As the *Course* says, and this is very important: "A sense of separation from God is the only lack you really need correct."[8] If that's the *only* lack, then all the others are simply symbolic of the first and only lack.

Incidentally, as well as not spending too much time describing us, I'd like to point out that you made the right decision in not taking pictures of us the first time around and also getting rid of those tapes, which you should also do this time.

GARY: It was very tempting for me to hold on to them, you know.

PURSAH: We know. But if they got out, then people would have been distracted. Instead of focusing on the teachings, now the conversation would become about whether or not the tapes are authentic. Who's really on the tapes? There are already too many distractions out there. Use the tapes for your own purpose of accuracy, and then get rid of them again. If somebody doesn't like it or doesn't think you're explaining your actions adequately, then so be it. The bigger picture is more important. Let's keep people's focus where it belongs, bro.

GARY: Bro? You're reminding me of Hawaii. I've still only been there twice, you know.

ARTEN: Take heart, bro. You'll be there two more times within the next year or so, once on the way back from Australia.

GARY: Australia! Are you serious?

ARTEN: Not too serious, but you *are* going to those places to share the teachings.

GARY: I don't believe it! When I was a kid, a place like Australia may as well have been Mars, it seemed so unreachable.

ARTEN: Well, it's not unreachable anymore. Just remember when you get there that it's all a mind trip. Also, people are basically the same everywhere. They may speak differently, but they think pretty much the same. Eventually you'll be going to places where you'll need a translator.

GARY: Let's hope they do a better job of translation than that computer gizmo we tried.

NOTE: After the publication of *The Disappearance of the Universe,* my first publisher, D. Patrick Miller, and I heard that there was some talk about the book on the Internet from other countries. One of them was Holland. We found a Web page where someone was talking about the book and tried to have a computer program translate it. However, a computer program only knows how to give a literal translation, and simply provides the words that are the closest to those being translated. The computer can't translate the meaning, which is what a real translator does. In describing how I said at the beginning of the book that I felt as though I had a relationship with Jesus, the translation came out, "The writer bathed with Jesus."

PURSAH: That bathing-with-Jesus idea might go over in Holland.

GARY: I'd rather bathe with you.

PURSAH: I'll be kind and overlook that. You're still freaked out from seeing all those bodies.

GARY: Yeah, and you know, some of them weren't bad.

ARTEN: How about if we move on and save people a few lifetimes here? We haven't finished our review of the teachings. For example, we've talked about the unconscious guilt that's in the mind and how it has to be removed by the Holy Spirit. Why? How did it get there? Would you like to share some more of your learning with us?

GARY: Sure, as long as you correct me, if necessary. Let's say you have God, and God is perfect oneness. There isn't anything else. God creates, but what He creates is exactly the same as He is. It's a sharing of perfect love that's beyond anything we can understand with a mind that isn't whole. Yet the experience of it is so great that it's totally awesome. Anyway, there's this thought that seems to occur. It's a meaningless thought that's over in just an instant. It's totally insignificant. It's a separation thought like, *What would it be like for me to go off and create on my own?* That idea implies an individual existence.

As you mentioned, God doesn't respond to it. He's no fool and keeps reality perfect and one, but that thought of separation makes something different appear to happen in *our* experience. Now here's the hard part: It doesn't *really* happen. It only appears to. Just like it's possible for a dream I have at night to seem totally real, this dream may also seem totally real, but it's not. In fact, other parts of the dream are made to seem less real so we'll think that the most clear part of the dream *is* real. That's a function of levels, which can't even exist in perfect oneness.

This different experience that appears to happen to us is occurring on a massive metaphysical level. We'll call this experience *consciousness*. As far as I know, *A Course in Miracles* is the only spiritual teaching in the world that exposes consciousness for what it really is. The *Course* says: "Consciousness, the level of perception, was the first split introduced into the mind after the separation, making the mind a perceiver rather than a creator. Consciousness is correctly identified as the domain of the ego."[9]

People think consciousness is really significant because we want what we made to be important. So we glorify it and measure it and attach specialness to it when it's really just a symbol of separation from our Source. It's separation, because in order to have consciousness, you have to have more than one thing. You have to have a subject and an object. You have to have something else to be conscious *of*. That's where twoness came from to replace oneness. That's what makes the resulting symbolic illusory opposites, polarities, and dualities.

So from twoness springs forth multiplicity, but it's all symbolic of the original idea of separation. Multiplicity breeds chaos. But underneath it all there are basic ideas, and these ideas can only seem to be real when you experience yourself as being apart from oneness—for example, the ideas of scarcity and death. There can be no scarcity in fullness, but once you have ideas like separation and opposites, then you have the possibility of all kinds of weird things showing up. *That's* why it says in the Book of Genesis, "You shall not eat of the tree of knowledge of good and evil, for on the day you eat of it you shall die." Well, good and evil are opposites, and once you have opposites then you have death. There can be no death in Heaven, where there is only eternal life, but once you have opposites, then you have a seeming opposite to life, which is death. It doesn't really exist. That's why the *Course* says, right in its Introduction that "the opposite of love is fear, but what is all-encompassing can have no opposite."[10] What is all-encompassing is true, and what's not all-encompassing, or perfectly whole, doesn't really exist.

ARTEN: The *Course* also says, about your salvation, that "it restores to your awareness the wholeness of the fragments you perceive as broken off and separate. And it is this that overcomes the fear of death. For separate fragments must decay and die, but wholeness is immortal."[11]

GARY: *Immortal.* I don't recall the *Course* using that word very much.

ARTEN: You'd be surprised. Please continue.

GARY: All right. As a response to the false condition of separation, real forgiveness denies what *isn't* true and accepts what's true. As J puts it in his *Course,* "It denies the ability of anything not of God to affect you."[12]

ARTEN: That reflects the *Course*'s knowledge that "what is immortal cannot be attacked; what is but temporal has no effect."[13]

GARY: Okay, immortal guy. For most of us, our experience that we are *here* seems very real, but to understand *why* that's the case, we have to go back to the metaphysical level, which is now unconscious to us. We'll see why in a minute. But on that metaphysical level, before the universe of time and space was made, we feel an absolutely terrible loss, and we experience it on a scale that we can't even begin to imagine now.

PURSAH: Very good. You need to understand that before that, everything was perfect in your experience. You were totally taken care of, totally provided for, with no problems and nothing but ecstasy. The perfect joy of this cannot be translated into words. But now, with this idea of separation, it's as though you've made a major blunder. It's like you've lost God, which means it's like you've lost everything! The only experience in this world that could come close to matching how you felt at that time of the original separation from God would be if the person you love most in this world died. What happens when that person dies? You're separate. You think you can never get them back. Of course that's not true because no one ever dies, but it feels and looks that way to you. It's really a symbol of the first separation being acted out in this world. And the original separation, which was from God on that metaphysical level, has you feeling terrible.

ARTEN: Because opposites follow as a result of division, there are now two possible ways of thinking about all of this: the right way, which we'll call the Holy Spirit's interpretation, and the wrong way, which we'll call the ego's interpretation. God did *not* send the Holy Spirit to rescue you. The Holy Spirit could be said to be your memory of your true home with God, which is the right part of your mind. The ego is the wrong part of your mind. At first people think that the *Course* is talking to them as a person, because that's what they think they are. But the "you" that the *Course* is addressing is actually your seemingly separated mind that needs to choose to listen to the right teacher instead of the wrong one.

That's not easy, because you feel terrible, and the ego is going to play on your fears. In this new experience of consciousness, you think you've lost everything, and the ego is more than happy to make you think you've done something wrong. "You're in for it, man. God's very angry at what you've done." Now, if you've done something wrong, what's that but the idea of sin? And if you've sinned, then that means you're guilty. And if you're guilty, that means that you're going to be punished. But on this level, you think you're going to be punished by God Himself! That results in the fear of God, which you still have, even though it's unconscious to you. The terrible guilt in your mind over this is still buried there, but with the mind being holographic, the experience of the truth is still buried there as well.

> **The Holy Spirit could be said to be your memory of your true home with God, which is the right part of your mind.**

PURSAH: Yes, and that truth, given to you by the Holy Spirit, is a completely different story. The Holy Spirit's message is: "What's your problem? You know God. You've been with Him forever. He gives you everything. What's He ever done except love you? All you have to do is forget about this silly idea and go home. Problem solved."

ARTEN: The ego has to come up with something fast. It *likes* the idea of having a separate identity. So it says, "Look, you've got to get away, and I have a place we can go." The ego knows you're hurting and wouldn't mind getting away if you could, but you don't know how. So the ego says, "If you come with me, you'll be free of this terrible pain you're feeling." That's exactly what you want to get away from, but you're still not sure about giving up on what the Holy Spirit is saying. So the ego has to throw in a bonus. It says, "Look, if you come with me, then *you* can be God. You can make up your own life. You'll have your own personal identity. You can call the shots. You can be *special."* That's the icing on the cake. Now, not only are you going to get away from this terrible feeling you have, but on top of it, you get to be God!

GARY: I thought I was doing the review!

PURSAH: Is that why you were just talking to yourself a little during Arten's presentation?

GARY: Hey, if I can't talk to me, then who can?

ARTEN: Let's briefly explain why all of this seems so real to you today. The ego has an ingenious plan. When you choose the ego on the metaphysical level we've been talking about, it's the same as joining with it. There is then a massive *denial* of everything that is in the mind that we discussed. However, when you deny something, it has to go somewhere. You think you're escaping from it by denying it, but you're not. You're really just pushing it underneath the surface and out of your awareness. This causes it to be unconscious. So all of the new ideas that couldn't exist in wholeness—ideas like sin, guilt, fear, scarcity, death, attack, that whole can of worms—are denied and then *projected* outward. Even on the level of the world, a psychologist will tell you that projection always follows denial. But here we're talking about something on an incredible scale. As J puts it in the *Course,* "You do not realize the magnitude of that one error."[14] He also says, "Listening to the ego's voice means that you believe it is possible to attack God, and that a part of Him has been torn away by you. Fear of retaliation from without follows, because the severity of the guilt is so acute that it must be projected."[15] Do you get the stunning implications of all this?

GARY: I can't believe I'm going to Australia.

ARTEN: Moving along, we see that everything you wanted to escape from, all the terrible things you thought were true about yourself, which can be summed up in just a couple of words, like *guilt,* as well as the *fear* of punishment for the retaliation that you believe is going to follow because you're guilty . . . all of it is denied, projected outward, and *seen* as being outside of you. This causes the making of the universe of time and space, starting with the big bang. The real purpose of that universe, although you've forgotten it through denial, is for you to appear to escape what you're feeling and believing about yourself. Now it's no longer in you, it's out there!

Of course there isn't *really* anything out there, but it looks that way. It's an optical illusion, but done on a multisensory scale that we'll get to in a second. The thing to remember here is what the *Course* says about the fact that "ideas leave not their source."[16] So, yes, it may *look* like you've escaped from those things by projecting them outside of you, but it's just an illusion, and they're still in your mind. It just doesn't seem that way because it's been denied and you're oblivious to it. So it looks like it's outside of you, and you've forgotten that when you joined with the ego, you made it. That brings up a very important principle from the *Course:* "Projection makes perception."[17] In fact, why don't you read just the first few sentences of that part from the Text?

GARY: Okay, teach. What page is it on?

ARTEN: 445.

GARY: Right at the top. "Projection makes perception. The world you see is what you gave it, nothing more than that. But though it is no more than that, it is not less. Therefore, to you it is important. It is the witness to your state of mind, the outside picture of an inward condition."[18] Wow. I never quite thought of it this way. I *made* what I'm seeing?

PURSAH: You got it, brother. But it doesn't feel that way because of the massive denial. That also applies to all of the bodies you see, including your own. The purpose of the body is to make the illusion seem real. But since the body is part of the illusion, it can hardly be counted on to tell you of the illusion's unreality. It was given form by the same decision to be separate through projection, which is what made the entire illusion in the first place. You wanted the separation so the guilt would be in other bodies and not yours, and thus outside of you and in them. But because projection made the perception of everything, the cause of it all is still right there in your mind, and minds can be changed. As the *Course* puts it: "The result of an idea is never separate from its source. The idea of separation produced the body and remains connected to it . . . "[19]

So now you feel stuck in a body that has to live with all these other bodies. All of your senses, not just sight, tell you that the world is completely real. It looks and feels totally authentic. From the moment you're born to the moment you die, it's all about the survival and success of your body, from attaining material comfort to receiving special love. It doesn't take too much power of observation to see that your society is crazed over bodies and the attainment of sex.

GARY: I can understand that. I had sex once, and it was one of the happiest minutes of my life.

PURSAH: Don't forget something, dear one. In a world of duality, even the good times have to turn bad eventually, even if it's merely through death. That's because what's really going on here is the reliving of the separation from God over and over again in different forms. It's like playing a DVD of the same thing over and over again, separation. The way J puts it about your life is, ". . . you but relive the single instant when the time of terror took the place of love."[20]

GARY: I like that Jesus. He really sticks to the *Course*. So it may look like all these things and people are out there, but they're not. They're not real people; it just looks that way. I made what I'm seeing, then I forgot. And I wanted it to be the way it is so what I secretly believed to be true about myself, what the *Course* calls "the secret sins and hidden hates"[21] that I have buried in my mind about me over the original separation are now seen to be in others and in the world. And what holds the whole thing in place is my judgment and condemnation of others.

PURSAH: Yes! Exactly. And it's all set up to ensure that you will judge and condemn and keep the whole vicious cycle going underneath the surface. That's how the ego survives, through the projection of unconscious guilt. It's never *your* fault that you don't feel happy and peaceful, it's *their* fault. You see it at work in relationships, whether individual or with countries. Unless they're one of your special loved ones, or an ally, it's always the other one's fault, and they're not even there! Not really, although it certainly looks and feels that way, which is testimony to how well you've been set up in the first place. And even if you *do* blame yourself, what is it that you're blaming? Just another body, because when you hold your hand up in front of your face and look at it, what is that? It's a body that's been projected. Of course you think it's a very special body because you think it's you, but it's not. It's just one out of all of the bodies you've projected. That body you see when you look in the mirror is no more real than the other bodies you see in the mirror you call the world.

GARY: And the world and all of its bodies are symbolic of the separation, and the massive, ontological guilt we felt over it, and thus the need to escape from it through denial and projection?

ARTEN: That's what the universe is, brother, your scapegoat. As J says in the *Course*, "That was the first projection of error outward. The world arose to hide it, and became the screen on which it was projected and drawn between you and the truth."[22]

Now your job becomes to undo it in your mind, so you can return home. Which brings up the one solution, forgiveness, to the one problem, separation. We'll talk more about forgiveness as we go along. It's way more important than most people think. It's vital that they stay focused on it.

True forgiveness means you don't judge and condemn another. There's not really any sin and guilt out there, because none of what we've been talking about happened except in a dream, and dreams are not real. So J counsels you in his *Course* not to make the ideas of sin and guilt real in the people, events, and situations you see in the world: "Call it not sin but madness, for such it was and so it still remains. Invest it not with guilt, for guilt implies it was accomplished in reality. And above all, *be not afraid of it.* . . . When you seem to see some twisted form of the original error rising to frighten you, say only, 'God is not fear, but Love,' and it will disappear."[23]

GARY: If only it were that easy.

ARTEN: We never said it was easy, Gary. But the truth *is* simple. It's what the ego made that's complicated. And that's what needs to be undone by your forgiveness. The more the ego is undone, the easier it will get for you. You're already doing well. We're going to explain forgiveness off and on throughout the visits in this cycle. By the time we're finished with you, you'll know what to do in every situation, not just intellectually, but experientially.

For now, remember that if ideas have not left their source, then what you're seeing has never left the mind. If it's in the mind, and if minds can be changed, then the mind is where real power is. What made J and Buddha who they were was that they were not tricked by appearances. The illusion exists to make you think you have put distance in between you and your guilt, but by making it real and judging and condemning it, you simply keep it in place. The ego has tricked you. In order to ensure its own survival, it has set you up to judge others. Now that you know the truth, it's time to put an end to all of that nonsense and go home where you belong. You're actually still there, but it's out of your awareness, although you are fortunate enough to have had lovely glimpses of it.

We call it true forgiveness because it's not the same as the way the world usually thinks of it, and you'll have unconscious resistance to this kind of forgiveness because the ego senses this is its end, and would rather kill you than have you kill it. There are teachers who will tell you to make friends with your ego or make peace with your ego as a way of dealing with it. All that will do is keep it in place. Besides, if you practice true forgiveness, which is the only way out, then the ego isn't interested in being your colleague. As J says, you "are threatening the ego's whole defensive system too seriously for it to bother to pretend it is your friend."[24] Your job is not to keep the ego in place; your job is to undo it through the dynamic of right-minded thinking, which we'll be talking to you about. As the *Course* says: "Salvation is undoing."[25] It's time for you to turn it up a notch, bro. Not just for you, but for everyone who is ready to listen. Are you ready?

GARY: Hell, yeah.

PURSAH: One of the most important things is not to make the universe of time and space real. You're innocent because it's not real. Don't spiritualize the universe. Don't spiritualize matter or energy. Energy looks like matter to you sometimes only because of the way you perceive it and perceive yourself. You perceive yourself as being in a body, and then the body tells you what to feel. But you should be the one who tells the body what to feel. You are not in the body; the body is in your mind. When you put the mind in its proper perspective, then you're taking charge of the cause instead of being at the mercy of the effect. Then you can choose the Holy Spirit and His answer instead of the ego's questions. Thus will you be returned to wholeness. Because of that, how you experience things will change on this level, and the Holy Spirit will take care of the job on the larger, metaphysical scale.

Make no mistake: There's a difference in levels between this and other teachings. The rest of them are moving things around in a universe that isn't really there. That's like moving the furniture around in a burning house. Yes, it might look nicer for a little while, but it's denying the real problem. *A Course in Miracles,* on the other hand, is the undoing of all of it, and the return to the only thing that is real. Remember what we've said so far and integrate it. There will be more. Use your speaking and traveling the best you can as lessons for forgiveness, and we'll be back in two months.

Then Arten and Pursah disappeared, and I sat there thinking about everything they had said, and the many twists and turns my life had taken over the years. I realized now what it was all for. It was to be used to undo that which made it, and return to our real Creator. For some reason, I remembered back to when I was a depressed teenager suffering from scoliosis and with nothing to look forward to. I could have certainly used the knowledge back then of what it was all for. But I had lived long enough to find the Holy Spirit, and turn a meaningless existence into a life with purpose . . . and ultimately, the only *real* purpose.

❦❧❦

3

LIFE OF GARY

No one who learns from experience that one choice brings peace and joy while another brings chaos and disaster needs additional convincing.[1]

In the weeks that followed, I would occasionally remember what Arten had said about the ego. Would it really rather kill me than have me kill it? I knew the *Course* itself said that the ego is "capable of suspiciousness at best and viciousness at worst. That is its range."[2] That wasn't a pretty thought. But I also knew that the *Course* said: "Do not be afraid of the ego. It depends on your mind, and as you made it by believing in it, so you can dispel it by withdrawing belief from it."[3] So I came to feel that Arten wasn't trying to scare me, but to simply let me know what I was up against. How can a problem be fixed if you don't know what the problem is? I also thought it was interesting that the *Course* used the word *dispel,* because I was realizing that's exactly what the universe of time and space is, one gigantic motherfreakin' spell that I'd put myself under. Now my job was to dispel it by giving up my belief in the ego, a teacher I had listened to for much too long. My belief was now in the Holy Spirit, but that didn't mean I wouldn't be tempted by the ego.

I had been tempted all of my life. In fact, the *Course*'s idea of the ego's form of temptation was to regard myself as a body.[4] To that end, like everyone else, I was born as a perfect little victim. I forgot what came before birth and sincerely believed this was my beginning. Now I was totally at the effect of everything and not the cause. Now I was a body that was caused by other bodies. That way, it wasn't my fault. I didn't ask to be born. It was my parents' fault. They did it. Then this whole story got going about why things were the way that they were. But of course the truth was that I did ask to be born, and the world I found was exactly what I asked to be born into.

I was born in Salem, Massachusetts. Don't read anything into that. There were no witches in Salem 300 years ago—they all moved there in the 1970s. Now it's a really good tourist thing. My teachers had told me that the Salem witch trials were "a classic example of the projection of unconscious guilt." Somebody else has to be found who's the cause of the problem, and any excuse will do, as long as it's them and not you. But what goes around comes around, and your turn always arrives eventually.

My mother was a virgin. She just wasn't very good at it. All right, she wasn't a virgin. Of course, J's mother wasn't a virgin either, but it's a cute story. I was born two months premature. I weighed less than three pounds and wasn't expected to live. Babies that small didn't usually live back then. They shoved me in an incubator, stuck me in the corner as if to say, "Good luck, kid," and that was it for a while. Mothers didn't always bond right away with their infants like they do today. It was perfect. I had every excuse in the world to be screwed up.

I was born with scoliosis, a very noticeable curvature of my spine, yet I didn't find out about it until I was 31 years old. We didn't have any money. Back in the '50s, people who didn't have any money or health insurance didn't get good health care, and it's nice to see that some things don't change.

In hindsight, I can see that the scoliosis robbed me of all my energy. When the spine is malformed like mine was then, the energy can't circulate. It's as if the brain is sending a signal to the body, but the telephone line is down and the message can't get through. I didn't know at the time that it's the mind and not the brain that tells the body what to do. I was still at the effect of things.

As a result of that, by the time I was a teenager I didn't have much energy at all. I went to school only because I had to. Even then I missed about 30 days one year, and they threatened to kick me out. After school I'd usually just sit there in front of the TV and not want to do anything. My parents were starting to get worried: All of my friends were out finding jobs, getting girls, and having a good time, and I was sitting there with no desire or ambition. This made me feel different, like there was something wrong. That's right up the ego's alley. What's guilt but the feeling that there's something wrong with you? I'm sure I was depressed, but people didn't care about depression in the '60s. Now everybody's depressed, and you have the doping of America going on. But back then it was like, "Depressed? What do you mean you're depressed? Get a job."

Fortunately for me, a group came over to America from England called the Beatles. I remember walking one day in Beverly, Massachusetts (the town where I lived most of the first half of my life), which is just north of Salem, right on the seacoast. I went into a store called Hayes Music, which put records on so people could listen to them and decide whether or not to buy them. Somebody asked the owner to put on a record by this new group that was getting a lot of publicity and was going to be on *The Ed Sullivan Show.* The song was "She Loves You." After listening to that two-and-a-half-minute song, I was never the same. The guitar work by George Harrison sent shivers up and down my spine, which was really cool because I never felt anything in my spine. I knew right then exactly what I wanted to do. I was going to be a guitar player.

I *did* become a guitar player. The idea wasn't that much of a stretch. My father, Rollie, played guitar, and my uncle Doug was one of the best guitar teachers in New England. He had played on national radio (NBC), back before television, when radio was the big deal. If he had been willing to tour, he could have made it big. The same was true of my father, who was a fine singer as well. They were both in a famous group in the '40s called the Moonlight Serenaders, but they chose not to tour due to family considerations. They ended up making a living the best they could in the New England area, both as soloists and in various bands together.

My future uncle introduced my parents to each other. They were gentle souls, both Pisceans, and hit it off immediately. I was born a Pisces as well. My mother, Louise, and my grandfather were also musicians, but until the Beatles, I didn't have the desire to become one myself. George Harrison, God bless him, was my first false idol. I modeled my guitar playing after him, even though I learned the basics from Uncle Doug. I didn't become a *great* guitar player. It takes a lot of drive, energy, and ambition to be great at anything, no matter what it is. Natural talent isn't enough. It takes work to develop it. I did become a *good* guitar player, though. I had enough musical ability, which I had inherited, and enough taste to make myself sound good. Eventually I was even successful at it.

When the time came to graduate from high school in 1969, I found myself in a tough situation. I didn't want to go to college. I hated school. I couldn't imagine how they could take such fascinating subjects and somehow manage to make them boring, but they did. I also couldn't stand the cliques and the dynamics of belonging to one group and not another. I wanted out. All I wanted to do was play my guitar. But there was this thing going on called the war in Vietnam. There were about a hundred American men getting killed every week there, and that didn't even count the ten times that many who were getting wounded and maimed.

I wasn't excited about the idea of going to war, but America had a military draft. I also didn't want to go to college, but if I didn't, then I wouldn't get a college deferment, and I'd be classified 1A, which would mean I could be drafted and sent to Vietnam at any time. I didn't have enough political conviction to want to go to Canada or actively avoid the draft in some other way. My scoliosis wouldn't keep me out of the military unless I was rich or politically connected enough to have influence. After all, I could walk. I was classified 1A in March of 1970.

Fortunately for me, a man had been elected President of the United States in 1968, and took office in 1969, whose name was Richard Nixon. I despised him and his campaign promise that he had a "secret plan" to end the war. When he got into office, he sure knew how to keep a secret. I wondered how the American people could possibly be so stupid. (It would eventually take longer to withdraw our troops from Vietnam than it took the United States to win World War II.)

However, after taking office, Nixon did one of the biggest favors anybody has ever done for me. He got Congress to switch over to something called the "draft lottery system." The way a draft lottery works is they draw these little balls with dates written on them like it's a lottery. They draw all 365, or 366 days if it's a leap year, that they're doing the drawing for, and whatever order the days come up determines the order in which the people with those dates as their birthdays will get drafted. The order in which your birth date is drawn is your draft lottery number. If your birthday is drawn in the top one-third, say from 1 to 122 or so, you're almost certain to get drafted. If you're in the middle third, from 122 to 244, it's kind of iffy. *But* if your birthday is drawn in the bottom third, from 244 to 366, then you have almost no chance of getting drafted.

On July 1, 1970, the draft lottery was conducted for my birth year. I remember praying the old-fashioned way, "Please, God, have my number come up around 300 so I don't have to worry about this crap." When my birthday, March 6, was drawn, I was number 296. At the age of 19, I was free. I had played by the rules and lucked out. I didn't have to worry about being drafted. I was free to just play my guitar and live happily ever after, right?

That's not the way things work in this world. If you solve one problem in the universe of time and space, then what you get is another problem. That's the way it's set up so you'll keep looking for answers in the wrong place out there in the world where the problem appears to be instead of where it really is, which is in the mind that caused

If you solve one problem in the universe of time and space, then what you get is another problem.

the one real problem in the first place. The next problem I cooked up was that I started to drink. Then I started to drink some more. Then I started to smoke a lot of grass. And that pretty much covers the 1970s.

I knew that wasn't a good thing and that I was ruining my life. I didn't play my guitar very much, and I was drunk a lot. I was a lousy son, and I only lived for my next chance to get wasted. Both of my parents died during the '70s, and I felt terribly guilty over the way I had acted and some of the things I had said to them.

During this dismal time in my life, I tried to find ways to deal with my drinking and smoking, although I certainly didn't see pot as the main problem. I never got into trouble if I only smoked grass. It was when I drank that the dark side took over. For some reason, I never felt comfortable with AA, even though I knew it worked for a lot of people. I was a binge drinker. I didn't drink all the time, so I used that as a reason why I wasn't an alcoholic. Still, I at least recognized that I had a problem.

In one attempt to handle it, I decided that I was going to become a born-again Christian. I did, but it wore off after a little while. Later on I tried it again. I was actually born again a couple of times in the 1970s. The good thing about it was that I read the Bible, and it was actually a very interesting experience. There were a lot of things in the Bible I could agree with; for example, the idea that "God is love." That made sense to me. At one point it even said, "God is perfect love." That made perfect sense to me. The only problem was that if I looked someplace else in the Bible, He was a killer. He was wrathful and vengeful and getting even with people. That didn't make sense to me. How could He be both?

The Bible was too conflicted to ring true for me; however, when I looked at the parts where Jesus spoke, like in the Sermon on the Mount, which contained so many beautiful passages about love and forgiveness, it *did* ring true for me. But it was more than that. There was something about the nature of J's voice that seemed familiar to me. I felt as though I knew him. I couldn't quite put my finger on it, but for some reason I felt like he was my friend and that I could talk to him. It wasn't a religious thing. I've never been religious. I like to joke that in the winter I'm a Buddhist, and in the summer I'm a nudist. But even though I couldn't stick with Christianity, I never gave up on this relationship I felt with J, and it continues to this day.

Even after Arten and Pursah started appearing to me, it was still J whom I would talk to in between visits. He's the manifestation of the Holy Spirit for me, even though Arten and Pursah are also certainly manifestations of the Holy Spirit. I wouldn't realize exactly why I felt such a strong connection to J until Arten and Pursah explained it to me at the end of their first series of appearances.

After my foray into organized religion, which included two baptisms, I went back to drinking. I don't know if I ever would have stopped if it weren't for the opportunity to participate in a two-weekend experience that came to New England from California called the *est* training. Developed by Werner Erhard, "the training," as we called it, borrowed from other disciplines, including Zen and Scientology. It was a brilliant fusion of advanced metaphysical ideas, a sophisticated knowledge of how the mind works, and exercises that were designed to produce an *experience* on the part of the participants. I did the training at the Ramada Inn in East Boston in December of 1978. That was the turning point of my spiritual path in this lifetime. In the '70s and '80s, I didn't think in terms of spirit, but looking back, I can see that the Holy Spirit was working through my mind the whole time. The *est* training itself was eventually sold and evolved into other forms.

One of the themes of *est* was taking responsibility for your life. It was about *not* being a victim. It contained a couple of ideas I would see explained in more detail later in the *Course,* like the great Workbook lesson, "I am not the victim of the world I see."[5] *Est* also explained what the ego was, from a Buddhist perspective, how the mind is a survival machine and reality is not what we assume it to be. In fact, it explained how what we see with our eyes is not real, and the unseen is more real. It was a very auspicious introduction to spiritual and metaphysical themes, as well as an experiential breakthrough.

It was while doing *est* that I had what I would describe as my first mystical experience. A group of 20 of us at a time were told to get up on the stage in front of the other 200 people, be silent, stand still, and just look at the crowd. After a couple of minutes, I did a double take and looked at the people again. It was as though everyone in the room was moving in slow motion. I've found with many such experiences that there's an intuition associated with them that tells you, in an unarticulated way, what they mean. Somehow you just know.

In this case, even though it only lasted a minute or so, when I saw the crowd moving in this surrealistic, slow-motion sort of way, the experience associated with it was that I was the one who was doing it. Now I was the one in charge of time and space. I could make it speed up or slow down. Time wasn't something that was being done *to* me, it was being done *by* me. It wasn't coming *at* me; it was coming *from* me. This was a reversal of cause and effect. That was just the beginning of a learning process on the subject, but a fascinating one. It was also the first of a series of mystical experiences, usually very visual, that would apparently last for the rest of my life.

As a result of doing the *est* training and taking responsibility for my life, something shifted in my unconscious mind. People think it's the beliefs that they have in their conscious mind that runs them, and that they can control their mind by changing their thoughts from negative to positive ones. That's not true when it comes to the big picture. It will only have a temporarily helpful impact. What *really* runs us are the beliefs we have that are unconscious to us, the things we can't see. *A Course in Miracles* presents a way to actually heal and remove the things that are hidden in the deep canyons of the unconscious mind. Very few spiritual teachings do anything on that level. The *est* training, by recognizing the difference between cause and effect, did have an impact on the unconscious mind of many of its participants, including me. This was despite the fact that the training, like almost all other disciplines, did *not* understand the total picture or include the relatively rapid method of undoing the ego that I would learn over a period of years from my ascended friends.

NOTE: *Est* was developed by 1974, and *A Course in Miracles* was published in 1976, 11 years after its scribing began. I never saw a copy of the *Course* until the first week of 1993.

Just getting a taste of real power created a situation where I made an unconscious decision that I was going to change my life and get well. Although that decision was out of my awareness at the time, it did show up as an *effect* in the form of my conscious thoughts and behavior. As a result, within a few years I became almost the opposite of myself. My friend Dan Stepenuck and I started a band together. Dan was a great singer, and we had worked together in other bands before, but this time we had commitment and discipline. It was Dan who had introduced me to the training. Our group was excellent, and I went from being a guitar player who didn't work very much to one who was eventually working five or six nights every week, often twice a day on weekends. I also organized the band's jobs, and after a few years I had us booked two years in advance. We started to become well known in New England, and I was making good money. It was fun to be successful. People were recognizing me on the street from seeing me play, and my relatives didn't think I was a jerk anymore.

I made up for lost time and lived two meaningful decades in the 1980s to make up for the ten years I'd blown. I was going out and doing everything that time permitted: walking on hot coals, jumping out of airplanes, and having all the fun I felt I had missed. I still didn't know it was a dream. I thought it was real, and I was determined to make the most of it.

After a couple of years in the band, I met a woman named Karen. She was my type (female), but I had been painfully shy around women for years. When I turned 14 years old, a very bad case of acne destroyed my confidence. From then on, it would be impossible for me to just walk up to a woman and talk to her. For some reason, Karen and I hit it off. We felt comfortable with each other, and we were married within a year and five months from the time we met. The marriage was often difficult, and I would later say in public that we were each other's best forgiveness lesson.

It was a year later that my decision to get well would bring into my "space," as we called it in *est*, another way for that decision to play itself out. I heard about a chiropractor named Bruce Hedendal who had a practice in Gloucester and also was the chiropractor for the Boston Ballet. He was a genius at what he did. I went there with still not enough energy to do the things I wanted to do in life, and he told me about my scoliosis. He took out a mirror and showed me the curvature in my spine, which I had never seen. Bruce worked on me, and within two months most of it was gone. Not all chiropractors are created equal, but I had found a great one. Two years later, much to my chagrin, Bruce moved to Florida. But he helped turn my energy level around enough so that I could do what I needed to do without suffering. My scoliosis was not completely cured. To this day I'm still not a high-energy person and probably never will be, but by 1982 I could function satisfactorily, which to me seemed like a miracle.

During the '80s, my spiritual path began to accelerate. To show you how new I was to spirituality at the beginning of the decade, I remember doing an *est* seminar at the Bradford Hotel in Boston. They broke us down into small sharing groups of four people so we could relate our experiences. I was sitting across from a very sophisticated and highly intelligent woman who was a professor at Harvard, and I must admit that I was intimidated by her success and education. All of a sudden she started talking about a woman named Jane Roberts and how she was "channeling" this ancient being named "Seth," who was thousands of years old. Seth would speak and give enlightened information through this woman.

I remember looking at this professor and incredulously thinking to myself, *Is she serious? Does she really believe that? Does she really think that could happen?* Twenty-three years later, I'd find myself standing in front of groups of people and telling them that two ascended masters appeared to me in person on my living-room couch. I couldn't help but feel that there was probably someone out in the audience who was thinking, *Is he serious? Does he really believe that? Does he really think that could happen?*

I read a few spiritual books in the next few years. I wasn't much of a reader, but I enjoyed some of them. When I read about things like Buddhism, Hinduism, and Taoism, I realized that I already knew most of the things that were being taught. Studying reincarnation brought home for me the idea that the reason I already knew most of these things intuitively was that I had studied them before in other lifetimes. My spiritual memories were reawakening in my mind.

In 1983, four years after my mother had passed and seven years after my father had, I had a dream that was nothing like a dream. It was real, or at least as real as any other experience I've ever had. Both of my parents came to me. There was no need to say anything. The two of them walked up to me, and we all hugged very closely for a long time. It was an experience of total love. I felt them there with me; their touches were real, and they were saying not with words but with their love that everything was all right. They were absolving me, forgiving me, and loving me. It was so real that I knew they were fine, and as far as they were concerned, everything was forgiven. That's not to say that I had completely forgiven *myself,* but this experience was both a symbol and a bridge for me to cross, and the realization that I didn't have to spend the rest of my life in guilt. I understood that all my parents ever wanted for me was happiness and love, and the beautiful and liberating realization of that would always stay with me on the road ahead.

I also experimented with meditation. Rather than learning what others were doing, I seemed to know what I should do and developed my own technique. However, I didn't really take the time to practice enough and perfect it. That would come later.

In the next few years, there was a heightening of my visual mystical ability. It got to the point where I would go to bed at night and close my eyes, and while lying there still awake, I'd see scenes, like a movie, parading in front of my eyes. The images I saw appeared to be from past lifetimes, often with sound. Once in a while I would make a connection between a person I was seeing in my "third-eye movie," as I came to think of it, and a person whom I knew in this lifetime. The scenes were often visually stunning. One would involve American Indians hunting, talking in a group, or walking along a river. Another would be on a ship, another in front of a fireplace in a small house.

Despite popular myth, the Holy Spirit doesn't always spell things out for you.

I didn't always understand what I was seeing or where and when the events were taking place. Despite popular myth, the

Holy Spirit doesn't always spell things out for you. It's like Spirit is leading you, giving you hints until you yourself are ready to have the "Aha!" experience you're being led to. You're shown pieces of the puzzle, whatever is best for you at the time, and then usually you put it all together later when you're ready, exactly when you're supposed to.

Such experiences were enthralling at times, and I wanted to develop my spiritual life. After seven years of being in the band, which was called "Hush" (not to be confused with another band of the same name that exists today), I realized that I wasn't really happy, which was a shocking realization for me. I had done almost everything I wanted to do in the previous few years, but it wasn't fulfilling. Something was missing. I didn't know what, but I knew I had to find out. This was disturbing because not doing anything didn't make me happy, and now doing everything didn't make me happy either. Would I *ever* be happy?

During the Harmonic Convergence in August of 1987, I made another decision to change my life. When an interplanetary alignment like the Harmonic Convergence occurs, it looks like it's happening out in the sky, but that's just a symbol. Where it's really taking place is in the unconscious mind. Then it shows up out in the sky. At a time like that, people are making decisions on a collective level that will change their attitudes and goals, and in some cases their places of residence and their careers. I realized that I wanted to quit my life in the fast lane and find a quiet place where I could think.

Because I had my name on many signed contracts, it took more than two years for me to get out of the band, but at the beginning of 1990 I found myself driving to the town of Poland Spring, Maine, with Karen and our dog, Nupey. This was only 120 miles from Beverly, Massachusetts, but a world apart. Once you get north of Portland, Maine, it's nothing like Massachusetts, which is fast and sophisticated. Northern Maine is slow and simple. It's the most heavily wooded state in America; 90 percent of the land is covered with trees. There's clean air, clean water, and the lowest crime rate in the country.

If I wanted peace and quiet, I'd come to the right place. If I wanted money, I hadn't. I had a vague idea of starting a business and making a living. When I got to Poland Spring, there were no sidewalks and not many people. I should have done more research, but my life in Massachusetts was too demanding of my time. I tried to be a trader of the financial markets, but no matter how much I learned, my knowledge of the markets and how they worked didn't enable me to make enough money to pay expenses and make a profit. I was too undercapitalized, and it was all very frustrating.

A welcome breakthrough came in the form of meditation. I got to the point where I could shut off all interfering thoughts and achieve absolute stillness. With a quiet mind, I sometimes felt as if I were getting in touch with something deeper, that vast collective unconscious that's underneath the surface, just as most of an iceberg is underneath the surface of the ocean. The magnitude of these experiences was far greater than I would have ever expected. It was as if I were connecting with something huge and amazing. I didn't completely understand it, but I did experience it. I was onto something, and practiced every day.

My meditation always provided a welcome break from the rest of my life, which was in turmoil. After a while, I realized that I didn't really like Maine and its hard, cold winters. I was a city boy. Sometimes I'd ask, "What am I doing here?" I didn't know that Maine was exactly the right place for me to be in order to facilitate what was to come. There was a great deal of financial stress during those first three years. My wife and I sometimes argued loudly. This was a bizarre counterpart to the quiet of my meditation. Nobody in the world could push my buttons in the way she could. Sometimes I was ready to say the hell with everything and go sleep on a beach in Hawaii. My life hadn't sucked this much since the '70s, yet there was an underlying feeling that kept me going. I couldn't confirm it with any evidence, but there was a thought that kept coming to my mind, the thought that this was all for a reason.

By the autumn of 1992, all of my spiritual learning of the previous 14 years came to a head. I had come to the conclusion that the only viable thing for me to do was to remove conflict from my life. Any drunk who's ever been facedown in the gutter and survived has said in some form to himself, "There's got to be a better way."

69

At the end of 1992, after three years in Maine, Arten and Pursah made their first appearance before me. Within a couple of weeks, I began to realize that yes, I had come to Maine for a reason. As time went on, I couldn't see how the events that transpired could have possibly happened for me anywhere else. There's no such thing as an accident, and what was to occur the rest of the decade and beyond gave me an appreciation for the fact that when things don't look the way I expect them to, it's time to stop questioning and start trusting.

In April of 2004, I made my second trip of the year to California. I visited both the San Francisco area and the southern part of the state. One day I was staying at the Hyatt on Sunset Strip in Hollywood when I was about to get in the elevator and go to the top of the building where the swimming pool was and take in the view. Suddenly four people came over. One of them, a woman, got in front of me and said, "You don't mind waiting for the next elevator, do you?" I was surprised, but then I looked over and saw that one of the individuals was none other than Little Richard, the iconic rock star. In the '80s, I had played my guitar at over 3,000 gigs, so I had enormous respect for great musicians. I said to the woman, "Sure, go ahead." I understood that it was her job to keep him from having to deal with fans and photographers, and I was happy to let them use the elevator first.

Then something very cool happened. Seeing that I was letting him go first, Little Richard came over to me and said, "Is this okay with you?" I said, "No problem. It's good to see you." Then Little Richard, a legend to anyone who knows the history of rock 'n' roll, looked me right in the eyes and said, "It's good to see you, too." As he got in the elevator, I thought, *Wow! This is the guy whose voice Paul McCartney imitated on "Long Tall Sally" saying it's good to see me, too!* It was a fun moment for me, and I soon thought of it as being a Holy encounter. Also, when I got home, I made it a point to rent and watch a movie I had seen once before called *Down and Out in Beverly Hills,* in which Little Richard was excellent as the rock-star neighbor.

At the end of April, it was time for Arten and Pursah's next promised visit. I knew that they wouldn't miss their appointment.

PURSAH: Hey, teacher of God. What have you been up to?

GARY: Oh, you know, the usual: heal a few sick, raise a few dead.

PURSAH: How'd ya like California?

GARY: I loved it! As I'm sure you know, I saw a lot more of it this time. It was great.

PURSAH: Good. You'll be going there many times. Enjoy.

ARTEN: We're going to stick to basics this visit because we want you to always be clear about where you should be coming from. For example, the Introduction to *A Course in Miracles* says: "Nothing real can be threatened."[6] What would you say that means?

GARY: Well, what's real is Spirit. And Spirit would be synonymous with God and Christ. In Heaven, there's no difference between you and God. We only need words as long as we think we're here to eventually lead us beyond all words. That being understood, spirit such as God would be immortal, invulnerable, and something that can't be threatened in any way by this world. It would be eternal and changeless, because it's perfect. It's something that literally can't be touched by anything in this world. That's our reality, and our reality is beyond anything that can be threatened. We can experience that reality even when we still appear to be here.

PURSAH: Okay. That same Intro says: "Nothing unreal exists."[7] What do you say?

GARY: That would be anything that *isn't* changeless, perfect, immortal, and invulnerable. Obviously the body would fall into that category. All those bodies I see out there don't really exist. That's because they're a product of my mind. It's only in my attitude that those bodies don't exist that I can experience that my body doesn't exist, and that what I really am is that which can't be threatened in any way.

ARTEN: Pretty smooth. You've been doing really well on the road, by the way. I couldn't have done any better myself. Well, yes, I could, but I'm trying to make you feel good.

GARY: Funny, you least famous of the disciples. I am having a good time traveling, though. I feel like Dan Aykroyd in that *Blues Brothers* movie. I'm on a mission from God.

ARTEN: Excellent, just as long as you remember not to take it too seriously.

PURSAH: The next line in that *Course* Introduction is: "Herein lies the peace of God."[8] That's self-explanatory. The reason we bring up the Intro is to stress the fact that when we're talking about forgiveness, we're talking about a choice. The choice is, what are you? Are you something separate from God? Are you an individual? Are you living in this world, really? Are you mortal? Are you a body? Or are you spirit, one with your Source, changeless and eternal, immortal and totally invulnerable? If you are the latter, then there's nothing to forgive. Only a body has grievances to forgive. So forgiveness is a choice of what you want to believe yourself to be by choosing what the other person is.

The *Course* puts it this way: "What is in him is changeless, and your changelessness is recognized in its acknowledgment. The holiness in you belongs to him. And by your seeing it in him, returns to you."[9] The ego, the part of your mind that wants to be special and have an individual identity, wants you to see others as separate bodies in order to perpetuate itself. The ego is not you, but as long as you see your brothers and sisters as bodies rather than perfect spirit, you are playing into the ego's desire to have you choose its thought system. As the *Course* also says: "You who believe it easier to see your brother's body than his holiness, be sure you understand what made this judgment."[10] What made it was the ego, and the Holy Spirit is now trying to get the part of your mind that chose the ego to choose once again. "Choose once again what you would have him be, remembering that every choice you make establishes your own identity as you will see it and believe it is."[11]

GARY: I hear you loud and clear, yet that's easier said than done.

ARTEN: Few have ever gotten to the point where they did it consistently through the discipline of a trained mind, up to and including forgiving the death of their body. That's why Nietzsche said, "There was only one Christian, and he died on the cross."

The key is mind training. How many people in the world really have a mind that is trained to think right-minded ideas? You'd have to meet thousands of people to find one. Because of Buddhism and the dissemination of *A Course in Miracles,* there are actually more of them now than at any point in history, but there are also more people.

That brings up the importance of doing the Workbook of the *Course.* The *Course* itself says that it's doing the exercises in the Workbook that makes the goal of the *Course* possible.[12] The mind will go to such lengths to avoid what the *Course* is saying and delay the clarification of it that people will read the Text and interpret it, usually incorrectly. They'll ignore the definitive statements of the *Course,* which we'll talk more about later, and start nit-picking and focusing on individual words or phrases that when taken out of context seem to support their interpretation. Yet everything the *Course* says *must* be put within the context of the *Course*'s larger teaching, which shows up unmistakably in those definitive statements.

Doing the Workbook helps the student focus on applying the larger teaching of the *Course* rather than giving in to the temptation to see the trees instead of the forest. It trains the mind to think along the lines of the theory that is *really* set forth in the Text. If people read the Text of the *Course* without doing the Workbook, then they have not done the *Course.* It's that simple. The *Course* itself says so. In the Manual for Teachers, J is talking about how much quiet time a teacher should spend with God at the beginning of the day, then he says, "This must depend on the teacher of God himself. He cannot claim that title until he has gone through the workbook, since we are learning within the framework of our course."[13]

GARY: Boy, I forgot about that. I did the Workbook, but only once. That's enough, right?

PURSAH: Yes, absolutely. You did all of the lessons and didn't do more than one lesson per day. Those are the only rules. I happen to know that you'll do the Workbook a second time, but for the most part all you need to do is read it once in a while after you've done it. It's always good to read the different parts of the *Course* as a refresher. That prevents the ego from bouncing back, which it will surely do without vigilance on your part.

ARTEN: Remember that what is immortal is permanent, and what is mortal is impermanent. The reason we talk about the disappearance of the universe is because when you wake up from a dream, the dream disappears. That's only possible because it was never real in the first place. Some people will think that means they're giving something up.

GARY: Just the universe.

ARTEN: Not the real universe. It's what you awaken *to* that matters. The universe of time and space was impermanent. What you awaken to is permanent. Your immortal reality is something that's constant. It never shifts or wavers. What people need to get is how much better their real life is than the one they thought was their life.

GARY: Well, according to what you've said, every time I choose to see people the way the Holy Spirit would have me see them instead of the way the ego wants me to see them is a step home.

ARTEN: Yes. Think of the Hindu analogy of undoing the ego. It's like peeling an onion. To adapt that analogy for our purposes, let's say you forgive someone, in the *Course*'s sense of the word. It's like peeling away a layer of an onion, or in this case, a layer of the ego. Maybe it will look to you like nothing's happened. Why? When you peel away the layer of an onion, it still looks like an onion. It still looks the same. But it's not really the same, because a layer of it has been peeled away.

Now, let's say you have perseverance. Maybe you occasionally have experiences of being very peaceful that encourage you. Or maybe something happens that would have made you feel bad in the past, and this time it doesn't make you feel bad. You realize that it's because you've been practicing forgiveness, and that the Holy Spirit is healing your mind at the level of the unconscious. So you keep going and you forgive again and again. What happens is another layer of the onion is peeled away. It may still *look* the same. So you go in the bathroom and you look in the mirror and you think it's the same old you, but it's not.

Maybe you're watching TV and you forgive a news story that you see. Another layer of the onion is peeled away, but you think nothing's happening. In the meantime, the Holy Spirit is shining your forgiveness everywhere throughout the mind that is projecting the universe, and thus through the projection as well. It cuts through unconscious guilt and its projections of karma like a laser beam. It goes through all of your past lives, all of your future lives, all through the different dimensions of time, everywhere in the universe of energy and form, and through every parallel universe that appears to exist. Incredible things are happening! The Holy Spirit is actually collapsing time as you sit there.

Because of your practice of forgiveness, there are lessons that you no longer need to learn, and the Holy Spirit is actually erasing the tapes, taking dimensions of time that held lessons you would have needed to learn if you didn't practice forgiveness, and making those dimensions disappear. And because you can't see everything that the Holy Spirit can see, you're sitting there thinking, *This is boring. Nothing's happening.* But something amazing *is* happening. More layers of the onion have been peeled away, and your ego is vanishing.

If you persevere and continue to practice forgiveness, then at some point you get down to the final layer of the onion. When you peel away that layer of the onion, then there's nothing left. The onion is gone. And that's the way it is with the ego. After your final forgiveness lesson, the ego is gone; it's been undone, and there's nothing left to interfere with your experience of what you are. There's no reason for you to reincarnate. Practicing forgiveness the way that we will continue to instruct you is how to break the cycle of birth and death.

GARY: Which ties in with that other part of the Introduction, where it talks about "removing the blocks to the awareness of love's presence."[14]

PURSAH: You got it. That's exactly what happens when you choose the Holy Spirit instead of the ego. Every act of forgiveness undoes the ego, and the Holy Spirit removes the blocks to the awareness of God, or spirit's presence. The blocks are those walls of guilt in the mind that keep you from your awareness of what you really are.

GARY: I've been using that Introduction before I go out to give my workshops. I join with J, and I say, "I am what you are. Nothing real can be threatened. That's spirit, which is what I really am. Nothing unreal exists. That would include all those bodies out there that I think I'm going to speak to. And if it includes those bodies, then it includes my body, too. And if I'm not a body, then I don't have anything to defend and nothing to worry about." I do that every time.

PURSAH: Very good. I also like it when you use that section from early in the *Course* about being there to be truly helpful. That invites the Holy Spirit to be in charge of the whole day, and it works very well.

GARY: Hey, you've been watching!

PURSAH: Why don't you recite it now? J gave it to Helen early in the scribing of the *Course,* but it was really meant for Bill at first. Of course, ultimately it was meant for everyone. But Bill had to get up and give this talk to a group of psychiatrists at Princeton, and he wasn't the kind of a person who would normally get up and speak. He was a lot like you; he was very introverted, which most mystical people are. They're used to going within, not being out there. So when Bill thought of J's words, it relaxed him, because he knew that the Holy Spirit was right there taking over.

GARY: Okay. It goes something like this. Actually it goes *exactly* like this:

I am here only to be truly helpful.
I am here to represent Him Who sent me.
I do not have to worry about what to say or what
    to do, because He Who sent me will direct me.
I am content to be wherever He wishes, knowing
    He goes there with me.
I will be healed as I let Him teach me to heal.[15]

ARTEN: So let's add the third way to be inspired, or in spirit. You join with the Holy Spirit. It's as simple as that. By putting spirit in charge, you are absolved of any responsibility and any guilt. Now it's the Holy Spirit's responsibility, which is also true of your books.

Of course, the more you do your forgiveness homework, the more free your mind will become from the blocks to hearing spirit. And the more you practice joining with God in the silent form of true prayer we talked about, the more clear you'll be to listen to spirit. Then, finally, there's the third method, which is the conscious act of joining with spirit whenever it's appropriate in order to help yourself or others in a situation that calls for it.

Remember this, also: The Holy Spirit will not always show up to you as a Voice. The Holy Spirit can show up in the form of intuition, an idea, or a feeling and can speak through another person you're listening to, and suddenly you may realize that what you're hearing is a good idea. Spirit can teach you in your dreams. There are numerous ways for the Holy Spirit to show up for you. Always be open to that.

GARY: Ah, yeah. I think I'm kind of open to that. Am I wrong, or did you guys just pop up out of nowhere? Hey! Do you remember the first time you ever appeared to me? I didn't know what the hell to think!

PURSAH: Yes, but we knew you were ready for it.

GARY: Both of you looked so peaceful, so it was reassuring, and the way you talked, well, I just kind of fell into it. What's strange is how normal it seemed. I'd get to talking to you and forget about the circumstances for a minute or two, and then all of a sudden I'd think, *Jesus Christ, these people just materialized out of thin air!* Then it would seem strange. Then you'd say something, and I'd start talking to you again, and it would seem normal. So we'd keep going for a while, and then all of a sudden I'd think, *Jesus Christ, these people just materialized out of thin air!* It was wild.

ARTEN: Maybe so, but the fact that we're appearing to you now is no more strange than the fact that you think *you're* appearing here right now. The appearance of our bodies is not happening in the way you're used to, but it's still no stranger than the appearance of other people's bodies. The main difference is that unlike other bodies, which are projected as a result of the thought of separation, our bodies are projected by the right part of the mind, where the Holy Spirit dwells. The purpose of them is to teach, in a way you can understand, that all separation is unreal. That *doesn't* mean that the Holy Spirit is projecting these bodies. It's the love of the Holy Spirit that is behind the appearances. Then it's the right part of the mind that gives form to that love. That's also true of the Holy Spirit's Voice. He may sound to you like some guy who speaks English. But the Holy Spirit is *not* some guy who speaks English. The *love* behind the Voice is the Holy Spirit's, but the form of it comes from the right-minded part of the split mind.

Speaking of the right part of the mind, we're going to give you two forgiveness thought processes that we want you to practice. We want you to use one of them on yourself, and the other one should be used to practice on the bodies that you see as being outside of you. They're really all the same, but we're giving you this idea so that you'll have someone to practice on when there's nobody else around. When you're alone, you can think of yourself while you say this first one. Or maybe when you're looking in the mirror. That would be a great time for you to say these words. Repeat after me:

I am immortal spirit.
This body is just an image.
It has nothing to do with what I am.

GARY: I am immortal spirit. This body is just an image. It has nothing to do with what I am. All right. I'll try it.

ARTEN: Good. You're a typical person in the sense that you have a tendency to project your unconscious guilt onto other people and make them wrong. But everybody has times when they blame themselves. This is for those times. When you're beating yourself up, remember this forgiveness thought process. Now, this will be especially useful for those who have a habit of blaming themselves. There are people who project their unconscious guilt onto their own body instead of others. That brings up a disturbing subject.

Suicide is the biggest problem in the world that the world is in total denial of.

Suicide is the biggest problem in the world that the world is in total denial of. It's the dirty little secret of the ego. Sure, people know about suicide, but they have no idea how widespread it is. *More people die from suicide than are killed by all of the wars and all of the crime in the world combined.* As just one example, more firefighters die from suicide than are ever killed in fires. Nobody wants to talk about it. Nobody wants to examine it. If someone is depressed, the system will put them on drugs and never look at the reasons. That's because the ego doesn't want to look at the issue of unconscious guilt, which is the real cause of suicide. The ego runs away from looking at it as fast as possible.

In Japan, there are groups of teenagers who meet on the Internet, go out in vans, and kill themselves together. That has also spread a little bit to Europe. I suppose you can imagine how parents in America would react to that kind of a situation.

GARY: Yeah. First they'd freak out, then they'd put more people on drugs. It's amazing how Americans don't have any problem with drugs as long as the right people are making money from them. The corporations and the government they run have everybody brainwashed. But I digress.

PURSAH: Remember, some of these drugs are necessary as a temporary measure for people. Not many can tolerate being healed all at once. That could be too threatening to their ego. Then feeling threatened, the ego could go ballistic and find another way to hurt them, perhaps a worse way. Don't forget that the nature of duality is that you have good and bad. Yes, the corporations have people brainwashed. People vote against themselves in your country. But at the same time there are a lot of new medicines that help people, especially older people, to not suffer the way they used to. Your parents could have used some of the medicines they have today. Their lives would have been more comfortable and less painful. They weren't quite ready to accept that it's all done by the mind. Don't just look for the bad. You don't want to be cynical. You want to be love.

GARY: Okay, beautiful. I can take a hint.

PURSAH: The long-term cure for all of this is forgiveness. As we've pointed out before, and this is very important, the *Course* says: "Atonement does not heal the sick, for that is not a cure. It takes away the guilt that makes the sickness possible. And that is cure indeed."[16]

GARY: It seems that you hear about suicides, but then that's it. There's no more discussion about it.

PURSAH: Yes. Given that the *Course* is the only teaching that not only addresses but completely explains the issue of unconscious guilt, it shows you how vital it is to make this teaching more available to people. Right now most of the people who teach it don't even understand it. And the ones who quote from it without teaching it certainly don't understand it. They take lines from it out of context to support what they're teaching. But what the *Course* is teaching is that you can undo the ego that's in your mind, have the Holy Spirit heal all of your unconscious guilt, and be free. The fastest way to do that is to change the way you look at other people, events, and situations. It also teaches you how to do that. Be grateful that you're one of the people who is privileged to spread this message. But don't stop there. The most important part of the *Course* isn't what it means. The most important part of doing the *Course* is applying it to your life.

ARTEN: That brings up the second forgiveness thought process we want you to do, and of course also share with others. This is how you should always think of another person. Memorize it and say it in your mind to others when it's appropriate. Obviously there will be times when you're carrying on a conversation with someone. Don't stop and think of this and then say it to them in your mind. Carry on a normal conversation. Always be appropriate. Don't be weird. When you don't have to talk, and you have a chance to send these words in your mind to another mind, think of the following. Repeat after me:

You are Spirit.
Whole and innocent.
All is forgiven and released.

GARY: You are Spirit. Whole and innocent. All is forgiven and released. Cool.

ARTEN: Yes, very cool. I used to say something very similar to my patients in my final lifetime. Saying those words in your mind to another is a way to have it be true about yourself in your own unconscious mind, and it allows the Holy Spirit to heal and release the unconscious guilt that binds you to the universe of form. The secret of reawakening to your immortality is in mastering not the *things* of this world, but the way you *look at* this world.

Let me give you an example. There are some people who have been studying *A Course in Miracles* for a long time who consider themselves to be very intelligent. They think they know what the *Course* means. In some cases, maybe they do; and in other cases, maybe they don't. Yet what's important is that you take your understanding of the *Course, whatever it is,* and apply it. The intellectual who uses his understanding of the *Course* to prove himself to be intellectually superior to others isn't really doing the *Course.*

I would contend to you that a person whom the world would judge as being mentally challenged, someone who has very little intelligence, who is going through life seeing people with love and nonjudgment, is making more spiritual progress in this lifetime than the intellectual who goes through life making himself right and others wrong about what *A Course in Miracles* means.

To repeat, it's not about impressing the world, it's about how you look at it. Mother Teresa was an excellent example. She looked at everybody with love and forgiveness. Ultimately, it didn't matter what her theology was. Most of the people she ministered to throughout her life weren't even members of her own religion. That didn't matter to her. She saw everyone as being completely worthy of God's love, without exception. Her love and forgiveness were not withheld from anyone. It was total and universal. She judged and condemned no one. So her mind was completely healed by the Holy Spirit. She became enlightened and broke the cycle of birth and death.

GARY: Excellent. So she doesn't have to come back, huh?

ARTEN: That's correct.

GARY: That would confirm that it's not the theology, but what you do with it. And you know, there's a school of thought that says J had to put the *Course* the way he did or else the intellectuals wouldn't have taken it seriously. If you give them something simple, they don't respect it! So he spelled it out with this lengthy intellectual, biblical, and scholarly presentation so it would be impressive enough for them to want to listen to it.

ARTEN: There's some truth to that, but it's not that simple. That's because, as we've said, the ego *isn't* simple. So it still takes a lot of work to undo the ego, and another reason for the *Course's* length and style is that it helps facilitate that. What *is* simple is that there are always really only two things to choose between, and only one of them is the truth.

GARY: You know some people might say that it's not very loving for God to let us dream a dream like this that always turns into a nightmare eventually. What would you say to that?

ARTEN: It's always amusing that those same people then want to turn around and say that God created the world! Talk about God not being loving. In answer to your question, God is not letting you dream this. In order to *let* you, He'd have to acknowledge a separation idea in the first place. We've already said that He doesn't. It's only because He doesn't that there is still perfect Oneness for you to wake up to.

GARY: Well, there are people who think that God couldn't experience Himself in Oneness, and the only way He could experience Himself was to make this world and live in it. A lot of them seem to listen to authors and teachers who say so, like the *Conversations with God* books.

PURSAH: If they looked deeper, they'd realize that they're regarding God as insane. You've had the mystical experience of what it's like to be with God in Heaven, right?

GARY: Yeah.

PURSAH: And how does Heaven compare to this world?

GARY: There *is* no comparison. In Heaven, you *are* God.

PURSAH: But it's an experience, like an awareness, isn't it?

GARY: It sure is! It's a far greater experience than anything this world has to offer.

PURSAH: All right, then. The idea of thinking that God would have to make this world in order to experience duality so he could appreciate and enjoy Himself is the equivalent of the idea that in order to experience and enjoy sex, you would have to also experience getting shot in the gut. No. Pain is the result of the guilt that came from thinking you separated yourself from God, and you *don't* have to experience pain in order to experience the pleasure of reality. But you do have to forgive pain and suffering and give it up in order to return to reality. J couldn't be any more clear about that in his *Course,* and he *is* the one you should listen to:

"From the ego came sin and guilt and death, in opposition to life and innocence, and to the Will of God Himself. Where can such opposition lie but in the sick minds of the insane, dedicated to madness and set against the peace of Heaven? One thing is sure; God, Who created neither sin nor death, wills not that you be bound by them. He knows of neither sin nor its results. The shrouded figures in the funeral procession march not in honor of their Creator, Whose Will it is they live. They are not following His Will; they are opposing it."[17]

GARY: Boy, he's gonna have to stop holding back and say how he really feels. So here are people saying that God made opposites so He could experience Himself, and here's J saying that what's all-encompassing can *have* no opposite, and that only the insane would think either that it could or that it should. Is that a fair statement?

PURSAH: Yes.

GARY: You know, sometimes people ask me why *A Course in Miracles* isn't more popular. Granted, the *Course* isn't obscure, and there *are* almost two million copies of it out there. But still, compared to some things, it's not that popular.

PURSAH: Actually, you're starting to change that, with our help, of course. One of the reasons the *Course* wasn't as popular as other approaches was because no popular teacher ever really explained it to people, so they'd start studying the *Course* and then not being able to understand it, they'd give up in frustration. Now, when they read your books and then go read the *Course* for themselves, they *can* understand it.

GARY: Cool, but getting back to what I was saying, when people ask me why the *Course* isn't more popular, I say that given what it's saying, it's a miracle that it's as popular as it is!

PURSAH: That's a good point. Remember, we never said that the *Course* is for everyone; in fact, it's *not* for everyone. But it *is* for a lot more people than have studied it so far, and the better people get what it's saying, the more likely they are to stay interested in it. And you have to keep in mind that this is just the beginning. It's always the application that leads to the experience the *Course* is directed toward.

GARY: Herein lies the peace of God, right?

PURSAH: You've got it, and that peace is an experience.

GARY: Beautiful. And I take it our review got finished somewhere along the way here?

PURSAH: Yes, you can always use a review. In fact, in between bringing in new ideas, the *Course* itself is a *constant* review. That quote I used a couple of minutes ago echoes the principle taught in the *Course*'s Introduction that you mentioned; the idea that what's all-encompassing can *have* no opposite. But it says it in a different way and on a deeper level. That's part of the method J uses to undo the ego.

GARY: Okay, I have a question. Every now and then I read about one of these Nazis who escaped to South America, and there will be a report that the guy died and he was like in his 80s or 90s or something. Now I've been told for the last 25 years that my thinking determines my health. So how come these jerks get to live to be a hundred? I mean, what kind of thoughts must *they* have been having most of their lives?

ARTEN: Get a grip, Gary. Your thoughts determine your *experience* of life, not *what* happens in your life. What happens on the level of form—how long you live, how rich or poor you are, whether or not you're faced with the challenge of heart disease, stroke, cancer, or what have you—was all determined before you ever appeared to be born. The instant you chose the ego on that metaphysical level, everything else was a done deal. That's why life here isn't fair. And don't ask why you should even bother! I just said you *do* determine your *experience* with your thoughts, and your experience is what's important.

The only real power you have here is the power to choose between the ego and the Holy Spirit. In the process, if you happen to change dimensions of time through the Holy Spirit's collapsing of time and thus have a different scenario play itself out within

> **The only real power you have here is the power to choose between the ego and the Holy Spirit.**

the fixed script, then you should consider that to be a fringe benefit. That's not what the *Course* is about, though. As for the collapsing of time, remember that only the Holy Spirit knows what's best for everyone. Put Him in charge of time and space. Put the one in charge who knows everything. If you're sick and your symptoms change through choosing forgiveness, then consider *that* to be a fringe benefit, also. The real goal is Heaven, but the short-term goal is peace, and the end of all pain and suffering. It's absolutely within your means to learn to end all pain and suffering, despite anything that appears to be happening in the world and regardless of what your symptoms appear to be. That's the Holy Spirit's answer to the ego's script of guilt, pain, suffering, and death.

GARY: So that Nazi would have lived to be 90, anyway, but the quality of his life and how he experiences those 90 years *is* determined by his thoughts, and that also goes for his spiritual progress and how many more lifetimes he has to come back for.

ARTEN: Exactly. Excellent. Now, it's just about time for us to take off. Be especially vigilant this next road trip, dear brother. You'll see why I said that. But have a good time, too!

GARY: Thanks! I'm doing my best.

PURSAH: We know, and that's all anyone can ask, teacher of God. Remember the two forgiveness thought processes we gave you! And sometime, when you're on a long plane trip and you're trying to take a nap but can't fall asleep because of turbulence or some other reason, think of these words from the *Course*. Then as you take your respite from the ways of Earth, you'll be reminded of the awesome truth that is within you: "The Son of Life cannot be killed. He is immortal as his Father. What he is cannot be changed."[18]

About three weeks later, I was returning from a trip to the Midwest, flying into Portland, Maine. I heard a loud bang on the right side of the aircraft and saw what appeared to be a flash of fire go by the window.

The flight attendant went running down the aisle toward the flight deck. The people on the plane, about 60 of them, became very quiet, wondering if something dreadful had happened to the plane's ability to function. I was nervous. I thought, *Damn it. Just when things were going so well.*

Then I remembered what Pursah had said just before she and Arten disappeared, and I repeated the words from the *Course* she'd told me to. I thought of the immortal nature of what I really am, and asked J to be with me and help me to see this situation differently. I felt better immediately, even though I still didn't know what was going on.

It didn't take long to find out. After what was probably no more than a minute, the flight attendant came on the intercom and said, "It's all right, folks. The plane was struck by lightning, but everything checks out okay."

All I said was "Thank you," and then I took a short nap while the pilot made his final approach into Portland.

❦❦❦

4

MURDERS WITHOUT CORPSES

Attack in any form is equally destructive. Its purpose does not change. Its sole intent is murder, and what form of murder serves to cover the massive guilt and frantic fear of punishment the murderer must feel? He may deny he is a murderer and justify his savagery with smiles as he attacks. Yet he will suffer, and will look on his intent in nightmares where the smiles are gone, and where the purpose rises to meet his horrified awareness and pursue him still. For no one thinks of murder and escapes the guilt the thought entails. If the intent is death, what matter the form it takes?[1]

On that same trip to the Midwest, I went to Wisconsin, where my friend Linda had arranged a workshop for me in Wisconsin Dells. It was a couple of miles down the road from a cult that uses *A Course in Miracles* for its own purposes. In fact, the leader of the cult refers to himself, incredibly, as "The Master Teacher of *A Course in Miracles.*" Hearing that I was doing a workshop near there, one of the teacher's cronies had invited me to visit. As Linda and I entered "Endeavor Academy," I had no doubt that it must be helpful to some of the people who were there. If they want to live or study somewhere, then there must be a reason that they believe serves them. What I found was an atmosphere that was highly unusual, especially compared to what one would expect from followers of a self-study course.

There was a room on the side where someone was reading the Workbook lesson for that day. There were around 40 people listening, and they would laugh at inappropriate times. Yes, the *Course* encourages laughter, but these people were laughing at serious lines they should have been thinking about and getting on a deeper level. It was as if they knew some funny meaning to the words that their thought system alone was privy to. What they were actually doing was ignoring the real meaning of the lines as a way of denying the *Course*'s message. Then the "Master Teacher" made his entrance down the stairway, and the crowd gathered around him. They followed him, as did I, into a larger room for what they called "Session."

The man spoke for about an hour. No one else was allowed to talk or ask questions. Because in the previous year the reading and sharing of my first book at the Academy had apparently contributed to a large number of people there finding out what the *Course* actually meant and then leaving, the man came up to me several times during the hour and confronted me, at one point bumping me and slapping me on the head. As he walked away from one of his confrontations, he called me a "dumb shit." I tried to look up this particular teaching style later in the Manual for Teachers of the *Course,* but I couldn't find it anywhere.

Through all of this, I didn't react to him, practicing the kind of forgiveness that's taught in the *Course.* My teachers had given me a heads-up that I would need to practice forgiveness in such situations. I thought of this man as being a projection I'd made up so that I could see what I secretly believed to be true about myself outside of me instead of on the inside. This reminded me that he wasn't really there, and so there wasn't really anyone to react to. An element of this is the knowing that only God is real and anything that is not of God cannot affect me. I then released him to the Holy Spirit in peace. At one point, the so-called Master Teacher appeared frustrated by my refusal to be rattled by him and exclaimed, "Look at him, he's smiling."

While I was there, I saw members of the group manipulated and pitted against each other. People were intimidated and verbally abused. Although this man was literally teaching a form of jibberish that had nothing to do with the *Course,* some of the participants were acting as though they understood it, at the same time turning him into their special teacher instead of listening to what the Voice of the *Course* was actually communicating. If you didn't understand what the Master Teacher was saying, and there was no reason why you should, then you'd be labeled as one of "the dead ones." If you went along with him, you'd fit right in. It was a classic cult atmosphere. Who doesn't want to fit in?

This teacher also mixed in parts of the Bible that weren't saying the same thing as the *Course.* He exhorted the virtue of "light bodies" and encouraged his followers to flip out on kundalini energy, apparently oblivious to the fact that according to the *Course,* energy is nothing but illusion and is not to be valued. By definition, anything that can change or be changed is not real.[2] In any case, the goal of the *Course* is the peace of God, not getting high on the ego's miscreations.

I stayed for an hour, listened, and forgave. Then the teacher put on a video of himself, and Linda and I left. I also visited the "Healing Center," which the cult has many branches of. In fact, they present themselves to most of the world through their more sane-looking Healing Centers as a way of inducing people to join.

The next day I did my workshop at a large hotel down the road. Many former members of the cult came who still resided in the area, as well as some who lived quite a distance away and traveled to be there. (Twenty current members also came over from the Academy, without permission.) Many of the former members of the cult, who are spread out all over the country, have a bond with each other and stay in touch. It was a pleasure to feel the love in the room and also share the message with them. One of my favorite parts of each workshop is the question-and-answer session, where I interact with the audience. But that's not the only time I interact with them. I like to meet people and talk with them all day, from the time I arrive until the time I leave, during my breaks, lunch, or whenever I have the chance. I also like to sign books. It makes me feel like an author.

The day after that, I found myself in the rural town of Kiel, Wisconsin, not far from Green Bay, to do another workshop, this time at a different *A Course in Miracles* teaching facility called "Pathways of Light." In the two days I spent there, I was struck by the similarity in approaches between the directors of the organization, Robert and Mary Stoelting, and what I had heard about the *Course*'s scribe, Helen Schucman.

When word had gotten out in the '70s that Helen was hearing the voice of Jesus, people would occasionally try to get her to ask him a question for them. Instead of doing that, Helen would sit down with them and ask them to listen with her. As an alternative to having them rely on her to hear the Voice for God, Helen's idea was to empower them to hear the Voice for themselves. I found that this was also the approach at Pathways of Light. Instead of telling people what to do, they were into teaching people how to hear the Holy Spirit's Voice for themselves so they could be guided by spirit without needing another human to mediate for them.

> It's also wise to remember that the "Voice" can actually show up in many different forms, not just as a Voice.

Of course, the best and fastest approach to making that happen in a permanent way is through the process of forgiveness, which undoes the blocks in people's minds to "hearing" that Voice. It's also wise to remember that the "Voice" can actually show up in many different forms, not just as a Voice.

I liked the Stoeltings very much, and I looked forward to returning to Pathways of Light.

I was speaking someplace different in the country almost every week now, and a month later, in May of 2004, I made my first trip to Canada to do an appearance in Halifax, Nova Scotia. As a way of illustrating how little traveling I had done before the book came out, I had lived in New England all of my life and had never been to Canada! I loved the people in Halifax. After the workshop, they had a celebration with music, drinking, and dancing. I found it refreshing that they didn't think being spiritual and having a good time were mutually exclusive.

While I was in Halifax I received the exciting news that Hay House, one of the most prominent self-help/spiritual publishers in the world, was interested in taking over the publication of *The Disappearance of the Universe*. Although I knew I'd have to talk about it with my original publisher, D. Patrick Miller of Fearless Books, I sensed that it was meant to happen, and I couldn't wait to acknowledge Arten and Pursah for their plan for the book. It suddenly dawned on me that they knew what they were doing all along, and that the path they had chosen was to have the book prove itself first through sales, which would enable it to find its way to a bigger publisher and a worldwide audience without the message in it ever being changed.

A couple of weeks later, Patrick and I were in Chicago to meet with Hay House at Book Expo America. It was an exciting event, and Bill Clinton gave the keynote speech. We came to an agreement with Hay House, and Patrick and I went out to dinner that night to celebrate. The next day I was due to fly to New Jersey for a workshop.

It was a beautiful, cloudless day as the plane took off and flew past the Sears Tower and out over Lake Michigan. The view was amazing. When we got to Newark, we flew down past the Statue of Liberty, and I could clearly see Manhattan, with the legendary Empire State Building dominating the skyline. Suddenly I thought, *My God, I'm getting paid for this?* It was then that I realized, in a good way, that my life was never going to be the same. I was overwhelmed with gratitude.

At the end of June, I had plenty to discuss with my ascended mentors. Arten and Pursah appeared and looked at me with their kind expressions and loving eyes. I expected them because I knew they were coming every two months, and when the time for their appearances drew near, I'd point my chair away from the television, which I found myself watching less and less the more I traveled, and toward the couch where they were scheduled to show up. Arten spoke first.

ARTEN: Hey, buddy. How was the game?

NOTE: I had been to a baseball game at Fenway Park the week before, on June 22. I had gone with a friend of mine from Naples, Maine, who treated me to the best seat I had ever sat in at a Red Sox game, just a few rows behind their dugout.

GARY: It was great! I must have been to Fenway a hundred times, but those seats were awesome. Curt Schilling pitched, they won the game, and I even got to see Nomar hit a grand slam.

NOTE: Red Sox shortstop Nomar Garciaparra was traded to the Chicago Cubs later in the season, which at the time outraged what we New Englanders call "Red Sox Nation."

GARY: And you know, I can't recall the Sox ever having pitching this good. Am I drunk, or could they go all the way this year?

ARTEN: Well, you're not drunk.

GARY: All right. I guess you wouldn't tell me something like that. But I have a feeling about it. I mean, if the Patriots can win these Super Bowls after coming up empty for 40 years, then anything can happen, right?

ARTEN: I can't argue with that. You've had developments outside the world of sports as well?

GARY: Oh yeah! The book's doing really well. Every month it does better than the month before. And I've been all over the place. Aside from spreading the word about the *Course,* I'm also using my traveling and speaking for what you said: forgiveness . . . at least when I remember. California was amazing, and that visit to Wisconsin was really good, except the session was a little hairy with that teacher you gave me the heads-up about. I did my job, though. The A.R.E. is really coming through, too. That's a breakthrough in many ways.

NOTE: At one time *A Course in Miracles* had been welcome at the Edgar Cayce group in Virginia Beach, the Association for Research and Enlightenment (A.R.E.). Hugh Lynn Cayce's friendship with

Helen Schucman and Bill Thetford helped get the *Course* off on the right foot there. In the previous ten years, however, the *Course* had fallen out of favor, as some students of the Cayce readings interpreted the *Course* as not always saying the same things as Cayce. They didn't want the *Course* at the A.R.E., and it hadn't been taught there in a long time. When *The Disappearance of the Universe* came out, it caught on quickly *before* these people got wind of the fact that it was about the *Course,* partly because *Disappearance* doesn't mention the *Course* on the cover. Before long, *Disappearance* was the number one book at the A.R.E., and the organization took that as a signal that maybe they should be more open to the *Course.*

I was invited to do an all-day workshop. I went in March for the first time and was very well received. This led to a new beginning for the *Course* at the A.R.E., and after that it was welcomed and studied by a lot of the members for the first time in many years. The inclusion of *Disappearance* in the organization's catalog, which went out to 200,000 people, and an excellent review of the book in their magazine, *Venture Inward,* didn't hurt either.

ARTEN: Excellent, and we saw your forgiveness process with that teacher in Wisconsin. Keep it up, wherever you go. Incidentally, you may sometimes find that it's harder to forgive on the Internet than in person. That's because a lot of people have a tendency to speak more freely there, and they'll sometimes say things about you online that they would never say to someone in person. Once you hit that "Send" button, you can't cancel a message. And it won't just be hard to forgive someone who condemns *you.* You'll have to be careful about not doing it to others. Judging and condemning someone else on the Internet, which of course is the projection of unconscious guilt, is a temptation for everyone nowadays.

GARY: I know. The Internet tends to bring out the worst in me. Not too often, but once in a while. Like I haven't been very appreciative of that woman who screwed over our book.

NOTE: *Disappearance* was quickly becoming the most talked-about, widely read, and critically acclaimed book about the *Course* in over a decade, yet the biggest organization within the *Course* community that carried other people's books, called Miracle Distribution Center, refused to even sell it! I couldn't believe it. Why not at least let the students decide for themselves what they want to read? The woman who founded this organization chose instead to attempt to prevent distribution of the book within the *Course* community.

No viable reason was offered, and given the success of the book, *Course* politics had to be the reason. The problem was compounded by the fact that the woman who refused to sell the book had lied to my publisher and me, saying that the reason for not selling it was that "the book just didn't speak to any of us here."

I later learned that the person who reviews books for this organization had given *Disappearance* an enthusiastic thumbs-up, and that his recommendation had been overruled by this woman. I also received evidence that she was working to help another *Course* author with a point of view different from what was expressed in my book, and any excuse not to carry *Disappearance* would do, including the fact that much of the information in it had come from "Ascended Masters." This from a seller of books about a *Course* that was channeled through a woman by Jesus! *Disappearance* was specifically about J and his *Course,* and rapidly increasing numbers of students were saying that it genuinely clarified *A Course in Miracles* and caused it to make sense to them for the first time ever. Many others were being introduced to it. The reinvigoration of energy and new excitement about the *Course* was undeniable.

This woman sold hundreds of books by other authors that didn't have any quotations from *A Course in Miracles* in them, and mine included *hundreds* of quotes from the *Course.* It was the first time in many years that any book had done so with the permission of the publishers of the *Course.* She also presented herself to the public as a "clearinghouse" for books about the *Course,* and she raised funds from those who thought they were giving money to support the *Course.* In fact, she openly encouraged them to leave money to her organization in their wills. And here she was, deliberately excluding a book that many people were learning about the *Course* from for the first time. Later, when some of those same individuals inevitably became customers of hers, she would also try to hit them up for money. I considered that to be unethical.

This was a classic forgiveness opportunity for me, but one I didn't accept easily. It wasn't that this woman's actions were hurting the success of the book. People simply bought it somewhere else, including members of her own staff. To not support a book is one thing. She could have offered the book for sale without supporting or advertising it. But to attempt to suppress it by not selling it at all was another thing. *Disappearance* was obviously the most visible *Course* book out there, and she was obviously the most visible seller of these books. To not even carry it was a public slap in the face.

> No matter how much it looks like you're right, and on the level of form you're certainly right, it won't bring you peace.

PURSAH: Gary, Gary, Gary. You're usually more aware of what's going on than what you're displaying in this situation. Don't you get it? You've been set up. It's a classic case of the ego laying its trap. No matter how much it looks like you're right, and on the level of form you're certainly right, it won't bring you peace. *That's* why the *Course* asks: "Do you prefer that you be right or happy?"[3]

What's the central thought the *Course* attempts to teach?

GARY: There is no world.[4]

PURSAH: I'm sorry. I didn't quite hear that.

GARY: *There is no world.*[5]

PURSAH: That's right. And it doesn't say, "There is no world, yeah, but maybe." It says, "There is no world! This is the central thought the *Course* attempts to teach."[6] That's a definitive statement, Gary. We'll talk about definitive statements shortly, but right now, do me a favor. Read that part of the paragraph from the Workbook. It's in Lesson 132. Read to the word *recognize* in the next paragraph. You've heard it before, but you'll get it on a deeper level.

GARY: All right. Usually when you have me read something from the *Course,* it makes me feel better about a situation.

". . . There is no world! This is the central thought the *Course* attempts to teach. Not everyone is ready to accept it, and each one must go as far as he can let himself be led along the road to truth. He will return and go still farther, or perhaps step back a while and then return again.

"But healing is the gift of those who are prepared to learn there is no world, and can accept the lesson now. Their readiness will bring the lesson to them in some form which they can understand and recognize."

PURSAH: Thank you, Gary. Now, you should always remember that whatever appears to happen is just a dream. The reason the *Course* says that reincarnation isn't true[8] is because it's an illusion. It *appears* to happen, but you never really go into a body, it just looks that way. It's an optical illusion. Why? Well, for one thing, the *Course* teaches that the body doesn't even exist![9] So how could you really be going into one? As the *Course* says: "The body does not exist except as a learning device for the mind. This learning device is not subject to errors if its own, because it cannot create. It is obvious, then, that inducing the mind to give up its miscreations is the only application of creative ability that is truly meaningful."[10]

GARY: Oh, great. The body doesn't exist and can't create, and all the mind can do is choose spirit instead of the ego and its projections, a projection being anything that appears to be separate from anything, and that would include the body, present company excluded, because you come through the right part of the mind, which is extremely rare for bodies. And if I'm hearing that quote right, it's saying that there's nothing meaningful in the concept of being a "co-creator" with God on the level of the world, because J is saying that the *only* meaningful thing the mind can do that involves any kind of creative ability is give up whatever appears to be separate. That doesn't mean you give it up physically, which would just make it real to the mind; you give it up by not believing in it, and choose perfect spirit as your identity instead. Am I in the ballpark here?

PURSAH: You got it.

GARY: Wonderful. Do you have anything else that's gonna help us sell a million copies?

PURSAH: That's funny, but on the practical side of things, if you want to make a million dollars, then it's apparent that you should write a book about how to make a million dollars. It won't matter if anybody actually *makes* a million dollars after they read it. You can just tell them they're not doing it right. But that's not the business we're in. We're in the business of undoing the ego and getting you home. If you want to undo the ego, then let's get down to business.

I said you've been set up. We mentioned earlier that you meet people in this lifetime whom you've had dealings with before in other lifetimes, whether through special love or special hate. Of course that's a linear perspective. It actually happened all at once as a hologram and then appears to act itself out in a linear manner. When you meet someone in this lifetime you've known before in other dream lifetimes, it's because you're orbiting each other. Just as planets orbit the sun, move away from each other in their orbits and then, after reaching their farthest point away, come back to their closest point again, people orbit each other in the hologram of time and space in a similar manner.

GARY: So opposites really do attract?

PURSAH: Yes, but the outcome isn't always pretty, because of the setup. Just as in the case of special love, people whom you've had special hate interests with in the past will come back to the closest point in their orbit with you, and because the unconscious mind has retained the memory of them, you'll have conflict, sometimes right away and sometimes later in the relationship. That shows up as a problem to you, but it's also a marvelous opportunity, if you have the mental discipline to use it. J is very eloquent about that when he says, "The holiest of all the spots on earth is where an ancient hatred has become a present love."[11]

Now, we've never said the *Course* is the only way home. We *have* implied that it's the fastest, and J makes a lot of statements about saving time in the *Course*. Some may scoff at that, but if they do, it's because they don't *really* get what the *Course* is saying. Still, the *Course* isn't the only way, as J points out in that quote you just read: "Their readiness will bring the lesson to them in some form which they can understand and recognize."[12] So it could be something else, like Buddhism, but we'll stick to the method J used in his final lifetime and that he's teaching in more detail through the *Course,* because people are in a position to better understand it now. Maybe there are some people who think there are other teachers in the world today who can get them home faster than J can. They are mistaken, but because the *Course* is not for everybody at the same time, then it doesn't really matter.

GARY: And that remark, "He will return and go still farther, or perhaps step back a while and then return again."[13] Does that mean in between lifetimes you can delay coming back again and hang out in the ether reading the Akashic Records and stuff?

ARTEN: Something like that. Maybe we'll give you a little tour sometime. But Pursah was saying?

PURSAH: That woman you mentioned who you said screwed over our book is a good example of someone coming back into your orbit. You've had lifetimes where you knew each other. You were even married once. She died fairly young, and you kind of blamed yourself for her death.

GARY: Why?

PURSAH: You killed her.

GARY: Oh.

PURSAH: It's a long story, but needless to say, there's a little unresolved conflict there. Today you have a book that a lot of people are reading, but the second she saw it, her unconscious mind had an aversion to it. The last time, she was the victim and you were the victimizer, but just so you won't feel too bad, you had times before that where you were the victim and she was the victimizer. Of course, you've switched genders at times. And so it goes. This time in your conjunction with her you get to be the victim. Congratulations! The question is, what are you going to use it for this time, freedom or bondage? Are you going to get that you're *not* a victim and take responsibility for dreaming, or are you going to make it real and stay stuck here?

GARY: But it's such a bitch. Not her, the situation.

PURSAH: Of course it is, or else it wouldn't be a setup! The two of you were supposed to come into each other's orbit. You can use your relationship for the ego's purposes or the Holy Spirit's. As J puts it, "Those who are to meet will meet, because together they have the potential for a holy relationship. They are ready for each other."[14]

GARY: Well, we couldn't have been too ready for each other that time I snuffed her.

PURSAH: First of all, she had killed you before that in another dream, so things aren't always as simple as they appear. More important, it's not *what* you do to each other that matters, it's how you think about each other. What you appear to do is just an effect of what you think. Because what you do is taking place within a dream, that's not the focus of the *Course*. Our focus is on the *cause* of the dream and undoing it. And if, as J also teaches, there are no degrees, aspects, or intervals in reality,[15] and levels only exist in the dream of separation, then that

Our focus is on the *cause* of the dream and undoing it.

means there are really only two things you can do. Every forgiving thought is an expression of love; every unforgiving thought is a murder. It doesn't matter if there isn't a corpse. Each day the earth turns is a day full of murders without corpses . . . people thinking unforgiving thoughts toward one another. As J says in no uncertain terms, "What is not love is murder. What is not loving must be an attack."[16]

GARY: So every unloving thought is the same, and how intense it appears to be is insignificant. But every thought of love is also the same. That's why it says right in that first miracles principle: "All expressions of love are maximal."[17]

PURSAH: Very nice. You *know* it's true, Gary. But we can't *make* you practice it. Doing it most of the time isn't enough. Sure, you're better off in many ways, but the only real ticket out of here is through universal application. If you remember it's really your own secret beliefs you have about yourself in your unconscious mind that you chose to see in her as a way of escaping from them, then you can get that *you* are the one being freed through your forgiveness. As the *Course* asks, "Would they be willing to accept the fact their savage purpose is directed against themselves?"[18]

GARY: I hear you. I'll do my best. I understand what you're saying about why some lessons are harder than others, and I'll try to remember that I set myself up from a higher illusory level! I made that woman up for a reason, and then we act out things here so it can look like my lack of peace is her fault, when the truth is my lack of peace, no matter what form it takes, is always a result of my own decision to not forgive. But decisions can be changed. I can recognize the truth, which is that nothing's really happening. It's just a dream, and I'm the *one* dreamer. It's like the *Course* says: "Awareness of dreaming is the real function of God's teachers."[19]

NOTE: I was still a little upset, but I realized that what Pursah said was true. Although I'd learned a great deal and often applied it, I didn't do it right away in every situation that came up in my daily life. And if I didn't, then I couldn't complete my lessons. I knew even more that if I only forgave partially, then I would be only partially forgiven. If I forgave completely, then I would be completely forgiven. It didn't matter *what* was being forgiven, and this was true of *Course* politics as well as any other forgiveness opportunity.

PURSAH: Excellent. So, we've been serious for too long. Say something funny.

GARY: Okay. Adam and Eve are lying underneath a tree in the Garden of Eden. Adam looks at Eve and says, "You know, I can't help but feel there's a book in this."

PURSAH: Cute. And you managed to work in an erotic touch.

GARY: Well, Pursah, speaking of erotic touches, when are you and I gonna hook up?

PURSAH: Hmm . . . let me see. Does never work for you?

GARY: Still playing hard to get, huh?

ARTEN: You know, buddy, that *is* the image of my wife you're talking to there, even if she is you.

GARY: Sorry, I forgot. It's hard to keep track of everybody. It's a good thing there's really only one of us, huh? Say, Pursah, do you remember the last series of visits, when you came once all by yourself? You're not by chance gonna do that again, are you?

PURSAH: Are you about ready to proceed?

GARY: Oh, all right. When you talked about definitive statements in the *Course,* I take it that the idea that *there is no world* would be one of them, right?

PURSAH: Yes. A definitive statement is an idea in the *Course* that's so clear it defines what the *Course* is teaching, and it encapsulates what the *Course* is saying. If there is no world, then there's nothing to forgive, and recognizing that fact in the events, situations, and people you see *is* advanced forgiveness, because now you're not forgiving other people for something they've really done, you're recognizing that they haven't really done anything. So you're actually forgiving yourself for dreaming them. That distinction is vital. Without it, you're doing the old-fashioned kind of forgiveness, which can't undo the ego.

GARY: How about another definitive idea?

ARTEN: Another one would be the idea that anger is *never* justified.[20] If you made the whole thing up, then who is there to be angry at? And a related definitive idea would be, "The secret of salvation is but this: That you are doing this unto yourself."[21] The two ideas fit together like a hand in a glove, and once you really *get* them then there's no getting away *from* them.

GARY: Cool. Give me another one.

ARTEN: Sure. "The world you see is an illusion of a world. God did not create it, for what He creates must be eternal as Himself."[22] And fitting perfectly with that idea, "Whatever is true is eternal, and cannot change or be changed. Spirit is therefore unalterable because it is already perfect, but the mind can elect what it chooses to serve. The only limit put on its choice is that it cannot serve two masters."[23]

GARY: Yeah, and it doesn't matter if you've heard that before, you just keep getting it deeper and deeper, if you keep practicing advanced forgiveness. And if anything that can change or be changed isn't true, then that must cover *everything* in the universe of time and space!

ARTEN: Yes, and it also includes anything that is used to measure, test, or calibrate anything in the universe of time and space. It's not true, which we'll talk about later.

PURSAH: One more definitive statement before we take off.

GARY: Go for it.

PURSAH: "Forgiveness recognizes what you thought your brother did to you has not occurred. It does not pardon sins and make them real. It sees there was no sin. And in that view are all your sins forgiven."[24]

I might add that *only* in that view are all your sins forgiven. If the world is real, then sins are real and they're guilty, which means you're guilty, or at least that's the way it will translate into your unconscious. Get it? If they're innocent because they haven't really done anything, then *you're* innocent because you haven't really done anything. Once again, that's the kind of an idea that's definitive. You can't get away from it. And making it a part of you will make you whole.

GARY: What does forgiveness do, then?

PURSAH: J has your answer, brother. "The miracle does nothing. All it does is to undo."[25] And when the ego is undone, the truth will be all that's left.

ARTEN: Next time we can talk a little bit about that movie you wanted to discuss. We'd also like to talk about a couple of the memories

> **If they're innocent because they haven't really done anything, then *you're* innocent because you haven't really done anything.**

you've had of your past lifetimes since the first series of visits. In addition, we'll talk about suffering, sacrifice, crucifixion, and death.

GARY: Wow. Popular subjects. Especially death. Oprah, here I come.

PURSAH: Somehow with you, Gary, it always ends up being entertaining. We love you for that.

GARY: I love you too, Pursah. Oh, you too, Arten. Thanks for talking to me through the Holy Spirit. It means a lot to me, including your guidance on what to do with the book. You keep everything on course, no pun intended.

ARTEN: No problem. Keep practicing, brother. We'll be watching.

With that, they appeared to be gone, and I appeared to be getting ready for another trip to Canada. The weather was warm, and I felt grateful for summer, for my two friends, and for all the new friends I was making because of them.

❦❦❦

5

THE "HERO" OF THE DREAM

Now you are being shown you *can* escape.
All that is needed is you look upon the problem
as it is, and not the way that you have set it up.[1]

The next two months were happy ones, seeing places I had never been to, such as Alberta, Canada; Santa Fe, New Mexico; and Lansing, Michigan. However, traveling had its drawbacks. Because of weather problems and cancellations, the trip from Portland, Maine, to Santa Fe involved four airline flights in one day. Yikes! Also, when my flight was canceled and I had to rebook at the airport, the computer would show that I'd just bought my ticket. It didn't take into consideration the fact that the airline had canceled my flight, which I had bought the ticket for a month and a half in advance. Because I was shown as having purchased my ticket in the previous 24 hours, that made me a security risk, and I was labeled a "selectee." A selectee is automatically pulled aside and searched, and your carry-on luggage is gone through with a fine-tooth comb, causing more delays, embarrassment, and frustration.

It was disconcerting to think that although most of the hijackers on September 11, 2001, were from Saudi Arabia, here was my government searching a frequent flyer like me, plus children and elderly women. Meanwhile, the entire bin Laden family had been allowed to fly out of America just a week after 9/11 without even being questioned for information, while almost everyone else in the country was grounded.

Later, upon going to other countries, I saw that their airports had more sophisticated scanning equipment, and I didn't have to take my laptop computer out of my bag and out of its case for it to be scanned the way I had to in America. Even the luggage gondolas were more technologically advanced. I was starting to think that the United States was falling behind because of an inability to shape intelligent policies, and that our country was run by corporate cronyism and corruption. I tried to see all of this as just another forgiveness opportunity (or JAFO, as we called it at our online discussion group), and I usually succeeded. But did that mean something shouldn't be done about my country's ineptitude? And if so, what? How likely were the American people to do anything in a national election except respond to fear? All it took was a cursory glance at the network news to see that the majority of my fellow citizens were being manipulated by experts who intended to do everything possible to capitalize on the 9/11 tragedy.

For the most part, though, the traveling was exciting for me, and the energy I got from the people who attended my workshops sometimes left me feeling better at the end of a long day than at the beginning. My experience was that something was being expressed through me, and occasionally the information would flow so smoothly that it was as if I were outside of my body, watching myself give the workshop, and I wasn't really the one doing it.

People would regularly report seeing lights around me of different shapes and colors, and occasionally someone would say that they saw my face changing, getting suddenly younger. At some point during the day, I met most of the people who came, and a common experience they reported was one of gratitude for both the day's event and the book. This made me very happy that I'd been guided to travel. If I hadn't gone on the road, I would have never known how much *A Course in Miracles* and *The Disappearance of the Universe* meant to people. Even when someone writes you a friendly e-mail, you can't see the expression on their face or hear the tone of their voice. In person, their real feelings show very clearly.

I was looking forward as much as ever to Arten and Pursah's next expected visit at the end of August. As usual, when they appeared, they didn't waste any time getting started.

ARTEN: You wanted to talk before about the movie *The Passion of the Christ*. A lot of the time Jesus in the movies, or J, as we'll continue to call him—

GARY: You could call him J dog.

ARTEN: A lot of the time J has been portrayed as a suffering, angst-ridden figure. That's not what he was like at all. He was a peaceful figure with a gentle smile. His eyes were clear and loving. There was no fear in him because he knew that there *was* nothing to fear. Nothing the world could do to him could affect him. He was not a body. He did not think of himself as being special. He was not the passion; he was a symbol of compassion.

PURSAH: You saw the movie. How did you feel about it?

GARY: Well, I got there and there were people lined up all the way around the block. They were really excited. It was like the second coming or something. The second coming of *what,* I didn't find out until I got inside. It was a bloody, horrific movie. Sitting there was like torture, but without the fun. They actually showed J's body being ripped apart. Even at the beginning of the movie, J is acting very much like a typical, fearful guy. He's angry. He steps on a snake and kills it, because Satan's supposed to be in the snake, and there's nothing to suggest the kind of a man Arten just talked about.

You know what? Early in the movie, Judas comes up to J in the garden and kisses him, and they have J say that famous line from the Bible, "Betrayest thou the Son of Man with a kiss?" Right away I remembered that section in the *Course* called "The Message of the Crucifixion," where J is teaching what the real message is, as opposed to what organized religion cooked up later, and at one point he says, and I'll grab it and read it here so I don't screw it up. He states, "I could not have said, 'Betrayest thou the Son of Man with a kiss?' unless I believed in betrayal. The whole message of the Crucifixion was simply that I did not. The 'punishment' I was said to have called forth upon Judas was a similar mistake. Judas was my brother and a Son of God, as much a part of the Sonship as myself. Was it likely that I would condemn him when I was ready to demonstrate that condemnation is impossible?"[2]

Throughout the film, J's body is made out to be *very* special. The presupposition is that he has to be sacrificed to atone for other people's sins. But the quote you gave me from Isaiah demonstrates that that idea was already as old as the hills, and the religion that came along later just superimposed it on to J. No thought is ever given to the fact that the whole premise gives us a God who is like humanity—in other words, insane. The movie, like the religion it's about, glorifies suffering and sacrifice. And people were bringing their nine- and ten-year-old kids to see this thing, and when they were coming out of the theater, you could just see the look on their faces, as if they were saying to the kids, "There, you see? You see what Jesus did for *you?* You see how he suffered and sacrificed himself for *you?* You guilty little bastards. Now what are *you* gonna do for *him?* You're gonna be a Christian, *right?*"

ARTEN: Yes, and *there* you have the makings of a very successful religion. Because if you want to get people to do something in this world, including impressionable children, make them feel guilty. You could make them believe in Santa Claus until they're 30 if you found a way to use guilt and nobody told them any better. And in this case, nobody's telling them any better. The whole thing also makes the body *very* real and the destruction of it important.

GARY: But if the guiltless mind cannot suffer,[3] as the *Course* says, then it wouldn't have mattered what they did to J. He wouldn't have reacted to what was done to him and felt all that pain the movie shows him suffering through.

PURSAH: Yes, and that's very important. That's another definitive idea in the *Course*. The guiltless mind cannot suffer. It blows the whole idea of glorifying sacrifice right out of the water. Because, as we've told you before, pain is not a physical process, it's a mental process, and if you healed all the unconscious guilt in the mind, then you couldn't feel any pain. That changes the message of the Crucifixion from the idea of worshiping suffering and sacrifice to a demonstration that if you were healed, then it would be *impossible* for you to feel any pain or to suffer. But suffering, like people now believe J did, is a hallmark of the religion that he had nothing to do with, but that was founded in his name.

GARY: They have a cruci-fixation.

ARTEN: Yes, but J's real message is the *opposite* of making the body real. In fact, if you want to be like J, then you want to eventually experience that the body is meaningless. Instead of believing in the body, you want to get to the point where you *can't* believe it.

GARY: I still can't believe the Sox traded Nomar.

ARTEN: A prerequisite for not believing in the body is an understanding of the dream and the body's place in it. I'm going to give you a couple of quotes from the *Course,* and then I want you to do a little bit of reading for me. First, we've talked about how the false belief that the suffering of the body, an idea that you now understand is caused by unconscious guilt, could have anything to do with J. In relation to that, listen to what he says in the section of the *Course* called "The Bridge to the Real World":

> **Instead of believing in the body, you want to get to the point where you *can't* believe it.**

"Be glad you have escaped the mockery of salvation the ego offered you, and look not back with longing on the travesty it made of your relationships. Now no one need suffer, for you have come too far to yield to the illusion of the beauty and holiness of guilt. Only the wholly insane could look on death and suffering, sickness and despair, and see it thus."[4]

The Holy Spirit will make an excellent trade with you, if you will accept it, as J says here in the section "The Obstacles to Peace":

"Your little part is but to give the Holy Spirit the whole idea of sacrifice. And to accept the peace He gives instead, without the limits that would hold its extension back, and so would limit your awareness of it."[5]

He goes on to say in that same section, "Why should the body be anything to you? Certainly what it is made of is not precious. And just as certainly it has no feeling. It transmits to you the feelings that you want. Like any communication medium the body receives and sends the messages that it is given. It has no feeling for them. All of the feeling with which they are invested is given by the sender and the receiver. The ego and the Holy Spirit both recognize this, and both also recognize that here the sender and receiver are the same. The Holy Spirit tells you this with joy. The ego hides it, for it would keep you unaware of it. Who would send messages of hatred and attack if he but understood he sends them to himself? Who would accuse, make guilty and condemn himself?"[6]

GARY: I think having that conviction, that you're doing it to yourself, is important, because when you remember it, then you don't want to hurt yourself, and the more you believe it, the more likely you are to remember it in everyday situations.

ARTEN: Exactly. And once you start questioning your old beliefs, some interesting things can take place, as you've heard from some of the book's readers.

NOTE: I would occasionally hear from readers who said they were experiencing symptoms of vertigo during or after reading *Disappearance.* A friend of mine, Reverend Doug Lee, taught a class on the book and said that several of his students reported the same thing. It reminded me of years earlier when I was doing the Workbook of the *Course.* There were a few times when I woke up in the morning, looked up, and saw that the ceiling was spinning around in a circle. I didn't feel sick or nauseated, but seeing the ceiling spinning like that was a mindblower. It didn't last more than a few weeks, and it never interfered with my ability to function. When I heard the reports later of similar things happening to people while reading *Disappearance,* I thought it was really cool.

GARY: Yeah, you mean the vertigo! Hearing about that made me feel like the book must really have something, if it was causing similar reactions in people as the *Course* did with me. I take it the symptoms are connected to questioning the ego thought system that our whole life has been based on?

ARTEN: Yes. Interestingly, there's another quote in the *Course* from a section I just recited from "The Bridge to the Real World," which addresses that very subject. You didn't make the connection before, but you will now. Here, J is talking about the process of crossing the bridge from your old experience of living as the ego to living in the real world with the Holy Spirit:

"The bridge itself is nothing more than a transition in the perspective of reality. On this side, everything you see is grossly distorted and completely out of perspective. What is little and insignificant is magnified, and what is strong and powerful cut down to littleness. In the transition there is a period of confusion, in which a sense of actual disorientation may occur. But fear it not, for it means only that you have been willing to let go your hold on the distorted frame of reference that seemed to hold your world together."[7]

GARY: Is that all? It only means that I've been willing to let go of what seemed to hold my world together? What the hell, I don't need anything to hold my world together.

ARTEN: The Holy Spirit is all you need. Then you can let go of the world you *thought* was yours, and exchange it for the real world.

GARY: I think I know what the real world is, but could you give me a refresher?

ARTEN: One succinct quote, brother, and it's this: "The real world is the symbol that the dream of sin and guilt is over, and God's Son no longer sleeps. His waking eyes perceive the sure reflection of his Father's Love; the certain promise that he is redeemed. The real world signifies the end of time, for its perception makes time purposeless."[8]

GARY: That must have been the condition J was in toward the end, right?

ARTEN: Yes, and his message was as clear as could be. He never compromised on it, and neither should you. If you give the ego an inch, it will take a mile. That's why we're happy to see that you stick to the *Course* and don't change the message. You have respect for the material. That's excellent, because one of the reasons we appear to you is to help prevent J's message from getting distorted the way it did 2,000 years ago. If enough people were to alter the meaning of the teaching, or even the words themselves, then after a century or two, you wouldn't even be able to recognize the *Course*.

GARY: Yeah, but you must already know if the message gets lost again. Does it?

ARTEN: We've said before that we weren't going to tell you too much about the future, for many reasons. What you want to do is take care of now.

GARY: Well, on the subject of the message getting distorted, seeing *Passion* reminded me of that series of books that's been going for a while: the *Left Behind* series. I had a little extra time in the airport, and I stopped at one of the bookstores and was looking at one of the recent books in the series. It's based on the Book of Revelation. I have a friend in Florida who *loves* that stuff. I think the series of books has sold around 60 million copies. Anyway, The Book of Revelation, which reads like it was written by somebody on acid or something, has J coming back and waging war against the nonbelievers. And in the *Left Behind* series, the narrator tells the tale of that war, which pits the forces of good against evil.

The recent book I was reading has J raising one of his hands, and this big chasm opens up and swallows all these nonbelievers, and they fall in, dying and screaming. In another part, J just speaks, and the bodies of the enemy are ripped open. The believers have to drive carefully to avoid hitting splayed and filleted bodies of men and women and even horses. I guess they weren't Christian horses. As Christians watch, the bad guys' flesh is dissolving, their eyes are melting, and their tongues are disintegrating. It's quite a scene.

It seems to me that what they've done here is take Jesus, the Prince of Peace, and turn him into their own personal hit man. Now he's killing their enemies for them. There's subtle racism involved, too, because the nonbelievers, which you may as well call the infidels, are recently being put in the context of the war on terror. It's the classic projection of unconscious guilt. We've got God, they don't, and they deserve to die.

Well, I'm sorry, but I don't see a damn bit of difference between this kind of insane fundamentalism and the fundamentalism that flew those planes into the World Trade Center on the morning of September 11, 2001. It's the same thing in a different package. It's the ego's thought system run amok. All it will do is lead to more tragedy, and it's the exact opposite of everything that J was all about. Somebody has to be willing to stand up and say enough is enough—not because the world has to change, but to encourage people to change their minds and choose forgiveness.

ARTEN: So why don't you be the one to stand up and say it?

GARY: I know. It took me a while to catch on, but I can see that one of the reasons you chose me was because I didn't have anything to lose. I could deliver your message and not worry about what people think. With nothing to lose, if someone doesn't respect me, so what?

PURSAH: Very good, dear brother. Keep putting it out there. Don't worry about what people will say. Dr. Georg (that's spelled without an *e* on the end) Groddeck once said, "Respect is just as hard to renounce as vanity." Just be yourself and speak the message.

> **"Respect is just as hard to renounce as vanity."**

As for results, everything happens the way it's supposed to anyway. If something isn't supposed to happen, you'll never be able to make it happen. And if something *is* supposed to happen, then there's nothing in the world you could do to stop it. So why not just be true to the truth of the Holy Spirit and let the rest take care of itself?

As for politics, now you know what politics is *for*. If you use it for forgiveness, your progress is assured.

GARY: Yeah. I slip a little sometimes, but I always remember the truth pretty quickly. It's interesting to watch peace activists and environmental activists. I know some peace activists who hate people. They're out there protesting against the war, which is cool, but what it's really about for them is getting their political opponents whom they hate, or the greedy corporate pigs who they think are exploiting everybody. But those corporate leaders are just people, like everybody else. Yeah, maybe they have an addiction to money, but almost everybody's after *something*. The interesting thing to me is, if you're against the war thinking about how much you're opposed to your political opponents, then you're doing it with the ego as your teacher. But you could do exactly the same thing with the Holy Spirit as your teacher, and it would be a totally different experience.

From that perspective, it's not about getting your political opponents or expressing your outrage at the powers that be. Now you're protesting against the war as an expression of what you are, which is love, with the idea of having a more loving world. That's a totally different place to be coming from. So it's not *what* you do that matters. Either way you could be out on the street protesting. Nobody else would be able to tell what's going on in your mind, but for *you*, it's now about love. It's not the form that matters; it's the content.

PURSAH: Hey, who's the teacher here? Just kidding. You're right. It's not *what* you do. It's whom you do it *with,* the ego or the Holy Spirit. Each choice leads to a totally different experience. People may think they can judge others by what they do, but that's not always the case. Somebody may have a job where they have to do things that may not appear to be spiritual to the world. Yet *anything* can be spiritual if you choose the Holy Spirit to guide you. So no job is really any more spiritual than any other job.

Now, even though what you do isn't the focus, we've also pointed out that what you do is a result of what you think. So sometimes you can tell a lot about people by the way they are. For example, if someone is angry a lot and they say rude things to people, what do you think that says about them?

GARY: Well, they probably hate themselves.

PURSAH: Yes. How you treat other people is a pretty good indication of how you feel about *yourself.* If you're looking at them with hostility, you're saying that you have a mind that's in conflict. If you're looking at them with kindness, it's a symptom of a mind that has peace. Not only that, but it will determine and reinforce how you feel about yourself. It's a cycle, either a peaceful or a vicious one. True, there are people who are very nice to others but don't necessarily feel good about themselves, but they're usually close to a breakthrough. If they express love, it's a symbol that they're on the right track, and they just need a little help in understanding the choice that's available to them. Once they do, then they're more likely than most to choose their strength, the Holy Spirit within them, instead of their own weakness, which is the ego.

GARY: I've heard great people, from the Dalai Lama to Ken Wapnick, stress the importance of being kind. I can see now what they mean. If how you look at other people says a lot about how you feel now, and also determines how you'll feel about yourself in the future, you're really doing yourself a favor by being kind and compassionate.

PURSAH: Very true. By the way, our compliments on how you treat people when you're on the road. Many teachers, under the pressure of travel and difficult schedules, have given in to the temptation to take it out on others. So far, you get an A-plus for your interactions with all those people you meet in person. You represent the *Course* very nicely.

GARY: Hey, thanks. I appreciate that. It's easy. I love those guys. And you know, what you said about no job really being more spiritual than any other job, that's right on. I mean, I've had people come up to me and say, "How come the Ascended Masters appeared to *you?* Why *you?*" And I tell them that first of all, how do they know that in a past lifetime they weren't one of those children who saw the Virgin Mary at Lourdes? Or maybe they've seen angels or other manifestations.

I think we all have the same kinds of gifts, but we don't have them all at the same time in the illusion. That's why the Manual for Teachers says, ". . . no one has any powers that are not available to everyone."[9] I used to think it would be really cool if I could be a spiritual healer; you know, go around laying hands on people and healing them and stuff. I thought that would be the ultimate. But that's not a gift of mine in this lifetime. If I try to heal somebody, I'm lucky if they don't die.

The point is that it's just not my gift this time around, but I know I've been a great healer in another lifetime. Everybody is at some point. And as far as seeing Ascended Masters, that's just what's meant to be for me this time around, and others do it at some other time. It would be kind of silly to have billions of people all going around seeing Ascended Masters. Then nobody would be using the other gifts.

Something I tell people that surprises them, and I don't mean any offense by this, is that seeing you two has *not* been the ultimate spiritual experience for me. The greatest experience I've ever had is what the *Course* calls revelation, which is direct communication or joining with God. That blows away anything in the world of perception.

PURSAH: No offense taken. J says in the *Course* that even though awe is a proper response to revelation, because you're having a direct experience of God, he also says, "Equals should not be in awe of one another because awe implies inequality. It is therefore an inappropriate reaction to me."[10] So not only should you not treat *us* like we're special, you shouldn't think of J as being anything special either.

GARY: Awesome. Sorry. So I tell people that revelation—that experience of their oneness with God—is the thing they *should* be going for, because it's an experience of reality, where seeing you guys is something that takes place within the realm of perception. And after revelation, everything in the world is just kind of like a dream that doesn't measure up to reality. But that doesn't mean you can't have fun while you appear to be here.

When I go to the movies I know it's not real, but that doesn't stop me from enjoying it. And that's what this world can be like. In fact, I'd say that if you have less unconscious guilt in your mind from practicing forgiveness, you can enjoy the world *more*. I mean I love listening to music today more than ever. So it's not about giving up the beautiful art and the romantic sunsets. I think if you get in touch with your innocence, everything is more enjoyable, because you're experiencing it with less guilt, and eventually with no guilt. Like how about sex? If you didn't have any guilt in your mind, wouldn't you enjoy sex more?

PURSAH: I take it that's a rhetorical question.

GARY: It is as long as Arten's here. Incidentally, people at my workshops are also surprised to find out that in between your visits, when I talk to the Holy Spirit, it's really J whom I think of and not you. He's always been the manifestation of the Holy Spirit for me, and I've always felt like I could talk to him and he'd help me. You don't mind that, do you? I know when I hear the Holy Spirit's Voice, it's also you.

PURSAH: As I said, we're not special. So whatever serves you best in between visits is all that matters. We know you think about us, and you know we're always with you, and so is J.

GARY: Ah, don't get all mushy on me now. But if we're all one, it doesn't really matter, does it? Oh, another thing. I was thinking about that spiritual job stuff. Let's say, for example, somebody's an accountant and they don't happen to think they have any particular spiritual gifts in this lifetime, not that accountants don't have spiritual gifts, but let's say this one didn't think they did. Well, if they gave their ability of accounting over to the Holy Spirit and used it under His direction, wouldn't that *make* it a spiritual gift? So a spiritual gift is something you give to the Holy Spirit. It doesn't matter what the gift is. Then by definition, if you use it under His Guidance, it's spiritual. And who knows, aside from keeping your day job, maybe you'll find a spiritual organization or individual who could use your help. And now your gift is helping people to spread the truth. What could be better than that?

ARTEN: Very nice, brother. You can translate that to any job. Maybe for some the Holy Spirit will want them to use their job to practice forgiveness. If they do, then it's a spiritual job. It doesn't matter what it is.

GARY: Hey, you told me we were gonna talk about death this time. I've been *so* looking forward to it.

ARTEN: All right, wise guy. We'll get to it shortly, but it's essential for you to understand, and also, as a result of your forgiveness, actually experience the dreamlike nature of this world. So it's time for you to do a little reading for us. Go to page 585 in the Text.

GARY: Ah, let me see here. "The 'Hero' of the Dream"? I haven't read this in a while.

ARTEN: Yes. I want you to read it again at least five times in the next couple of months.

GARY: Five times? It better be good.

ARTEN: It's better than good; it's the truth. I'm only going to have you read the first four paragraphs right now. Then read all four pages every two weeks or so, for a total of five times. Think about the ideas and consider what it means in regard to what you're seeing in your everyday life. But read those first four paragraphs for us now.

GARY: All right. Here it comes:

"The body is the central figure in the dreaming of the world. There is no dream without it, nor does it exist without the dream in which it acts as if it were a person to be seen and be believed. It takes the central place in every dream, which tells the story of how it was made by other bodies, born into the world outside the body, lives a little while and dies, to be united in the dust with other bodies dying like itself. In the brief time allotted it to live, it seeks for other bodies as its friends and enemies. Its safety is its main concern. Its comfort is its guiding rule. It tries to look for pleasure, and avoid the things that would be hurtful. Above all, it tries to teach itself its pains and joys are different and can be told apart.

"The dreaming of the world takes many forms, because the body seeks in many ways to prove it is autonomous and real. It puts things on itself that it has bought with little metal discs or paper strips the world proclaims as valuable and real. It works to get them, doing senseless things, and tosses them away for senseless things it does not need and does not even want. It hires other bodies, that they may protect it and collect more senseless things that it can call its own. It looks about for special bodies that can share its dream. Sometimes it dreams it is a conqueror of bodies weaker than itself. But in some phases of the dream, it is the slave of bodies that would hurt and torture it.

"The body's serial adventures, from the time of birth to dying are the theme of every dream the world has ever had. The 'hero' of this dream will never change, nor will its purpose. Though the dream itself takes many forms, and seems to show a great variety of places and events wherein its 'hero' finds itself, the dream has but one purpose, taught in many ways. This single lesson does it try to teach again, and still again, and yet once more; that it is cause and not effect. And you are its effect, and cannot be its cause.

"Thus are you not the dreamer, but the dream. And so you wander idly in and out of places and events that it contrives. That this is all the body does is true, for it is but a figure in a dream. But who reacts to figures in a dream unless he sees them as if they were real? The instant that he sees them as they are they have no more effects on him, because he understands he gave them their effects by causing them and making them seem real.

"How willing are you to escape effects of all the dreams the world has ever had?"[11]

Oh, wait, I'm supposed to stop. That's so profound I wanted to keep going.

ARTEN: You will, but that's perfect, brother. J goes on and talks about how the dream was made. Make sure you read that whole section later five times. You'll keep getting it on a deeper level, and you'll never be given a more amazing description of both the way into the dream and the way out of it. Near the end of that section, he says, "When you forgive the world your guilt, you will be free of it."[12]

GARY: Free of my guilt or free of the world?

ARTEN: Without one, you have no need for the other. Your guilt, which is now unconscious, is the reason for the world. Your job is to undo it. That's how to break the cycle of birth and death.

PURSAH: Speaking of death . . .

GARY: You should have had a drumroll just before you said that.

PURSAH: What I was going to say was, speaking of death, we'll be getting to that subject in a minute. But first, remember that the more you forgive, the less you're taken in by the ego's tricks. As J says late in the *Course* about God's teachers, "They watch the dream figures come and go, shift and change, suffer and die. Yet they are not deceived by what they see. They recognize that to behold a dream figure as sick and separate is no more real than to regard it as healthy and beautiful."[13]

> **Bodies, sick or healthy, are really all the same, because none of them are true.**

So bodies, sick or healthy, are really all the same, because none of them are true. And there's not really any difference between sickness and death either. They're just different illusory levels of the thought of separation from God.

GARY: So the only difference between a rut and a grave is the depth.

PURSAH: Yes, humorous one. And the depth is also an illusion. That last quote was from the Manual for Teachers, and this next quote is from the Text. We want to show you that the *Course* is saying the same thing all the way through. From the Text, to the Workbook, and through the Manual, the *Course* is a purely nondualistic teaching. It's consistent. And if that's true, and it certainly is, then it means there's only one authentic way to interpret it.

In the Text, J says, "Appearances can but deceive the mind that wants to be deceived. And you can make a simple choice that will forever place you far beyond deception."[14]

That simple choice is forgiveness, and it's applied the same way to everything, up to and including death. Consider these words from the Workbook: "You think that death is of the body. Yet it is but an idea, irrelevant to what is seen as physical. A thought is in the mind. It can be then applied as mind directs it. But its origin is where it must be changed, if change occurs. Ideas leave not their source. The emphasis this course has placed on that idea is due to its centrality in our attempts to change your mind about yourself. It is the reason you can heal. It is the cause of healing. It is why you cannot die. Its truth established you as one with God."[15] And he says at the beginning of the next paragraph, "Death is the thought that you are separate from your Creator."[16]

Later in that same Workbook Lesson, J says, "What seems to die is but the sign of mind asleep."[17] And a little later, "Its form may change; it may appear to be what it is not. Yet mind is mind, awake or sleeping."[18] And here's one more quote about the mind from that Lesson: ". . . it merely seems to go to sleep a while. It dreams of time; an interval in which what seems to happen never has occurred, the changes wrought are substance-less, and all events are nowhere. When the mind awakes, it but continues as it always was."[19]

GARY: So it really is all just a dream, and I take it that when we undo the ego and wake up, we *experience* that we never really left home. Then when the body is laid aside for the final time and there's no need to come back, the experience of being one with God becomes our permanent reality and never stops.

ARTEN: That's the fact, Jack. And remember, to wake up is to wake up completely. To sleep is to sleep. It doesn't matter if you're dreaming that you're alive or dreaming that you're dead. Neither one is true. As the *Course* says: ". . . the retreat to death is not the end of conflict."[20]

GARY: So there ain't no easy way out. You've got to do your forgiveness work, or else you'll keep dreaming you come back until you finish your lessons and wake up for good.

ARTEN: Yes, we're nearing the end of our visit, and we want to complete our discussion about death. It should be clear that death is no more real than life in the body. Neither one is true. Real life is total and permanent. As the *Course* says: "The curious belief that there is a part of dying things that may go on apart from what will die, does not proclaim a loving God nor re-establish any grounds for trust."[21]

GARY: So what some people think of as their soul that goes on after death is really a seemingly separated mind.

ARTEN: That's a brilliant observation, and very Buddhist. *Real* spirit is whole and permanent. That's your immortal reality. So no matter *what* appears to be happening, including death and the in-between-life, the truth is that there are only two things to choose from, your reality with God, or anything else. Now all you've got to do is use the mind to choose between God and anything else.

Real spirit is whole and permanent. That's your immortal reality.

PURSAH: You were kind enough to read for us, and now, before we leave, we're going to be kind enough to recite something for you that J says about death. I'll begin, and Arten will join in. This is meant to firmly fix the idea in your mind on the choice you have to make whenever the thought of death rears its ugly head.

The hero of the dream will always have an end to his or her story, and that's all it is, a story. Of course the hero will be back in another form, until you end your belief in all forms. Forgive, dear brother, and you'll have no use for the ego's dream of death. Exposing it, seeing it for what it is and forgiving it, will set you free. Listen to what J says here:

"Death is the central dream from which all illusions stem. Is it not madness to think of life as being born, aging, losing vitality, and dying in the end? We have asked this question before, but now we need to consider it more carefully. It is the one fixed, unchangeable belief of the world that all things in it are born only to die. This is regarded as 'the way of nature,' not to be raised to question, but to be accepted as the 'natural' law of life. The cyclical, the changing and unsure; the undependable and the unsteady, waxing and waning in a certain way upon a certain path—all this is taken as the Will of God. And no one asks if a benign Creator could will this."[22]

ARTEN: "The 'reality' of death is firmly rooted in the belief that God's Son is a body. And if God created bodies, death would indeed be real. But God would not be loving."[23]

PURSAH: "In this perception of the universe as God created it, it would be impossible to think of Him as loving. For who has decreed that all things pass away, ending in dust and disappointment and despair, can be but feared. He holds your little life in his hand but by a thread, ready to break it off without regret or care, perhaps today. Or if he waits, yet is the ending certain. Who loves such a god knows not of love, because he has denied that life is real. Death has become life's symbol. His world is now a battleground, where contradiction reigns and opposites make endless war. Where there is death is peace impossible."[24]

ARTEN: "Death is the symbol of the fear of God. His Love is blotted out in the idea, which holds it from awareness like a shield held up to obscure the sun. The grimness of the symbol is enough to show it cannot coexist with God. It holds an image of the Son of God in which he is 'laid to rest' in devastation's arms, where worms wait to greet him and to last a little while by his destruction. Yet the worms as well are doomed to be destroyed as certainly. And so do all things live because of death. Devouring is nature's 'law of life.' God is insane, and fear alone is real."[25]

As you can see, J doesn't hold back about the true nature of this world, and what it would say about God if He really were the one responsible for it.

GARY: Nice. You know, I could probably write a song out of that. But seriously, I get the picture.

PURSAH: I can see that. It's disturbing but true. And that "devouring is nature's law of life" quote reminded me; you've never been a vegetarian, have you?

GARY: Nah, but I *do* believe there's a place for all of God's creatures—usually right next to the mashed potatoes.

PURSAH: That's all right, brother, as long as you don't make it real. Like anything else, if being a vegetarian is done from a place of love and as an expression of love, then it's a beautiful thing. If it's done to make other people wrong for *not* being vegetarians, then it will imprison the mind. I say that because you're meeting a lot of people now who are vegetarians, and it might be good for you to help them keep things in perspective.

ARTEN: And on that note, it's time for you to be alone to think about all of this for a while. You might also want to start thinking about a title for our book. We're going to let you name it this time. The last time Pursah gave you the title right in the first four sentences she spoke to you on that first visit, but it took you years to get it! This time, we'll let you choose.

GARY: Cool. Thanks!

ARTEN: And remember your reading assignment.

PURSAH: We're going to give you a saying from the *Course* to think about just before you go onstage to speak during the next two months. You're doing fine with your forgiveness in that area. This will help to accelerate you. By the way, you're in for a big surprise before we come back. Enjoy.

GARY: Something good? I like *good* surprises.

PURSAH: Oh, you'll like this. You'll know what I mean when it happens. It'll play itself out the next couple of months. We'll see you after you get back from Texas. Be well, and think of these words for a minute or two before you walk out in front of the crowds. It will transform your experience.

I who remain as God created me would loose the
world from all I thought it was. For I am real because
the world is not, and I would know my own reality.[26]

Then Arten and Pursah returned to spirit, and I thought for hours about everything that had been said. I also looked forward to the surprise Pursah had mentioned. When it came, being vaguely warned about it didn't spoil it one bit, because I still couldn't believe it.

❦❦❦

6

IT'S THIS LIFETIME, STUPID

> If you are willing to renounce the role of guardian
> of your thought system and open it to me, I will
> correct it very gently and lead you back to God.[1]

On October 27, 2004, the impossible happened. That night it was said that pigs were seen flying over New England; hell froze over; and Elvis, who had passed away 27 years before, but had been previously contracted to give a concert in Maine the night after he died, finally left the building.

My father had been a Red Sox fan his entire life, but at the time he made his transition, he had never seen them win the World Series. Neither had I. Still, despite the team's track record, I had a good feeling about their prospects on that October night for two reasons: First, a total eclipse of the moon was scheduled to occur during the game, and if the Sox were actually going to win the Series for the first time in 86 years, it was bound to be then. Second, the team was red hot. After being down three games to none against their classic rivals, the New York Yankees, the Red Sox had pulled off the biggest victory in team history, beating the Yankees four straight to win the American League pennant. It was a comeback no writer could have made up because people would have thought it was too far-fetched.

A bunch of self-proclaimed "idiots," the Red Sox players had no cares about the so-called Curse of the Bambino that had supposedly plagued the team ever since Babe Ruth was sold to the Yankees in 1919. These guys played like nobody was watching. They loved the game and each other. It was a genuine pleasure to behold.

Not only did I really want the Sox to win, but I was hoping that they'd win that night because I was scheduled to fly to Austin, Texas, in the morning to do a three-day workshop at "The Crossings." I didn't know how the logistics would work in terms of seeing the rest of the games after I got there, so I thought it would be great if the Series ended that night. The Red Sox had won three straight against the St. Louis Cardinals, arguably the best team in baseball that year. After the Sox won the first game, a slugfest that could have gone either way, their starting pitchers took over and performed brilliantly. That was exactly what the team had lacked all those years. They always had great hitters, and this year was no exception.

But having more than one great pitcher on the team was a rarity in Red Sox history. In 2004, they had several, and when the Series came around, they delivered. It's been said that good pitching will always beat good hitting, and vice versa. But the fact is, pitching wins in baseball just like defense wins in football, as the New England Patriots had proven again that year in the Super Bowl. New England sports fans were beside themselves. Despite everything I knew about the world being an illusion, I was one of them. I was being normal.

When the last pitch of the Series was hit back to the pitcher's mound and the ball was tossed to first base, more than a game ended. It was the end of an era, or as I might wisecrack to Arten and Pursah, the end of an error. There never had been a curse. They lost because they lost, and they won because they won.

The game that night was in St. Louis. I was watching at home in Maine between packing things for my flight to Texas. When the historic moment for Red Sox Nation came, I jumped up in the air and yelled out, "Yes! Yes!" I was thrilled as I watched the joy of the players, and also the fans celebrating at the bars and in the streets of Boston who were being shown on national television. Then my thoughts turned to my father.

I thought back to when I was six years old and my dad took my brother, Paul, and me to Fenway Park for the first time. There's nothing like early memories of "The Green Monster" in left field and the crack of a bat against a baseball. Going to Fenway is a regional rite of passage that's passed on from one generation to the next. It's the stuff that childhood dreams are made of. Now, on a night New England would never forget, I joined with my father at the level of the mind and said, "That's for you, Dad. I know you were watching with me."

It was November 2, the night of the Presidential election, when Arten and Pursah appeared to me again. I was the one who spoke first.

GARY: You got me, Pursah. I was expecting a good surprise, but not *that*.

PURSAH: That's one of the reasons we don't tell you too much about your future, Gary. Not only do we not want to deprive you of your forgiveness opportunities, but there can be happy surprises, too. That's duality. You get both good and bad.

GARY: Well, I was thrilled. I've had a permanent smile on my face for six days. When I got to Texas, some readers of the book took me out to eat. I felt like doing something to celebrate. I'd never seen fried rattlesnake on a menu before, so I ordered some and I ate it. Yes, it tasted like chicken.

Anyway, it's been a lot of fun this week. A baseball fan and reader of *Disappearance* e-mailed me and thanked me for forgiving the Red Sox in the book so they could finally win! Remember when I said, "Any team can have a bad century"? Now all we have to do is get the White Sox and the Cubs to win, and we can retire that saying.

ARTEN: Stranger things have happened.

PURSAH: Enjoy, brother. So you got back yesterday and voted today?

GARY: Yeah. I don't suppose you're gonna tell me the outcome?

PURSAH: Well, maybe yes and maybe no.

GARY: Okay. I'll bite. Is Kerry gonna win?

PURSAH: Well, yes and no.

GARY: Come on. What does that mean?

PURSAH: I don't say this to be cynical, just to give you some facts in the dream for you to forgive. Since the 1980s, if a Democrat wants to be elected President of the United States, he or she has to win by *at least* two million votes. That's because across the country the Democratic candidate is routinely cheated out of at least one million and often two million votes in every national election. This time is no different. If someone wins by a comfortable margin, like Bill Clinton did, then yes, a Democrat can be elected President. But in this day and age, you can forget about a Democrat winning the close ones. If he or she *does* win a close one, it's because he or she actually won by a lot more votes than the count shows.

GARY: Are you telling me that Bush is gonna win *again* tonight, but that if every single ballot that was cast in the United States was fairly counted, he wouldn't?

PURSAH: Yes. Sorry. Of course a lot of it is racist. A million black votes are discarded in America every single national election. And there are plenty of tricks that are used that are too numerous to mention right now. As long as people are willing to allow it, then the only recourse your favorite political party has is to win the election by a few million votes. It may still look close, but at least they'll win.

You'll notice in Ohio the exit polls will show that Kerry won, because the people leaving the polls naively assumed their votes would actually be counted. But Kerry will be cheated out of 3 percent of the vote there, and Bush will win among the votes that actually *are* counted.

GARY: You're telling me that our close elections are fixed? That *sucks*. And I was so happy about the Red Sox!

ARTEN: Be of good cheer, brother. There is no world, remember?

GARY: You know, I'm actually feeling that way a lot of the time when there's something to forgive. It's like all I have to do is remember that. There is no world. Then the whole truth comes back to me, but it's not about words; the thought triggers an experience.

PURSAH: As you said when the Sox won, "Yes! Yes!" That's *it.* That's what it's like as you progress on the path. You get so good at forgiveness that it starts to get easier. Right-minded thoughts trigger the experience of the truth in you. I wouldn't have brought up the thing about the election tonight in the first place if I didn't know you were ready to forgive it. You *are* ready, right?

GARY: Yes, I am. I mean how can I take George Bush seriously anyway? Look at him. He's not real. He's like a cardboard-cutout poster boy for corporate corruption. In the dream story, they sent Martha Stewart to jail for doing less than the kind of insider stock deal he did when his father was President. And instead of the haves and the have-nots, he joked in public that his political base consists of "the haves, and the have-mores." It's nothing but a joke that this guy is President. Up until recently I forgot to laugh. I thought he was real. But he's not. I set myself up to hate this guy, and now I can see he's not even there. It was all a trick. I made him up so he could be the guilty one instead of me. He's the scapegoat. But If I release him, then I'm free.

ARTEN: Not bad for a rattlesnake eater, and very much in harmony with what J says here in his Course: "A simple question yet remains, and needs an answer. Do you like what you have made?—a world of murder and attack, through which you thread your timid way through constant dangers, alone and frightened, hoping at most that death will wait a little longer before it overtakes you and you disappear. *You made this up.* It is a picture of what you think you are; of how you see yourself."[2]

It's only after the ego is sufficiently undone that you can look back and see how crazy your ego thought system was. That's why J also says this: "You cannot evaluate an insane belief system from within it. Its range precludes this. You can only go beyond it, look back from a point where sanity exists and *see the contrast.* Only by this contrast can insanity be judged as insane."[3]

GARY: Yeah. Like I've been thinking about all that stuff about the body. I did my reading homework, you know, and then I observed a lot of the things that are going on. It's like everything in life, or what we call life, is about the body and connected to the body. If you win a game, or if you lose, or you're successful in your career or a failure, and I've been both, you get the girl or you get rejected, you're famous or scorned, you're hungry for food, whatever kind you like, you're horny for sex, whatever kind you like, you want a new place to live or a new car, or you just want a rest. What *is* it that gets all these things and wants all these things? What would *any* of them be without a body? And when we're horrified by tragedies, what is it that we see as dying? Who do we feel bad for? And when someone we love dies, what is that we think died? It's always about the body. Without the body none of it would mean a thing. That hero of the dream stuff is really true. And the more I forgive, the more the body *feels* like it's just a dream figure. It feels lighter. It's like it isn't me.

I started going to a study group in Leeds just a few months after you two first showed up. The last time I went, and I'd been going there for 11 years, one of the regulars told me that I look younger today than when I first started going. That's fun. I'm not saying that the benefits are gonna show up the same way for everyone. But if all thought produces form at some level, then we know the forgiveness is doing its work somewhere.

> **The more you forgive, the more you become aware that you're just dreaming.**

ARTEN: Excellent. You can't wake up from a dream as long as you're stuck in it. Awareness of dreaming breaks the hold. And the more you forgive, the more you become aware that you're just dreaming.

PURSAH: We're going to do a time-travel exercise that will help you understand the nonlinear nature of things and help you get even more that this is all something of your own making. Are you game?

GARY: Absolutely!

ARTEN: You've got a lot of interesting trips coming up. We know that you're excited about going to Australia, and we noticed that you just happened to arrange a workshop in Hawaii on the way back. We may as well start calling you bro all the time, brother. You'll be going there three times within the next year and three months or so.

GARY: Three times! I've only been there twice in my life!

ARTEN: Have a good time. You have great people you're supposed to meet there. There are no accidents in salvation. It always looks like something else, and it always comes back to relationships. But to stay on the subject of our time-travel exercise, another place you'll be going to in about six months is St. Louis.

GARY: Cool. Hey! Cahokia! I should go there!

ARTEN: Because time is holographic and not linear, your trip has already been made. We're going to transport ourselves six months into the future. You won't see us until you get near the mound of the Great Sun. You'll be with two people you've already met by the time you go to Cahokia with them six months from now, but because you're being transported there from this place and time with your present awareness, you won't know them this time. That doesn't matter. You don't talk much on this trip because all three of you are respectful of where you're going. We'll think you into the hologram at the point where you arrive at Cahokia.

At times you'll notice Pursah and me walking around at a bit of a distance from you three. Of course you won't say anything to your friends about us. They've read the book, but they won't connect us to it because we'll be just far enough away for them to not think about us. Without realizing it, you'll do everything exactly as you will six months from now. It's just that six months from now, you'll be doing it a second time. When we transport you back here this time, it will be as though you have a memory of something that hasn't really happened yet in your linear time frame, but has already occurred in holographic time. Then six months from now when you go to Cahokia, we want you to observe what it's like and report your experience back to us. Are you ready?

GARY: Are you kidding? Let's go!

NOTE: I was stunned when I immediately found myself in a car that was stopping in a parking lot. The person sitting in the driver's seat shut off the car, got out, and so did I. There was a modern-looking building near us as we walked out of the parking lot. We headed down a narrow road toward what appeared to be the main road and then crossed it. There were two men with me whom I didn't recognize. The second one had been sitting in the backseat. We didn't say too much, but talked in general, almost hushed tones about Cahokia. I had an eerie feeling of déjà vu as I crossed the road and entered a field. I could see a giant mound of earth and immediately recognized it as the home of the Great Sun, the American Indian spiritual master of a thousand years ago. The people had built a house for him on top of the mound, and I had dreamed, seen visions of, and thought often about the lifetime I lived here at the time the Great Sun ruled.

We walked toward the mound. It was a warm, sunny day, but it felt more like spring than summer. When we got there, I saw that it would be a climb up two different levels of stairs to get to the top. There were signs saying that the area was a state historic site, and they explained details about what I was looking at, but I was too amazed by what was happening to read them. It was then that I also noticed Arten and Pursah about a hundred feet away, dressed in jeans and talking to each other. They were inconspicuous, and the two guys I was with didn't seem to notice them. I noticed *them*, though, because Pursah had her shirt tied up and was exposing her tummy. *What a tease,* I thought, because she knew I had this thing for a woman's belly button, but I wouldn't be close enough to see hers.

I was surprised when the two men I was with stopped and motioned for me to go ahead by myself. It was as though they were showing respect for my privacy, and it was only then I realized I had a desire to go to the top of the mound alone and experience being there. I took it as a sign of respect that the two men would do that for me, and I felt another familiarity, this time with the men themselves, and realized that they had been there a thousand years ago, too, even though they didn't look anything today like they did back then. There were other people in the area, but no one else was going to the top of the mound right at that time.

I began my ascent up the mound, slowly walking up the stairs and looking around. Once I was up about 20 feet to the top of the first level, I could see the skyline of a city not too far in the distance. I realized that it must be St. Louis, although I wasn't sure exactly how far away it was. I guessed from five to ten miles. The surrounding area was very flat and green, but there were also a lot of trees and a very peaceful feeling.

After looking over the countryside I went up the next flight of stairs to the second level, which was the peak of the mound. It had a flat top, but the house where the Great Sun lived was gone. After the visit to my place in Maine years earlier by Arten and Pursah when they first talked about the Great Sun and me, I began to have numerous fascinating memories of him and what life was like in Cahokia. I could remember visiting him here in his house on top of the mound. Although we were friends, it was still considered an honor among Indians to be invited to go to the top of the mound and enter the home.

As I surveyed the area, I realized that something else was missing. The river! Where was the river? Then I remembered hearing that there had been a continent-altering earthquake some 300 years ago in this very area, and it had caused the Mississippi River to reflow several miles away. I knew from my memories that the river was important to Cahokia a thousand years ago, because it was a place of large gatherings and commerce. I also knew if that big an earthquake were to happen today in this same area, the toll in human lives, damage, and suffering would be way beyond what most people could imagine.

I went to all four corners of the top of the mound, staring in different directions and taking in the experience of being there. I could see the two men I had come with, whom I hadn't been introduced to yet, standing and talking a little bit in the distance below me. Arten and Pursah stayed far enough away to not be noticed by the two men, and I felt amused by being the only one who knew they were there. I also made a mental note to give Pursah a hard time about her choice of wardrobe.

Then, as I stood alone on top of the huge mound and glanced at the tranquil surroundings, I had a vision. Like most visions, it only lasted a few seconds. Suddenly I saw many people, *thousands* of them. There was a large communal plaza where people walked and greeted each other. There were also tables in a huge marketplace, and a large, pillared village with many houses. There was a bustling, festive atmosphere. Men were playing games, but I couldn't see exactly what they were doing because they were surrounded. Then, just as suddenly as it began, the vision was over.

I sensed that the house on top of the mound had been next to me, but I didn't have time to look at it. Still, I was astounded by how real it all seemed. It wasn't *just* a vision; I was *there*, in the Cahokia that's both legendary and sacred to the American Indians. I was home again, if only for a few seconds.

There was more than one "Great Sun" leader over the years in Cahokia, but the one who lived there a thousand years ago was like no other. He was not only a genius at governing people, he was the spiritual equivalent of Buddha and J. When he ruled, Cahokia was one of the most peaceful places anywhere or anytime in history, even if that particular phase of it only lasted for a couple of decades. I had many wistful memories of this place, and of my life as an Indian who traveled the rivers and was a trader of furs. But I always came home to see my family, my friends, and a city of peace that couldn't last indefinitely because it was part of a world that was based on separation.

After I came down from the mound, I told the two men about my vision. They understood completely and didn't seem the least bit surprised. Then we walked back to the parking lot and went to a building called The Interpretive Center. We walked through the door of the Center, but as I did, I was astounded once again, this time to find myself instantaneously sitting in my chair looking at Arten and Pursah, just as I had been before the visit to Cahokia began.

ARTEN: Well, what did you think?

GARY: Unbelievable, in many ways. The place itself was amazing, but the *vision*—that was one of the most incredible experiences I've ever had. It seemed so *real,* just like being there in Cahokia this time seemed real. But it couldn't be real. You transported me there. It was an event that hasn't even happened yet. And the vision I saw at the top of the mound was of a thousand years ago. Now it looks like I'm here, and this seems real. My God, I'm not really here either, am I? You didn't send me there so I'd think it was real; you sent me there to make me realize that *none* of it's real!

ARTEN: Yes, and you'll experience that on an even deeper level now. Let it unfold in your awareness. You're not a body, and no body you ever saw was real. Nothing that passes away can be true. As J says in the *Course:* "Can you paint rosy red lips on a skeleton, dress it in loveliness, pet it and pamper it, and make it live? And can you be content with an illusion that you are living?"[4]

PURSAH: The next time you get upset with someone's behavior, think of their body as being a wind-up toy. If you really *knew* that the body was just a wind-up toy, then it couldn't upset you, no matter *what* it said or did. If you really understood that what you were seeing wasn't true, then it wouldn't bother you at all. That's the way you should be with people who give you a difficult time.

Nothing that passes away can be true.

GARY: Wow, I can see that. I'll try it. Really, but hey, what was with that outfit at Cahokia? Were you trying to give me ideas?

PURSAH: My little joke, Gary. Forgive me. Remember, everyone has preferences. This isn't about giving them up, because the *Course* isn't about behavior. At the same time, it's helpful to remember, when you can, that none of what you see with the body's eyes in this lifetime is true, and *everything* is for forgiveness. Many of the desires people have, as well as the relationship intricacies, both good and bad, are continuations of themes from past dream lifetimes.

For example, you lived a lifetime in what is now Syria where you were in a position of power. You developed and carried over into this lifetime the same belly-button fetish you have now. In that other lifetime, you made sure you got your share of belly-dancing entertainment. You shouldn't feel guilty about that. Belly dancing is an exquisite and beautiful art. Of course, it's also inescapably sexy. You were also quite spiritual in that lifetime, and you were well spoken. The Syrian language is actually the closest language you have today to Aramaic. In very recent history, Syria pretty much committed suicide with its civil war. It will recover, though.

My point is that you can choose to forgive anything in *any* lifetime because, as we just demonstrated to you, time isn't linear, but holographic. For that reason, there's *no* difference between choosing the Holy Spirit right now and choosing the Holy Spirit at the exact instant of the separation! People don't realize that history is happening right now, and so is the future, and the *only* thing that matters is choosing forgiveness now. When you had that vision in Cahokia, you were just breaking through some of the blocks in the mind. But it's really always about now. So don't be concerned about whether or not you're going to come back for another lifetime. Don't be concerned about your past lifetimes. It's *always* about now, and it's *always* about forgiveness. It's this lifetime that matters, always, and then you learn that every instant is really always the same instant anyway.

Do you remember that political campaign you were into once when the economy was bad, and the winning candidate kept reminding the people in his campaign, "It's the economy, stupid"? They stayed focused on what mattered and they won. And guess what? When it comes to spirituality, it's this lifetime, stupid. If you stay focused on forgiving it and everything that happens in it, then you can win, big time, and not just in illusions. So we use the body and past lifetimes to illustrate for you that there's only one purpose for everything, and if you stay focused on what really matters, then you *will* win.

GARY: And helping me and other people stay focused is why you came back?

PURSAH: Yes. It's about true forgiveness and staying focused on it in this lifetime. What you're *really* forgiving is always the instant of separation from God, no matter what the forgiveness opportunity may look like. And the purpose is always to be free of the false universe and return to the real Universe, Heaven, by forgiving what's right in front of your face. It's not about whether or not you come back for another lifetime in the future, and it's not about history.

GARY: I like history, but I don't empathize with the historical figures that much. I mean, it's like they're a bunch of people who happened to be in the right place at the right time, then they just did what had to be done, and now they're given *way* too much credit. Hey, wait a minute. That sounds like me.

PURSAH: Helping people stay focused isn't as easy as you might think. For example, the most popular teacher of *A Course in Miracles,* at least before you came along, has repeatedly put people's focus on fixing up the dream instead of waking up from it.

GARY: Yeah, I heard her talking to someone who saw an apparition of a split mind who had gone on to the other side, and she said to the person who saw it, "That's reality." Well, according to the *Course,* that's *not* reality. She's confusing people. It obscures the choice that needs to be made. Reality is perfect oneness with God, and nothing else exists—nothing that changes, nothing that appears separate. *Nothing.* I've also gotten e-mails from her where she tries to get people to take certain actions in the world, like stopping genocide, and she actually included a quote from Dante, the one that says, "There is a special place in hell reserved for those who, in times of moral crisis, remain neutral." I mean, talk about trying to get people to do something in the illusion by making them feel guilty! What does *that* have to do with *A Course in Miracles?*

The *Course* says about the body: "Of itself it is neutral, as is everything in the world of perception."[5] Yes, the *Course* teaches there are no neutral *thoughts,*[6] because it's a *Course* in cause, which is the mind, and not effects, which is the world. And she says things like you have to fix up the world, and that's what turns it into a "happy dream," which isn't what the *Course* means by that at all, but she puts the emphasis on fixing it up first and *then* you can be free of it. Well, *no.* The happy dream doesn't have *anything* to do with what's going on in the world. When you reach a state like J or Buddha and you're having a happy dream, then you're completely peaceful *regardless* of what appears to be happening in the world. She's distracting people from the truth by putting their focus on the wrong place, the illusion, instead of on the right place, which is the decision in the mind to forgive what isn't really there. As the *Course* says, our task is *not* to give truth to our illusions, but to bring our illusions to the truth.

PURSAH: The exact quote is: "When you try to bring truth to illusions, you are trying to make illusions real, and keep them by justifying your belief in them. But to give illusions to truth is to enable truth to teach that the illusions are unreal, and thus enable you to escape from them. Reserve not one idea aside from truth, or you establish orders of reality that must imprison you. There is no order in reality, because everything there is true."[7]

So, is there anything you'd like to add?

GARY: I could, but I'm being polite. I mean, obviously there's nothing *wrong* with trying to stop genocide. But if you want to move around the furniture in a burning house instead of focusing on the real problem, then why confuse people by telling them you're teaching *A Course in Miracles?* Why not just admit that you're doing your own thing? If you're gonna teach the *Course,* then teach the *Course.* If you're gonna teach something else, then teach something else, but don't *call* it the *Course.*

> A successful relationship is one where you are forgiving, or have forgiven, the other person.

PURSAH: The reason I brought her up was because *she* isn't really there either. So remember something. This isn't about being right in regard to what the *Course* means. If you want the experience the *Course* is directed toward, then it's about *using* what you know to forgive. Is that clear to you?

GARY: Yeah. You're right. I get caught up in things too much sometimes, and *that's* making it real, too.

PURSAH: Since you realize that, we'll let you practice forgiving it. That's good. Your forgiveness lessons are whatever's going on in your life. That's why we talk to you about these things. We said that we were going to focus more on your professional forgiveness lessons this time than your personal ones, and we have.

Obviously it doesn't really matter whether it's professional or personal. You just happen to have a whole new kind of life in the last couple of years. Whether professional or personal, I'll give you the definition of a successful relationship. Listen carefully. It doesn't matter who it is or what it looks like. You got that? Even if the relationship appears to be a bad one and things are terrible on the level of form, it doesn't matter. *A successful relationship is one where you are forgiving, or have forgiven, the other person.* That's what it takes to transform it into a holy relationship, and that's *all* it takes.

As the *Course* says, "To heal, then, is to correct perception in your brother and yourself by sharing the Holy Spirit with him. This places you both within the Kingdom, and restores its wholeness in your mind. This reflects creation, because it unifies by increasing and integrates by extending."[8]

ARTEN: J also says, "The extension of truth, which *is* the law of the Kingdom, rests only on the knowledge of what truth is. This is your inheritance and requires no learning at all, but when you disinherited yourself you became a learner of necessity."[9]

GARY: Very clear, man. I read quotations like that from the *Course,* and I wonder how anyone can come up with a different interpretation of it than what you've taught me.

ARTEN: People can only accept what they're ready to. So some people will learn a great deal from our books and use them, and some people will say you're crazy, or some people will say you lied about us and you were trying to make money.

GARY: That's ridiculous. It's not money that I love; it's the sex I can buy with it.

ARTEN: Actually, you haven't gotten that hard a time from people on the road, have you? No real confrontations, and people haven't really stood up and said you're crazy either. Not that you won't

> **People can only accept what they're ready to.**

get a heckler once in a while. That goes with the territory. But in general, you're doing great.

GARY: Yeah, that's really true. Hey! You probably already know this, but I've been given an advance peek at an article that was written about me by a psychiatrist from New Hampshire, Dr. William Evans. It's called "Mystical Experiences: Is Gary Renard and *The Disappearance of the Universe* for real?" Let me grab it and read you a cool excerpt. It started out with Bill kind of interviewing me, but we became friends, as the article shows. Not only is he a psychiatrist, he has a lot of experience with spirituality and mysticism. He's given me permission to use his article as I please. Dig this:

"Gary and I developed an extensive e-mail relationship, and I spent the day after Thanksgiving, 2003, having an enjoyable lunch alone with him in Maine. Later, he asked me to fly to Virginia Beach, Virginia to attend a lecture he gave at the Association for Research and Enlightenment at Edgar Cayce's organization last March, and we had dinner there afterwards. I have since been to more of Gary's functions and have had a couple of other intimate dinners with him.

"Recently, I began to get the strong intuition that this was no accident, indeed it may be a major part of my purpose in life, that I was in a position of being a psychiatrist knowledgeable of Yogananda's documentation of experiences similar to Gary's, and friendly with Gary in a personal manner. Certainly, being a psychiatrist with some special interest in diagnosing clinical delusional disorders and distinguishing them from other clinical psychotic disorders, I am in an expert position to assure you that Gary is not delusional when he relates his story of the actual physical manifestations of the ascended masters, Arten and Pursah (not their real names, as many of you who have read his book now know.)"

Pretty neat, huh? I'm not delusional.

ARTEN: What does he know? Just kidding. So that only leaves two possibilities: You're either telling the truth in regard to your experience or you're lying. No offense, but you're not smart enough to have written *Disappearance* on your own. You're not a dumb shit, as Master Teacher said, but you're not capable of writing a book that succeeded in doing what other people have been trying to do for 30 years: make *A Course in Miracles* truly understandable to the everyday person.

GARY: An English teacher friend of mine from New Jersey told me that I'm the one who brought the *Course* into the vernacular. I'm gonna look that up.

ARTEN: Good boy. We're going to be going soon, so don't forget your number one priority, which is forgiveness. You did a good job last week when that car on the highway cut you off and sped away. You felt like yelling at the driver and giving him the finger. You didn't, even though you were taken aback by what he did.

GARY: Yeah. Those cops think they own the road.

PURSAH: Keep forgiving on the Internet, too. Sometimes people appear to attack, and you have to remember what your job is.

GARY: Yeah, some of those people online can be pretty mean.

PURSAH: Don't assume malice for what stupidity may be able to explain.

ARTEN: We're going to leave you this time with two quotes, one from the *Course* and one from Shakespeare.

GARY: I never asked you, was Shakespeare enlightened?

ARTEN: Yes, he was.

GARY: Cool. I knew it.

PURSAH: Remember, it's through your own choice for the Holy Spirit and His thought system instead of the ego's that your mind is returned to peace. That has to happen *first* in order for you to go home. You can't skip your forgiveness homework. Everybody wants to skip to the end and be enlightened now, but it doesn't work that way. If peace is the condition of the Kingdom, then the mind must be at peace in order to fit in. And in order for the mind to *be* at peace, you have to forgive. It's as simple as that.

With that in mind, think about this quote from the *Course* in the light of all we've discussed. Then take it with you in your heart wherever you go, and remember that we love you:

"Faith in the eternal is always justified, for the eternal is forever kind, infinite in its patience and wholly loving. It will accept you wholly, and give you peace. Yet it can unite only with what already is at peace in you, immortal as itself."[10]

ARTEN: As you continue the process of experiencing the meaninglessness of the body, looking past it and thinking of people as they really are, which is perfect spirit, you may want to consider this quotation from *The Tempest*. There's a striking similarity between what we've been saying, the quotations we've used from *A Course in Miracles,* and these lines. The truth is the truth, and nobody has a monopoly on it. After I speak these words, just sit here silently for a while. We know you'll enjoy Australia and Hawaii. Stay too cool for school, bro.

Our revels now are ended. These our actors,
As I foretold you, were all spirits and
Are melted into air, into thin air
And, like the baseless fabric of this vision,
The cloud-capp'd towers, the gorgeous palaces,
The solemn temples, the great globe itself,
Yea, all which it inherit, shall dissolve
And, like this insubstantial pageant faded,
Leave not a rack behind. We are such stuff
As dreams are made of, and our little life
Is rounded with a sleep.

PURSAH'S GOSPEL OF THOMAS

> I am constantly being perceived as a
> teacher either to be exalted or rejected, but
> I do not accept either perception for myself.[1]

Later that month I went on a 20,000-mile trip. I flew five hours to California, and then a thirteen-and-a-half-hour nonstop flight to Australia, where I got to speak in four different states and do a national radio show. It was all very much like a dream, not just because I couldn't believe I was there, but because of all that my teachers and I had been discussing. I liked Australia very much and got to see some of Sydney, Melbourne, Tasmania, the Gold Coast, Brisbane, and a beautiful place at the easternmost tip of the continent called Byron Bay. In general, the people in Australia seemed more laid back than Americans, and not as materialistic. I took delight in the little things, like seeing a sky full of stars with a completely different configuration, including the Southern Cross, which I had wanted to see since I was a child, and watching the water spin down the drain counterclockwise instead of clockwise because of the change in magnetism from being in the Southern Hemisphere. My hosts, Raj and Suzanne, pointed out that I'm not very hard to please.

It was another long flight to Hawaii. I was sleepy when I got there, but I couldn't help but notice when I looked in the mirror in the airport men's room that I had a smile on my face. I was in

Hawaii, or at least it sure looked that way, and I was very happy. Arten was right, there were great people I was supposed to meet there. I did, and I was sure I'd meet many more. I loved the Aloha spirit of Hawaii, the friendliness of the people, the beauty of the islands, and the gentleness of the climate. I didn't have any illusions about Hawaii being perfect, because no place is. But it had taken me 35 years to get there the first time, and I greatly appreciated any chance I had to be in this wonderful place. With all the traveling I was doing, it didn't seem practical to live there yet, as it would add five hours on to every flight to do a workshop in America. Still, I had ideas of moving to the islands when the timing was right.

Overall, my life had taken on a surreal quality. It was hectic, but I always seemed to have just enough time and energy to do what had to be done. Given that I was a low-energy guy who didn't even have a personal assistant, I could only attribute my logistical success to the guidance of the Holy Spirit.

When it was December 21 again and I was back home, I looked forward to Arten and Pursah's next visit. Even though they hadn't specifically said they'd appear that day or night, they'd chosen that date many times over the previous 12 years. I went to the movies in the afternoon and saw an exciting and somewhat sexy movie. When I got out of the theater, it was unusually cold, even for Maine, and I realized I wasn't looking forward to winter. Fortunately, I was scheduled to go back to Hawaii (this time to Kauai on my birthday in March), to do another tropical workshop. Somehow that made the winter seem more tolerable. Also, I'd joke with J about the cold, and he'd remind me what it was really for.

When Arten and Pursah appeared that night, I felt an immediate connection of love. The words the two of them used just before they left the last time had touched me deeply. I was genuinely grateful to be with them. Pursah spoke first.

PURSAH: Hey, buddy. How was the movie?

GARY: It was very titillating.

PURSAH: Nice. And we saw that you had a great time in Australia and Hawaii. Congratulations. You deserve it.

ARTEN: Absolutely, and Mele Kalikimaka.

GARY: Thanks! Merry Christmas to you, too. Hey, wait, is that politically correct?

ARTEN: Who cares?

GARY: You're right. But just in case, Happy Hanukah, Kwanzaa, Ramadan, Wiccan Festival of the Yule, Gita Jayanthi, Feast Day for St. Thomas, and National Canada Day. Just kidding on that last one.

It's great to see you two again! And yes, I loved the whole trip. You know what was strange, though? When I was flying across America on the first leg, everybody was so uptight—the security is so personally intrusive and illogical. I mean, they don't even check the most likely place for a bomb to go on board, which is in the cargo, because that might cost a corporation a few bucks, or do anything to stop a potential surface-to-air missile attack, and in the meantime there's just a depressed kind of a feeling hanging over most of the people, who are treated like they're criminals or something.

It's not about the TSA [Transportation Security Administration] doing anything that actually works; it's about using fear to gain political power and control the country, which, of course, is about money. Then, when I got to California and switched over to the Australian airline, Qantas, it was like a total breath of fresh air. The employees were light and playful with the passengers and each other, having a good time, there was a festive atmosphere, the security was less invasive and more high tech, and it was like it was okay for life to be fun again. America has become a sad place, and I have to think it's been caused by this hidden agenda of wanting to own and run the world, and the resentment that comes back to us as a result. Hey, I'm sorry. I don't mean to get into politics again. Let's talk about something else.

ARTEN: What you say about the difference in attitude between the two countries is very true. In America it's become *all* about the money. There's a saying that different countries have about each other, but in the case of America, it's true. You could say that in America, people live to work, but in most other countries, people work to live. Living to work is exactly what the corporations want, because that's what's best for profits. But when it's all about the money, it makes for a different kind of a life. True, it's all illusion, but in that illusion, you should always ask the Holy Spirit what kind of a life is best for *you.*

GARY: Thanks, I appreciate that. So, I have other questions.

ARTEN: We have answers. What's up?

GARY: First, I've noticed that there's still a little controversy about the fact that the final, published version of *A Course in Miracles* was slightly abridged, mostly in the first five chapters, from the earlier versions, which are referred to as the Urtext, meaning original Text, and the one that's called the "Hugh Lynn Cayce Version" of the *Course,* which is the copy Helen and Bill gave to Edgar Cayce's son, Hugh Lynn, during a visit to Virginia Beach. Those two early versions weren't published, and The Hugh Lynn Cayce version doesn't include the Workbook or Manual for Teachers. The Hugh Lynn Cayce version was obtained illegally, I guess meaning it was stolen, by someone who put it on the Internet. That's why it's available. In any case, I want to be confident that the words I'm reading in the *Course* are the ones that J *meant* for me to be studying.

For example, there's a small minority of students who accuse Ken Wapnick of editing the *Course* and changing it to his own liking after it was scribed. When I was in Fairfax, Virginia, one of them showed me the Hugh Lynn Cayce version and said, "Here, you see what the *Course* looked like before Ken Wapnick got his hands on it and altered it?" They say about 25 percent of the first five chapters that are in the Hugh Lynn Cayce version are missing from the published version. They also say that J told Helen in the Urtext that Bill should be in charge of what goes in the *Course,* and that Bill's opinion is reflected in the Hugh Lynn Cayce version, but he wasn't consulted for the final version. They say that's why its meaning is different. They say the term *Sons of God* is used a lot, and they *know* this means that God *did* create separate individuals. They also contend that the *Course* says you should do certain things in the world. There's an early quote that says: "Listen to my voice, learn to undo error, and do something to correct it." Can you shed some light on these things for me and other students? I'm not saying I don't already have an opinion on this. I do. But I'd like to hear what you guys have to say about this on the record.

ARTEN: Pursah is going to have a lot to say this visit about J's words, so I'll let her answer.

PURSAH: Sure. What was your question again? Just kidding. I can say in no uncertain terms that the words of J you are studying in the authentic, published version of *A Course in Miracles* are *exactly* the right words of his that you're supposed to be studying. That blue book you have right there is the right one. I'll briefly address what you just said so you'll know why you're betting on a winner.

First, before I begin correcting the misinformation, let's get one thing straight: From the very beginning of the scribing of *A Course in Miracles* in 1965, all the way through to the publication of the *Course* in 1976, there was only *one* editor of the *Course,* and that was Helen Schucman. Bill Thetford was *never* an editor of the *Course.* Ken Wapnick was *never* an editor of the *Course.* By *all* accounts, Bill included, Helen was very protective of the material and considered it to be her "life's work," with the understanding that she was the scribe and not the author. Helen would never have let *anyone* mess around with the *Course* unless they were suggesting something that she totally agreed with and felt inspired by Jesus to do. I hope there's nothing about that you don't understand.

Yes, J told Helen very early that if there was ever a disagreement, then Bill should be the one to decide what should go in the *Course.* Bill never saw any reason to exercise that option. At the time J said that, toward the beginning, Helen was very fearful. That's why it was said. But as time went on, Helen got more used to the process and became more comfortable with it. You can see the *Course* flowing more and more smoothly as the years went on, being increasingly given in iambic pentameter and culminating to the point where the last couple of chapters are given completely in Shakespearean blank verse.

As for Bill, we pointed out earlier that he knew what the *Course* meant. That's why he referred to it as the "Christian Vedanta." He understood that it was a purely nondualistic teaching. We'll talk more about Bill shortly.

Ken Wapnick came on the scene with Helen and Bill after the *Course* had already been scribed. The first version of the *Course* he saw was the Hugh Lynn Cayce version. Obviously, Ken could not have been responsible for any of the changes that were made from the Urtext to the Hugh Lynn Cayce version. He did suggest to Helen that the *Course* could be more professional, with better chapter titles, subsections, more consistent capitalization and punctuation, and the like. Helen, in the meantime, wanted to omit certain things that Jesus said that were more personal and clearly meant for her and Bill, or were more professional and would only be properly understood by those in their field. She even makes reference to these omissions in the Preface of the *Course*. There was never any attempt to hide it. It was always completely innocent, and none of it had any effect on what the *Course* means. During the editing, Helen was inspired by Jesus. J did not dictate the editing, but it was certainly a case of Helen being in spirit along with him.

GARY: There's a scholar named Richard Smoley who wasn't connected with any of the controversy, so he didn't have an ax to grind, and he wrote a report about the differences between the three versions of the *Course* and came to the conclusion that the differences were, and I quote, "Very minor." Like a better way of saying the same thing?

PURSAH: That's correct. These minor differences didn't change the overall meaning of the *Course* one bit. So let's continue to look for a minute at some of the things that are being said by people who want to spend their time convincing others that there's something wrong with the published version of the *Course* instead of spending their time learning it. For example, you mentioned that about 25 percent of the first five chapters are missing. Well, 25 percent sounds like a lot, doesn't it? But is making a statement like that honest, or is it intentionally deceptive? There are not 5 chapters in the Text, there are 31. Put in the context of the entire Text, Helen did not omit 25 percent of it, but only 3 percent. She had the equivalent of a 692-page Text which, when published, still retained 669 pages, or 97 percent. And the Text is just one part of the *Course!*

There are 1,248 pages, including the Workbook and Manual for Teachers. So if we look at the situation honestly, then we find that what Helen omitted from the entire *Course* was not 25 percent, but

1.7 percent. That's *1.7* percent, and most of it from the first five chapters that were scribed during the first few difficult months of a seven-year process. Why are some people focusing so heavily on a few changes during the first five chapters? Could it be because by doing so they don't have to learn the *Course,* and can simply make up their own? It's nothing more than an ego distraction designed to keep people away from the truth.

You mentioned that the term *Sons of God* is used a lot, and that some people see this when reading the first five chapters and just "know" this means that God *did* create individuals. But what they actually "know" is a totally misinformed beginner's interpretation of the *Course.* The fact that the *Course* uses the term *Sons of God* is hardly a revelation. It is used throughout the *Course* to refer to the seemingly split-off parts of the Sonship, the ones who *think* they are separate. The *Course* also uses the term *Son of God,* singular, to describe Christ, which is perfect oneness with God, and which is what they *really* are. The *Course* is so consistent about that all the way through all three books that to ascribe any other meaning to the terms is, in a word, inept.

You also brought up those who contend that the *Course* says you should do certain things in the world. There's an early quote that says: "Listen to my voice, learn to undo error, and do something to correct it." Well, what you *do* is give it to the Holy Spirit, who is in the mind. It's *never* about doing anything in the world. Never! If you're inspired to do something after you forgive, fine. But that's never the *focus* of the *Course.* To teach people otherwise is completely inaccurate.

Ken Wapnick, a fine scholar and now the *Course's* greatest teacher, came on the scene in 1972, after Helen and Bill had already been working with the *Course* for seven years. Ken hadn't been working with it at all at that time. He was much younger than they were, and they had higher positions than he did at work. So I have a question for you: Does it make any sense to think that Helen and Bill would let Ken change the *Course?* Why would they do that? You can probably think of a dozen reasons why they *wouldn't* let him do that, but can you think of one reason why they *would?* Ken read the *Course* in 1973 and assisted Helen in editing it the next two years. Helen herself went over every single word of the published version to make sure it was right. She was the editor and made the decisions.

Now let's talk about Bill Thetford. The critics of the published version always seem to invoke his name, as though he was never consulted in the final editing. Let's be generous and say that this position is caused by ignorance and not dishonesty. It was Bill who insisted that there be 50 principles of miracles at the beginning, not 43 or 53, as there were in different retypings by Helen. Thus, there were 50 in the final version at Bill's insistence. No material was added or deleted from the Text in order to accomplish this. It was simply rearranged. Bill was also adamant that the final paragraph of the Text should appear on one page and not be broken up. That's the way it appears.

Does that sound like a man who was left out of the loop, didn't know what was going on, and wasn't consulted or allowed to give his opinion? No. The truth is, Bill wasn't the kind of a man who liked to pay attention to a lot of details, which is required in editing. But he was shown the editing whenever anything was changed, such as a paragraph being moved around, and when he thought something was important, he spoke up. *That's* the way it really was. So now let's ask our own questions to those who try to find something sinister in normal editing decisions instead of doing the *Course.*

Weren't both Helen and Bill satisfied enough with the final edit of *A Course in Miracles* to publish it (along with Ken Wapnick, Judy Skutch, and Bob Skutch) under the name of the nonprofit organization the Foundation for Inner Peace? Weren't they the five original members? Didn't Helen appear in person in California with Bill, Ken, and Judy sharing the newly published *Course* with people? Didn't Bill appear on camera on more than one occasion and quote from the published version, and also use it himself in study-group meetings in the San Diego area during his retirement? Did Helen, in the five years that she lived after the *Course* was published; or Bill, in the ten years that he lived after the *Course* was published; *ever* do anything or say anything to suggest that the final published version of the *Course* wasn't the right version that people should be studying?

It's inaccurate at best and dishonest at worst to present Bill as being anything but completely behind the final, published version of the *Course*. And I don't think it's going too far to say that both Bill and Helen would be completely supporting it if they were here today. So whom are you going to believe, the people who were there, or people who came along later and wanted the *Course* for themselves, apparently so they could have it mean what they want it to mean instead of having to do it?

GARY: I love your rhetorical questions. Thanks, Pursah. That's a real help for me. As for others, let them decide. But you know, the arguments of the people who spread the controversy never rang true for me. I mean, if the Holy Spirit can see all of time, do they expect me to believe that J didn't know what he was doing when he gave his *Course* to Helen and Bill? And are these critics saying that J didn't know that Ken and Judy would be coming on the scene? Are they saying that J would go through all of that scribing with Helen, and have her go through everything she had to while taking down the *Course* for seven years, knowing that his message wouldn't be given the way he wanted it? That doesn't make any sense. In fact, it sounds like crap. Actually, it sounds like a huge, steaming pile of crap.

PURSAH: Don't overdo it. The point is that you have the right version of the *Course*. And certainly J knew everything that was going to happen when he chose to work with Helen and Bill. If he knew it wasn't going to come out the way he wanted, then why would he do it? He can see everything that ever happened or ever will happen from the end of time, just as the *Course* teaches.[2] He also says, "I do not choose God's channels wrongly."[3] Those who suggest that another version of the *Course* is needed rather than the authentic one are falling into a trap. As J says right in the *Course,* ". . . those who seek controversy will find it. Yet those who seek clarification will find it as well. They must, however, be willing to overlook controversy, recognizing that it is a defense against truth in the form of a delaying maneuver."[4]

The seekers of controversy, and those who champion them, accomplish one thing and one thing only. They manage to distract potentially good students who otherwise would *do* the *Course,* get them to focus on the trees instead of the forest, and thus delay their experience of the truth. If that's the desired vocation of these people, then they're welcome to it. But the truth is still there to be found by anyone who seeks clarification and is willing to use the technology of forgiveness. They will also find the experience that goes along with it, which is the goal of the *Course*.

ARTEN: Now, a word about splits. Dividing is what the ego does. Everything in the world separates, even if only through death, because everything here is symbolic of the thought of separation. Don't fear that. It will always happen as long as there appears to be any kind of form. There has never been a church or spiritual organization that didn't undergo some kind of a split, usually sooner rather than later. Your job is to forgive it. Do the *Course*. If there appear to be divisions on the level of form within the *Course* community, understand that the way out of it is *not* on the level of form, it's through the forgiveness of the level of form. And *that's* done at the level of the mind, which has *nothing* to do with the level of form.

> **The truth is still there to be found by anyone who seeks clarification and is willing to use the technology of forgiveness.**

I'm sure you remember the line about Carl Jung who, surveying all the different variations of his work that were being done by students of his near the end of his career, remarked, "Thank God I am Jung and not a Jungian." Well, if everything splits and changes, whether it be a church, a philosophy, psychology, spirituality, or organization, then what form of the approach is likely to be the most accurate?

GARY: I don't know. What?

ARTEN: Think, Gary. If something undergoes a split, what form of the approach is likely to be the most accurate?

GARY: I know! The form of the approach that would be the most accurate would be the one that existed *before the first split occurred!*

ARTEN: Very good. Remember that fact if you ever have any doubts about whom you should believe when it comes to what the

Course is saying. You have the original members of the Foundation for Inner Peace: Helen, Bill, Ken, Judy, and Bob. They were there before the first split occurred, which by definition means that their take on what it's all about is bound to be the most accurate.

By the way, you might want to notice that Ken, Judy, and Bob are all still friends; and if Helen and Bill were here, they'd still be friends with all of the original members of the Foundation. That's a lot more than you can say for the early members of some spiritual organizations. In fact, if you want forgiveness opportunities, I'd recommend that you hang around with spiritual people. You're bound to find plenty of them.

PURSAH: There's a corollary here. Just as the *Course* splitters will probably never acknowledge that the version of the *Course* used by Helen and Bill is the correct version, the Church will never admit that the Gospel of Thomas existed before the other Gospels. It did, and it's another excellent example of how the approach that existed before the first split occurred is always the most accurate one.

> **If you want forgiveness opportunities, I'd recommend that you hang around with spiritual people.**

After the Crucifixion, some of the disciples were inspired by the fact that J didn't suffer. Others were demoralized because the Master was gone. Thaddaeus and I started a sect based on the teachings of J, and eventually we had several scrolls made of what would become The Gospel of Thomas, although at the time we simply referred to it as "The Sayings." At least that's the word in English. There was one other Gospel based on J's words that was accurate. It was called "Words of the Master." I told you before that this is the famous "Q" Gospel, the source that the three so-called Synoptic Gospels: Mark, Matthew, and Luke, all borrowed from. They left out the parts they didn't agree with, the parts that didn't fit with the later theology of Paul.

Eventually, both "Thomas" and "Words" were wiped out by the church, never to be seen again, except for the flawed version of Thomas you have today that was dug up in 1945 in Nag Hammadi.

I've said that one-third of those sayings were added on during the 300 years in between the Crucifixion and the time the Gospel was buried in the fourth century. The Gospel of Judas is actually a later Gnostic document that doesn't reveal very much and has J saying many things he never said.

Not only did the Church destroy those Gospels and many others, it tried to eliminate from history some of the first teachers of J's message. Because of that, the best of those teachers are not well known to Christians or the rest of the world. Yes, I'm known, and by "I" in this case I mean Thomas (although you are just as much Thomas as I am, Gary), but I'm known as the so-called Doubting Thomas. The way that story was told in the New Testament was an attempt to make me look bad because the Church felt threatened by the Thomas Gospel. I was too famous to be eradicated, so a revised history was needed. The stories of others almost vanished. I'll mention two of these because they were among the finest teachers of J's message.

The first was Stephen. He was an early church leader and one of the scribes of "Words of the Master." While the more conservative types gravitated to J's brother, James the Just, the more mystical followers—and J was certainly mystical—tended to want to be with one of three teachers. I was one of them.

Stephen was my equal as a teacher, and he had a fine Gospel, although we didn't call them Gospels in those days. He was pretty well known because he built up a following in many of the places J had visited. He had the right interpretation of J, and was a very big influence in the years after the crucifixion. But by the time the New Testament was written and revised by the Church over the centuries, Stephen's place in the overall scheme of things had been greatly reduced. Yes, he is written about in the New Testament. There's actually a hint of what a great teacher he was in the Book of Acts, Chapters 6 and 7. But the amount of space given him doesn't do justice to the role he played. Still, I'll give you a brief quote from Acts, which is a fairly accurate account of the death of Stephen:

"And Stephen, full of grace and power, did great wonders and signs among the people. Then some of those who belonged to the synagogue of the Freedmen [as it was called], and of the Cyre'nians, and of the Alexandrians, and of those from Cili'cia and Asia, arose and disputed with Stephen. But they could not withstand the wisdom and the Spirit with which he spoke."

It goes on and describes how they killed him over his "blasphemous words." Incredibly, Saul, who would later be called St. Paul, was there, and as the Book of Acts itself puts it: "Saul was consenting to his death." Remember, Saul persecuted Christians until his guilt got the better of him. Also, the event being described took place a good 20 years after the Crucifixion, and Saul had not yet taken up J's cause, which he eventually converted into a theology. Stephen had a fine ability to communicate J's message to people. But by the time Christianity was established as an organized religion, it had become a set of beliefs rather than a new way of looking at the world and everything in it. And by "looking" at the world I mean spiritual sight. J's teaching on vision is that you *look past* the world to reality. That was Stephen's message, also, and the church had no use for it.

J's teaching on vision is that you *look past* the world to reality.

Of all the fine teachers who were written out of or revised by history, none was greater than Mary Mag'dalene. We made it clear during the first series of visits that Mary was not the prostitute J saved from being stoned to death, and we repeated that during this series because it's obvious that some people still don't get it. Mary was J's wife. Jewish rabbis were not bachelors. But J treated Mary like an equal, and we never saw any reason to think she wasn't. Because of that, there was some jealousy. That's the way of the world, and the disciples were human, although Mary *was* enlightened.

Like "Thomas," the Gospel of Mary isn't perfect. It was changed over the centuries. But you can still get a glimpse of J and Mary. Mary Mag'dalene was probably the clearest of the teachers of J's message, possibly because she understood him so well on a personal level. It was as though she had become one with him. Interestingly, a lot of J's following consisted of women. Women hadn't been allowed to express themselves spiritually as well as men in the

Jewish culture of 2,000 years ago. But J treated everyone the same, and it became apparent to women that they were welcome in his presence, and the word got around. Women became a very important part of his ministry. They were the advance people, arranging future food and shelter in the houses of other women. The men just went from place to place, and they were usually provided for.

After the Crucifixion, Mary knew that J was all right. She was the first to see him appear as a body afterward. Of course the purpose of this was to teach the unreality of the body. Mary understood that. Stephen, Thaddaeus, and I did to a certain degree, but not as well as Mary. The other disciples didn't understand the lesson very well at all, and some of them used it as a reason to glorify J personally as a resurrected body.

Mary was a glorious teacher of J's message. Sometimes people would just sit there with their mouths open, listening to her. It so happened that a pretty high percentage of the people who went to her gatherings were women. Women have always been more spiritually advanced than men in general because they tend to be more mature. That doesn't mean that there aren't men who are just as advanced or more advanced; there just aren't as many of them. In the culture of that time, the women were joyous to hear Mary instead of the same old ideas they'd been given, seemingly forever.

Mary was a glorious teacher of J's message.

I'm not going to get into Mary's teachings, which were J's, or her Gospel. I like to stick to the Thomas Gospel, which was the biggest part of my personal experience. There are and will be many people talking about Mary. I would like to correct one misperception, though. J and Mary didn't have any children. And even if they did, the concept of a so-called bloodline would be totally meaningless to J. It misses the point entirely. If you found a person who inherited J's genetics, so what? His whole point was to teach the *meaninglessness* of the body, not glorify it. And even if someone was a descendant of his, that wouldn't give them any extra spiritual ability, any more than most children have all of their parents' abilities.

The focus should always be on doing your forgiveness lessons and going home, not on the level of form and the body, which *cannot* be spiritualized. People are always looking for vicarious salvation. They want to be enlightened by following an enlightened one and having it bestowed on them. It doesn't work that way. In addition, there are so many people out there presenting themselves as some kind of a master and saying they're going to teach you "mastery," that it's comical. If you drove a nail through the wrist of these people, it would hurt like hell. J really *was* a master, and he could feel no pain because the guiltless mind cannot suffer. As for the bloodline, there is no bloodline. And if there were, it would merely put people's attention exactly where it shouldn't be.

GARY: Cool. So Mary, Stephen, and a very humble Thomas . . . sounds like quite a group. Did you guys get along with each other? Just kidding.

PURSAH: Actually, we did. I know you're joking, because since the last visit in the first series you've had quite a few memories of being Thomas and of your life with J, right?

GARY: You know it, related one.

PURSAH: Maybe we can talk about that a little sometime. But I know you have something else you'd like to do right now.

GARY: Yeah, there's no hiding anything from you. I'd like to try a little experiment, because I have something I'd like to read. It's connected to the *Course* and the Gospel of Thomas. Would that be okay with you?

PURSAH: You're messing with my head, Gary. Just kidding. But tell a joke first. We shouldn't go too long without a funny. You make the people laugh in your workshops, and it's perfect. Incidentally, *your* clarity when you teach in person is pretty impressive, also.

GARY: I have some good teachers and a lot of help. But thanks. I can always use a little encouragement. So here's my joke. Jesus is walking down the road 2,000 years ago. Of course his name wasn't Jesus, but we'll call him that for the purposes of this joke. All of a sudden he comes up to a group of people who are about to stone a prostitute to death. That was the law back then. If you caught a prostitute, you stoned her to death, even if you were with her like an hour ago. These guys see Jesus coming, and they have an idea. You see, they didn't like Jesus; he was kind of a renegade rabbi, and he didn't bow down to their precious rules. So they figured they'd trick him. They'd get him to say they shouldn't stone the prostitute to death. In those days, it wasn't enough to just follow the law; you had to agree with it. If you spoke out against one of God's laws, it was blasphemy. That would be just as bad as disobeying the law itself. So when Jesus came up to them, one of them said, "Rabbi, we have a prostitute here, and we're going to stone her to death. That's what we're supposed to do, *right?*"

Well, you've gotta get up pretty early in the morning to pull one over on old Jesus. He just looked at the group of them and said, "He amongst you who is without sin, let him cast the first stone." And they all just dropped their rocks one at a time because they couldn't picture themselves as being without sin. And Jesus got to save the prostitute's life, teach a lesson, and not get stoned to death himself in the process. It was the perfect solution to say, "He amongst you who is without sin, let him cast the first stone."

But then all of a sudden this woman comes walking along. She has a great big rock in her hand. She walks up to the prostitute and drops the rock right on the prostitute's head. Knocks her out. Jesus looks at the woman who just did this and says, "Come on, Mom. Will you give me a little space?"

ARTEN: That's a good one. And it's appropriate that you don't always take your spirituality so damn seriously. Many people today would be surprised at the irreverent humor J would occasionally display. And the experiment you were talking about?

GARY: Yeah. I'd like to read a question that was asked online at the discussion group that talks about *Disappearance,* and then read how it was answered by one of our members, not just because I agree with what's being said by the person answering, but because I think it's a great demonstration of a turning tide, a new way of looking at J. After all, he's an enlightened being who people have been receiving new information about from the *Course* and from Gospels like Thomas, which were lost to the world for 1,600 years. I think what's said here puts a focus on a new way of looking at the world, which is a modern counterpart to many of the ideas that were expressed in those early Gospels that were wiped out by the Church. What do you think?

ARTEN: Go for it.

GARY: All right. First, here's a statement by an anonymous, traditional Christian at the online discussion group for *The Disappearance of the Universe.* He wrote:

> The truth is the Gospel of Jesus Christ. The Gospel is that Christ came into the world to save it through his death on the cross and resurrection.
>
> Christ didn't come to share divine truths or secrets with us. He came to die for our sins so that we might be saved and share eternity with God.
>
> I'm not posting this to debate or anything like that. I have a relative who introduced me to this book, *The Disappearance of the Universe,* and wanted me to read it. That is how I came across this message board.

That's the end of the message.

So that's the typical Christian take on the J guy. The writer even has part of the Apostle's Creed in there. Now, I'm gonna read the response that was given by Rogier F. van Vlissingen of New York, the author of *The Gospel as a Spiritual Path,* and the translator and publisher of the work of a Dutch author on spirituality named Jan Willem Kaiser. It's published in English under the imprint of Open Field Books. Rogier, whom I met when I did my first workshop in Manhattan, is working on a new translation from the Greek, as well as an introduction to The Gospel According to Mark. By the way, I'm gonna substitute the letter "J" for Jesus. I have Rogier's permission to use what he wrote here. I think it describes something fascinating I've noticed happening ever since our book came out. This is Rogier's response:

> Hi. Just consider that different people have experienced J in different ways. Christianity explains J in a certain way, and if that works for you, you should stick with it. However, those explanations do not work for a lot of people, nor did they for my parents,

who left their church when I was two and a half. One of the realizations they had, which was prevalent in Protestant theology since the middle of the 19th century, was that Christianity was a creation of Paul, and did not represent the teachings of J. Subsequently, I was raised with a notion of the living presence of J in my life, in the form of our ability to call on him as "God's Help." So for me, the idea of J dying for our sins was always phony baloney—it was a theology about J, as opposed to a teaching of J.

Then, when I found *A Course in Miracles,* where J explains in detail why the meaning of the Crucifixion is NOT the sacrifice of God's son for our sins, but is rather a teaching of infinite love, I knew that this was the J for whom I had been looking all of my life. There was a profound recognition. All my life I had studied scripture quite intensely, including studying the Old Testament in Hebrew, and the New Testament in Greek, so as not to have to depend on translations I did not trust; plus, I frankly always focused on the words of J, and not on the interpretations of others, Paul, and even the apostles. Even from the stories in the New Testament, it seemed clear to me that the apostles were struggling to understand, and were by no means clear about his meaning. The apparent certainty and seeming clarity of Paul for me always seemed to be a cover over a profound uncertainty concerning his own experience on the road to Damascus. So for me, Paul always seemed unreliable in the extreme. He writes beautiful passages, but it's framed within a lot of hateful stuff about sin and guilt, not to mention the biggest one, his interpretation of the Crucifixion as J dying for our sins.

In short, for me J worked, Paul didn't, and in *A Course in Miracles* and later *The Disappearance of the Universe,* I found the voice of J free of the later theologies about him. Also, I was aware very early of the Gospel according to Thomas, from which J speaks to us in terms that are very clearly nondualistic, and that produce great difficulty in harmonizing them with Pauline theology, though there is potentially less of a problem with other Gospel materials, depending on how you read it. The church initially dismissed Thomas as being rather late, but internal evidence has led many scholars to believe that it is rather early, and in fact probably ca. A.D. 50, or *before* Paul or the other Gospels were even written. In which case it offers interesting additional evidence of the teachings of J free of the later Pauline theologizing.

So, speaking strictly for myself, this makes sense to me, and can be understood completely within a fairly orderly revisionist history of early Christianity. In this context it should be clear that J had no intention whatsoever of founding a religion, but that rather he was a universal spiritual teacher, though appearing in a Jewish world. Seen in that light, Christianity was merely one attempt (even if it was to become historically dominant for 2,000 years), of framing those teachings into an organized religion. Looking at it this way, there is room for a different way of understanding J. This was represented by the many forms of Christianity that were ultimately suppressed, destroyed and forgotten. This is represented today by a living tradition of *A Course in Miracles* and *The Disappearance of the Universe*. And there are many other schools of thought as well.

Generally the best idea will be to stick with what works for you. The model of *A Course in Miracles* works for me, and it is the topic of *The Disappearance of the Universe*. It is what's being discussed on this list. So if you're interested, hang around, but if not, that's fine, too. No one here is interested in repeating any of the 2,000 years of infighting and splits that is the history of the Christian church. We simply focus on an alternative view of the matter, which again is represented by *A Course in Miracles*.

The Disappearance of the Universe adds to this by providing the bridge between the modern formulations of the teachings of J as presented in *A Course in Miracles* and connecting them to the central teachings of the Thomas Gospel. This is intriguing, since Thomas clearly does not fit comfortably within the Pauline tradition, and presents major challenges of theology. So at a minimum, one would have to conclude that it represented a different understanding of J than what orthodox Christianity developed.

GARY: Makes sense to me.

PURSAH: He's right on the money, bro. And that actually makes a good introduction to a little surprise I have for *you.*

I've said that two-thirds of the sayings in Thomas are authentic, and one-third were added on later. In all, there are 114 sayings in the version of The Gospel of Thomas you have today. Forty-four of those were added on during the 300 years in between my execution in India and the time the copy you have today was buried in Egypt. I'm not going to explain different sayings this time. I'm going to actually recite the 70 authentic sayings from The Gospel of Thomas as they should be spoken in English, and I'll simply leave out the 44 that were added on later. People can use the thought system of the Holy Spirit to interpret the meaning for themselves. They also have the explanations I gave for 22 of the sayings at various times during the first series of visits to help keep them on the right track.

As I did before with those 22 sayings, which are also included here, but without the explanations, I'll use my own kind of revised-standard-version way of putting things in order to closely match what J said at the time. Remember, though, I said that those 22 were the most relevant to your culture. Some of the others are very Eastern and may seem a bit odd to Westerners. Nevertheless, no matter what scripture they're reading, people should eventually become their own ministers and interpreters, using the Holy Spirit as their guide. That's actually part of the process of returning to, or re-becoming Spirit, which is what they really are.

It's not necessary to understand every saying right away. And of course, further readings of the three books of *A Course in Miracles,* as well as the *Disappearance* books, are always highly recommended. That's the *present* way that J is giving his message. Remember, he has to talk to people in words and symbols that they can understand and accept at the time. He spoke the way he did in Thomas for certain reasons. He speaks today the way he does in the *Course,* and we assist him in the *Disappearance* books, for other reasons. As J himself puts it in the *Course,* "The Holy Spirit has the task of undoing what the ego has made. He undoes it at the same level on which the ego operates, or the mind would be unable to understand the change."[5] Thus, even though the content of the message, the love of the Holy Spirit, *doesn't* change, the form *does*. Also, the messages of both Thomas and the *Course* are purely nondualistic and should always be viewed in that light, even when metaphor is used to describe the separated world and those who believe in it.

These are the 70 correct sayings, or logia, in the current Gospel that I'm personally willing to vouch for. If you want, you can even call it "Pursah's Gospel of Thomas" to distinguish it from the Nag Hammadi version. This is Y'shua 2,000 years ago. Because the sayings are in a different language, they're not exact quotations of J's words, but they're the closest possible in English. Have a good time with them.

It's a pleasure to see these words of J being examined today by those who have two good ears to hear. It wasn't so easy to share these sayings 2,000 years ago. But since time isn't real, that doesn't matter.

Although the original version didn't have numbers, I'll use the numbers that correspond to the current numbered Gospel to help people if they choose to compare this corrected version to other versions and translations. The numbers for the previously mentioned sayings that were added on by others, but which are being omitted here, will simply be skipped. Those who may wish to re-number the Gospel later to 70 sayings are welcome to do so.

I've combined numbers 6 and 14 from the Nag Hammadi, Coptic-language version, because they got mixed up over the years, but parts of them contain a true saying. In saying 13, I didn't speak in the first person because J was talking with other people at the beginning of it and not just me. Also, in regard to the last saying in the Nag Hammadi version, number 114, which says you have to make a female into a male before she can enter the Kingdom, I'd like to observe that it was so clearly added on later and so obviously contradicts earlier sayings in the Gospel that it's absolutely incredible anyone could have ever taken it seriously.

Incidentally, a good translation into Aramaic of the words I'll speak for you tonight will give you the only complete Gospel in existence that has just the original words of J in his own language. These are not his *only* words from that time period, but they are the authentic ones from my Gospel. It would take many more words to capture everything helpful that J said in the last several years he appeared to be in a body.

I consider it an act of completion to have J's words in The Gospel of Thomas recorded accurately by a later incarnation of myself. I recorded J's words 2,000 years ago, and now you will record them again. Thus will the Gospel be corrected and passed along in its original form.

NOTE: I inserted the title below. Pursah spoke all 70 of the sayings. They were recorded for accuracy.

PURSAH'S GOSPEL OF THOMAS

These are the hidden sayings that the living J spoke and Didymus Judas Thomas recorded:

1. And he said, "Whoever discovers the interpretation of these sayings will not taste death."

2. J said, "Those who seek should not stop seeking until they find. When they find, they will be disturbed. When they are disturbed, they will marvel, and they will reign over all."

3. J said, "If your teachers say to you, 'Look, God's Divine Rule is in the sky,' then the birds will precede you. If they say to you, 'It's in the sea,' then the fish will precede you. Rather, God's Divine Rule is within you and you are everywhere. When you know yourself, you will be known, and you will understand that we are one. But if you don't know yourself, you live in poverty, and you are the poverty."

4. J said, "The person old in days should not hesitate to ask a little child the meaning of life, and that person will live. For many of the first will be last, and they will become a single one."

5. Know what is in front of your face, and what is hidden from you will be disclosed to you. For there is nothing hidden that will not be revealed.

6. The disciples asked him, "Do you want us to fast? How should we pray? Should we give to charity? What diet should we observe?" J said, "When you go into any region and walk in the countryside, and people take you in, eat what they serve you. After all, what goes into your mouth will not defile you; rather, it's what comes out of your mouth that will reveal you."

8. J said, "A wise fisherman cast his net into the sea. When he drew it up it was full of little fish. Among them he discovered a large, fine fish. He threw all the little fish back into the sea, and he chose the large fish. Anyone here with two good ears should listen."

9. J said, "Look, the sower went out, took a handful of seeds, and scattered them. Some fell on the road, and the birds came and ate them. Others fell on the rocks, and they didn't take root and didn't produce grain. Others fell on the thorns, and they choked the seed and the worms ate them. And others fell on good soil, and it produced a good crop; it yielded sixty per measure and one hundred twenty per measure."

11. The dead are not alive, and the living will not die.

13. J said to the disciples, "Compare me to something and tell me what I'm like." Simon Peter said to him, "You are like a just angel." Matthew said to him, "You are like a wisdom teacher." Thomas said to him, "Master, my mouth is utterly unable to say what you are like."

    And he took him, and withdrew, and spoke three sayings to him. When Thomas came back to his friends, they asked him, "What did J say to you?"

Thomas said to them, "If I tell you one of the sayings he spoke to me, you will pick up rocks and stone me, and fire will come from the rocks and consume you."

17. J said, "I will give you what no eye has seen, what no ear has heard, what no hand has touched, and what has not arisen in the human heart."

18. The followers said to J, "Tell us how our end will be." He said, "Have you discovered the beginning, then, so that you are seeking the end? For where the beginning is, the end will be. Fortunate is the one who stands at the beginning: That one will know the end and will not taste death."

20. The disciples said to J, "Tell us what God's Divine Rule is like." He said to them, "It's like a mustard seed. It's the smallest of all seeds, but when it falls on prepared soil, it produces a large plant and becomes a shelter for birds of the sky."

22. When you make the two into one, and when you make the inner like the outer and the outer like the inner, and the upper like the lower, and when you make male and female into a single one, so the male will not be male and the female will not be female . . . then you will enter the Kingdom.

23. I shall choose you, one from a thousand and two from ten thousand, and they shall stand as a single one.

24. The disciples said, "Show us the place where you are, for we must seek it." He said to them, "Anyone here with two ears had better listen! There is light within a person of light, and it shines on the whole world. If it does not shine, it is dark."

26. You see the speck that is in your brother's eye, but you do not see the log that is in your own eye. When you take the log out of your own eye, then you will see clearly enough to take the speck out of your brother's eye.

28. I stood in the world and found them all drunk, and I did not find any of them thirsty. They came into the world empty, and they seek to leave the world empty. But meanwhile they are drunk. When they shake off their wine, they will open their eyes.

31. A prophet is not acceptable in his own town. A doctor does not heal those who know him.

32. J said, "A city built on a high hill and fortified cannot fall, nor can it be hidden."

34. J said, "If a blind person leads a blind person, both of them will fall into a hole."

36. Do not worry, from morning to night and from night until morning, about what you will wear. The lilies neither toil nor spin.

37. When you take your clothes off without guilt, and you put them under your feet like little children and trample them, then you will see the son of the living one and you will not be afraid.

40. A grapevine has been planted outside of the Father, but since it is not strong, it will be pulled up by its roots and shall pass away.

41. J said, "Whoever has something in hand will be given more, and whoever has nothing will be deprived of even the little they have."

42. Be passersby.

45. Grapes are not harvested from thorn trees, nor are figs gathered from thistles.

47. A person cannot mount two horses or bend two bows. And a servant cannot serve two masters, or that servant will honor the one and offend the other.
    Nobody drinks aged wine and immediately wants to drink young wine. Young wine is not poured into old wineskins, or they might break, and aged wine is not poured into new wineskins, or it might spoil. An old patch is not sewn onto a new garment, since it would create a tear.

48. J said, "If two make peace with each other in a single house, they will say to the mountain, 'Move over here!' and it will move."

49. Fortunate are those who are alone and chosen, for you will find the Kingdom. For you have come from it, and you will return there again.

51. The disciples said to him, "When will the rest for the dead take place, and when will the new world come?" He said to them, "What you are looking forward to has come, but you don't know it."

52. The disciples said to him, "Twenty-four prophets have spoken in Israel, and they all spoke of you." He said to them, "You have disregarded the living one who is in your presence, and have spoken of the dead."

54. Fortunate are the poor, for yours is the Father's Kingdom.

56. Whoever has come to understand this world has found merely a corpse, and whoever has discovered the corpse, of that one the world is no longer worthy.

57. God's Divine Rule is like a person who had good seed. His rival came during the night and sowed weeds among the good seed. The person did not let the workers pull up the weeds, but said to them, "No, otherwise you might go to pull up the weeds and pull up the wheat along with them." For on the day of the harvest the weeds will be conspicuous, and will be pulled up and burned."

58. J said, "Congratulations to the person who has forgiven and has found life."

59. Look to the living One as long as you live. Otherwise, when you die and then try to see the living One, you will be unable to see.

61. I am the one who comes from what is whole. I was given from the things of my Father. Therefore, I say that if one is whole, one will be filled with light, but if one is divided, one will be filled with darkness.

62. J said, "I disclose my mysteries to those who are ready for my mysteries. Do not let your left hand know what your right hand is doing."

63. There was a rich person who had a great deal of money. He said, "I shall invest my money so that I may sow, reap, plant, and fill my storehouses with produce, that I may lack nothing." These were the things he was thinking in his heart, but that very night he died.

66. J said, "Show me the stone that the builders rejected. That is the keystone."

67. J said, "Those who know all, but are lacking in themselves, are completely lacking."

70. J said, "If you bring forth what is within you, what you have will save you. If you do not have that within you, what you do not have within you will kill you."

72. A person said to him, "Tell my brothers to divide my father's possessions with me." He said to the person, "Brother, who made me a divider?" He turned to his disciples and said to them, "I'm not a divider, am I?"

75. J said, "There are many standing at the door, but those who are alone will enter the bridal suite."

76. J said, "God's Divine Rule is like a merchant who had a supply of merchandise and then found a pearl. That merchant was prudent; he sold the merchandise and bought the single pearl for himself. So also with you, seek the treasure that is unfailing, that is enduring, where no moth comes to eat and no worm destroys."

79. A woman in the crowd said to him, "Lucky are the womb that bore you and the breasts that fed you." He said to her, "Lucky are those who have heard the word of the Father and have truly kept it. For there will be days when you will say, "Lucky are the womb that has not conceived and the breasts that have not given milk."

80. J said, "Whoever has come to know the world has discovered the body, and whoever has discovered the body, of that one the world is not worthy."

85. J said, "Adam came from great power and great wealth, but he was not worthy of you. For had he been worthy, he would not have tasted death."

86. J said, "Foxes have their dens and birds have their nests, but human beings have no place to lay down and rest."

87. J said, "How miserable is the body that depends on a body, and how miserable is the soul that depends on these two."

88. J said, "The messengers and the prophets will come to you and give you what belongs to you. You, in turn, give them what you have, and say to yourselves, 'When will they come and take what belongs to them?'"

89. J said, "Why do you wash the outside of the cup? Don't you understand that the one who made the inside is also the one who made the outside?"

90. J said, "Come to me, for my yoke is comfortable and my lordship is gentle, and you will find rest for yourselves."

91. They said to him, "Tell us who you are so that we may believe in you." He said to them, "You examine the face of Heaven and earth, but you have not come to know the one who is in your presence, and you do not know how to examine the present moment."

92. J said, "Seek and you will find. In the past, however, I did not tell you the things about which you asked me then. Now I am willing to tell them, but you are not seeking them."

94. J said, "One who seeks will find. And for one who knocks, it shall be opened."

95. J said, "If you have money, do not lend it at interest. Rather, give it to someone who will not pay you back."

96. J said, "God's Divine Rule is like a woman. She took a little leaven, hid it in dough, and made it into large loaves of bread. Anyone here with two ears had better listen!"

97. J said, "God's Divine Rule is like a woman who was carrying a jar full of meal. While she was walking along a distant road, the handle of the jar broke, and the meal spilled behind her along the road. She didn't know it; she hadn't noticed a problem. When she reached her house, she put the jar down and discovered that it was empty."

99. The disciples said to him, "Your brothers and your mother are standing outside." He said to them, "Those here who do what my Father wants are my brothers and my mother. They are the ones who will enter the Father's Kingdom."

100. They showed J a gold coin and said to him, "The Roman Emperor's people demand taxes from us." He said to them, "Give the Emperor what belongs to the Emperor. Give God what belongs to God."

103. J said, "Congratulations to those who know where the rebels are going to attack. They can get going, collect their Divine resources, and be prepared before the rebels arrive."

106. J said, "When you make the two into one, you will become children of Adam, and when you say, 'Mountain, move from here!' it will move."

107. J said, "God's Divine Rule is like a shepherd who had a hundred sheep. One of them, the largest, went astray. He left the ninety-nine and looked for the one until he found it. After he had toiled, he said to the sheep, 'I love you more than the ninety-nine.'"

108. J said, "Whoever drinks from my mouth shall become like me. I myself shall become that person, and the hidden things will be revealed to that person."

109. J said, "God's Divine Rule is like a person who had a treasure hidden in his field but did not know it. And when he died he left it to his son. The son did not know about it either. He took over the field and sold it. The buyer went plowing, discovered the treasure, and began to lend money at interest to whomever he wished."

110. J said, "Let one who has found the world, and has become wealthy, renounce the world."

111. J said, "The Heavens and the earth will roll up in your presence, and whoever is living with the living one will not see death. Did not I say, 'Those who have found themselves, of them the world is not worthy'?"

113. The disciples said to him, "When will the Kingdom come?" He said, "It will not come by watching for it. It will not be said, 'Behold here,' or 'Behold there.' Rather, the Kingdom of the Father is spread out upon the earth, and people do not see it."

NOTE: We sat there for a few minutes and said nothing. I felt transcendent from the experience. Then finally, I asked a question.

GARY: Whoa, Pursah. That was incredible. It really rang true for me. And the whole thing has a much better flow to it now, too. I could picture J saying the words. In fact, the first time I really heard his Voice, he said a few of the words to me that you said near the end there, at number 110. It was only later I could see there was more than one reason he did that. He was reintroducing himself to me on a much deeper level.

One question: I've checked out the Gospel myself a little, and I noticed something just now about your corrections. It seemed to me that some of your sayings were shorter.

PURSAH: Just as there were sayings that were added on later, there were also *parts* of sayings that were added on later. I left them out. Also, a couple of the ones I gave you last time were longer this time, because I *always* gave you the whole saying.

GARY: Why didn't you last time?

PURSAH: I did usually. But the purpose then was to give you a feel for the Gospel, where this time the purpose was to give you the *entire* Gospel the way it was intended.

GARY: Thanks. I appreciate it.

PURSAH: So now you get to give the correct version of The Gospel of Thomas *again*. I appreciate *that*.

GARY: My pleasure.

ARTEN: Now's a good time for us to disappear for a while. I'm sure you'll have no trouble finding things to do while we appear to be gone.

GARY: Yeah, my little dance card is all full.

ARTEN: Five days from now, the day after Christmas, there's going to be a terrible natural disaster, and I use the word *natural* loosely. Even the ego wouldn't be depraved enough to have this happen on Christmas day, so it will happen the day after. Most of the people affected won't be Christians, but the Christian world will be watching, which is why I mentioned the holiday. Use this calamity to teach people that God has nothing to do with this world, and that the real God is not one of fear but one of Love.

We'll be back in two months. We know that you'll be practicing forgiveness.

GARY: I love you guys.

PURSAH: And we love you.

NOTE: And then my couch was empty. Five days later, one of the most powerful earthquakes in history rocked the Indian Ocean, causing a tsunami that would kill between 200,000 and 300,000 people. At first, as in many natural disasters, it wasn't clear how bad it was. But as time went on, the cost became well known. I found it interesting that as soon as Arten said most of the people affected wouldn't be Christians, I wasn't that worried about the coming natural disaster. Knowing it would be in a faraway country made it seem less threatening. In America, we regard the taking of American lives as *very* important. The seeming "special-ness" of certain bodies over others plays its role in every kind of event, situation, and relationship.

That's not to say that I didn't care after it happened. I *was* concerned, but I noticed that because of the teachings, my experience of the tsunami was different from that of most people. It wasn't that I *did* anything different from others. It felt right to give money and try to help. But as I did, there was a dominant part of me that knew that what I was seeing was a dream I was projecting. There was no world, only a dream of one, and I could more clearly relate to the people trapped in the tsunami as being what they really are, perfect spirit, rather than as bodies. What the body's eyes seemed to be showing me was a dream of separation, and I was the one ego that thought it was here. It was *my* dream, and the purpose of it was to make me think I was a body, because if the tsunami victims were bodies, I was one, too.

I started the New Year knowing that it would be even busier than the previous one. Somehow that didn't matter. The years that had been different were now all the same. They were all untrue, and underneath that realization was freedom.

ᘓᘓᘓ ᘓᘓ

8

LOOKING INTO THE FUTURE, PART II

> Your ego is never at stake because God did not
> create it. Your spirit is never at stake because He did.[1]

Two months later, *Disappearance* had become much better known, and I found my days crammed with activity from the time I woke up in the morning until the time I went to bed at night. It was interesting to me that people never see most of the things a well-known author does. The writing (in my case, the narration for the books, various articles, and other projects); the e-mails and phone calls; scheduling; traveling; speaking; publicity; magazine and radio interviews (which are mostly recorded); meeting people; preparing talks and workshops; and a half dozen other things are all done behind the scenes. It's only when you step out in public at talks, workshops, and book signings—and during certain kinds of media participation—that the public actually gets to see you.

This was fun most of the time, but there were always forgiveness opportunities involving what I went through with the traveling and occasional attacks from people, most of whom were misinformed in regard to what they said about the book. I wasn't complaining, because I figured that it came along with the package, and if the book wasn't successful, then nobody would be saying anything good *or* bad about it. Still, it was difficult not to respond in kind, especially when someone was saying things that simply weren't true. Should they be allowed to misinform the public without accurate information also being presented? This was a problem, especially on the Internet, where easy access made it possible for anyone with an ax to grind to have a forum for the presentation of false information.

> **If you feel that some kind of action is required, then *always* ask the Holy Spirit.**

It was a difficult issue to deal with. Arten had already told me to forgive on the Internet, but it was very hard to stand by and watch people being presented with lies about our work. I also had a couple of questions nagging at me about things Arten and Pursah had said during their first series of visits, plus I personally wanted to know more about the future of the planet, illusion or not. The next time my teachers appeared, I felt inspired to ask about these issues.

PURSAH: How you doing, bro?

GARY: Still too cool for school. Welcome to my humble abode.

PURSAH: It's nice to be here.

ARTEN: Yes, it is. So have you thought of that title for our next book yet?

GARY: Yup.

ARTEN: All right, I'll bite. What is it?

GARY: I'm gonna call it *The Hidden Messages in Beer.*

ARTEN: Not bad, but that's not it. Keep joining with God. It'll come to you.

GARY: So, first question: If someone is saying something factually inaccurate about me or our book or anything else connected with our work on the Internet, am I supposed to just stand by and let them?

ARTEN: I told you to forgive, but it's time to add something. Yes, you *always* forgive. Then after you forgive, if you feel that some kind of action is required, then *always* ask the Holy Spirit if there's anything you should do. Remember, the Holy Spirit doesn't do anything in the world, *ever*. But He *can* inspire you as to what you should do.

GARY: So a good rule of thumb would be that the Holy Spirit doesn't create a parking space for you, but He *can* inspire you to find one.

ARTEN: Yes, I like that. It's exactly correct. And the important thing is that by putting Him in charge, you're undoing the idea of separation rather than reinforcing it.

GARY: So I forgive and then ask.

PURSAH: Yes, if there's time. Sometimes, in an emergency, there may not be time to ask. For example, if someone is attempting to rape a woman, she doesn't have time to join with the Holy Spirit and ask for guidance. In that case, she should do whatever is appropriate. That's *not* the time to be applying that Workbook Lesson, "If I defend myself I am attacked."[2] Remember, the *Course* is done at the level of the mind. If you're a woman, and a man is trying to rape you, kick him in the balls.

ARTEN: Thank you, Pursah, the voice of experience. So if someone attacks you and there's time, forgive. After you forgive, if you don't feel any need to respond, then don't. If you do feel a need to respond, put the Holy Spirit in charge. The guidance could be, "Forget it. Don't do anything." Or it could be that you should do something. But if it is, don't do anything until you feel you've been told, or inspired, as to what it should be. Got it?

GARY: Got it. Now I want to ask you about a couple of things you said before. Somebody from England pointed out that if Shakespeare was an earl, then that would make him nobility, not royalty, but you referred to him as royalty. Did you screw up?

ARTEN. No. Sorry, buddy, but you did. We referred to the queen, thinking at that time that writing plays, especially comedies, would be beneath the dignity of nobility, and you mistakenly said royalty later. Of course it would be beneath the dignity of royalty, too. That part on the tape wasn't clear, and you got a word wrong. Don't feel bad. Overall, you did a tremendous job. But as you said in your Author's Note, you're not perfect.

GARY: All right. I can live with that. How about the Jefferson Bible? You said it would be made available soon for people who want to see it. Now it's true that the actual Jefferson Bible itself was put on display at Monticello awhile after you said that, but the Text of Jefferson's Bible was published and known before that. What do you say?

ARTEN: About what?

GARY: Weren't you wrong?

ARTEN: No. In fact, the Jefferson Bible had become mostly unavailable at the time we made that statement. It was after we made that statement that the Jefferson Bible became widely available.

GARY: All right. Just asking. Those weren't the biggest questions. The one that really got a couple of people up in arms was the idea that humans migrated here from Mars and didn't evolve on Earth. Grant you, most of the people who've read the book don't seem to have a huge problem with that, but the two I mentioned were quite indignant! They pointed out that human DNA is 97 percent the same as that of apes, and that fossil records show we evolved from them. What say you?

> In the universe of form, the seeds of life hobnob between far-flung celestial locations.

ARTEN: We stand by what we said. Human life migrated from a distant planet to Mars. Eventually it also migrated from Mars to Earth. Your fossil records are evidence, not proof. They're incomplete, and they don't really prove anything. They're simply evidence of one possibility, which happens to be incorrect. As for human DNA being 97 percent the same as ape DNA, so what? It doesn't prove that you evolved from apes! There are several types of aliens who, if they crash-landed here on Earth again like some did in Roswell, and if you studied their DNA and the public knew about it, would be shown to everyone to have DNA that's very similar to yours. What would you expect from other humanoid-type life-forms? The reasons for this are actually explained by one of your other scientific theories. That's right, evolution isn't the only scientific theory when it comes to explaining how you appeared to get here on the illusory level of form.

In the universe of form, the seeds of life hobnob between far-flung celestial locations. RNA and DNA were actually seeded, or imported from beyond your solar system. It existed in other places simultaneously. The scientific theory that explains this is called *panspermia*. But don't use that or any other theory as an excuse to take your eye off the ball. Instead of looking out into the universe, you should be remembering where that universe came from.

Obviously, the people you're talking about are very committed to the idea of human evolvement from apes being a fact. It's all rooted in having the body as your identity and proving it's real by demonstrating where it came from.

GARY: Yeah, a lot of people are committed to the idea of evolution. It's passed down through the school systems, and people just accept everything about it.

ARTEN: Monkey see, monkey do.

PURSAH: Don't forget something. Virtually everything that has *ever* been accepted by people as being true has eventually been proven to be false. This year's scientific fact is the next century's debunked old theory. That's because every theory is part of the carrot-and-stick syndrome. Its purpose is to keep people looking at effects instead of looking at the cause. Don't take it seriously. Yes, science can be helpful, especially when physics demonstrates that you can't really separate one thing from something else. People need to take such ideas and apply them for themselves, because very few scientists are willing to take ideas like that to their logical extension. They know that the universe is an illusion, yet they're not willing to tell anybody that it's not real! That's what happens when you need to make a living as a scientist. *You* don't have to, so give it to 'em straight.

ARTEN: You have a great teaching to share. Many people are dispirited and apathetic. A message like the one in *A Course in Miracles* is a cure for apathy.

GARY: Yeah, but what if you have a cure for apathy and nobody cares?

ARTEN: Enough of them will care. You don't need the world's agreement. There is no world. Just share the message with those seemingly separated aspects of your own mind that are ready for it.

GARY: That's what I do, man. But I have a few questions about the future, if you don't mind. I know, it's not really happening so it's not important, but you did talk about it with me last time, so I was wondering if you would again?

PURSAH: We always talk to you about the things you're interested in, Gary. That's one of the ways we make forgiveness relevant to your life. These aren't theories. They're supposed to be applied to whatever you're interested in and whatever's happening in your dream. That's how true forgiveness works. It's like the *Course* says about applying the ideas in the Workbook: "It is their use that will give them meaning to you, and will show you that they are true."[3]

ARTEN: On that note, ask away.

GARY: Okay. A lot of people are pointing out that the Mayan calendar ends in the year 2012, and they say that means that the end of the world is gonna happen at that time. You didn't mention anything about that in your first series of visits. So I was wondering if in telling me about the next century you neglected to mention the end of the world?

ARTEN: No. Sorry, but we have no end of the world scheduled for that time. The year 2012 is the end of a cycle, not the end of the human race. What happens at the beginning of a new cycle is that a new phase starts. The reason we didn't mention it is because it's a cycle, which means that it's, well, cyclical. That means it repeats. That's what cycles do. So you get that which has already happened before in a different form.

What will happen in the new cycle is a lot of good mixed in with a lot of bad.

And then people make a big deal out of it when all it really proves is that the more things change, the more they stay the same. What's happening is always a seemingly new and different form of the same old thing. Thus, the wise saying, "There's nothing new under the sun." It's true.

GARY: So there's no apocalypse, no shifting of the earth's axis to instantly freeze people to death or stuff like that?

ARTEN: No. What will happen in the new cycle is a lot of good mixed in with a lot of bad. That's duality. On the good side, you'll start to see more cooperation from the United States in trying to end global warming. Your country has put itself in an unexplainable position to the rest of the world on that issue. In the meantime, the climate is already displaying symptoms of the effects of warmer ocean waters. You'll have a record 27 named tropical storms and hurricanes in the Atlantic this year. Every time the water warms by a tenth of a degree, you have more storms, and they're also more powerful on average. That trend will continue, and your country will eventually get the message . . . after you have a change of leadership.

Scientists will also notice more fresh water runoff into the ocean from the melting of glaciers and the extra rain. That also has an effect. Within a few years, there will be so much concern about the environment and so many warnings from mainstream scientists that action will be taken by your country in cooperation with others for the good of the many, as opposed to your current policy of "to hell with the world for the good of the few and their profits." Instead of selling out the future of the children, it will actually become fashionable at the level of government to hand over a decent planet to the children.

When you have such a high concentration of opinion among scientists that heat-trapping gases from burning fossil fuels is leading to rising temperatures that, if not stopped, will melt ice caps; raise sea levels by three feet by the end of the century; swamp coastal communities; and bring even more floods, droughts, and storms; even the government has to listen eventually. Keep in mind that it will take time to turn this around, and people will still be frightened by the extremes in weather conditions, both hot and cold. Global warming leads to extreme weather in different forms. Still, it will be turned around eventually, and the global cooperation will make people more optimistic about the future.

This may be a good time to point out that despite all the terrible things you hear on the news every day, people are better off today than they've ever been. A hundred years ago, the average life span was 49. Now it's 75. By late in this century, the average life span will have risen to 100. It won't be that uncommon for people to live to 130. They may not feel it, but the truth is that people are safer than they've ever been. If that isn't true, then why are they living longer?

GARY: I'm sure it's true, but obviously the preferred method of gaining power is to play on people's fears. Then they'll want to rely on the government to protect them, even if the government isn't logical in its policies. Hey, that reminds me of a line I always got a kick out of. About a hundred years ago, there was this Republican U.S. senator from Massachusetts named Henry Cabot Lodge. His grandson was also a senator, and the vice-presidential running mate for Richard Nixon in 1960. The first Lodge a century ago was on the floor of the U.S. Senate during a big economic crisis, and he said to his colleagues, "Is there anything we can appear to do?" I always thought that was pretty funny.

PURSAH: Yes, it was. Of course in the age of television, he might be a little more careful about his public statements. But getting back on the subject, don't forget we told you before that the world is set up to undergo the biggest economic expansion in human history. We haven't changed our opinion.

GARY: So you guys are saying that people will live even longer, things are getting better in general, and yes, we're screwing up the environment, but things are gonna change around 2012 with the beginning of the new cycle. That sounds like a lot of good news. So what's the bad news?

ARTEN: Well, for one thing, you'll start hearing more this year about the new leader of Iran. On the level of form, this guy is bad news. He's the one Nostradamus was *really* talking about when he described a man who would be the biggest threat to the cities of the West. He's an extremist who is not to be fooled with or dismissed lightly. The man is insane.

GARY: You said before that terrorists would succeed in setting off a nuclear device in a major city. Is he the one responsible?

ARTEN: Yes, in the sense that he'll play an important part in it. But it won't be just him. Still, it couldn't have happened without him, which makes him responsible.

GARY: I noticed in reading the transcript from the last time that when I asked that question I just used the phrase "major city," not "American city." So it doesn't necessarily have to be an American city that gets hit, right?

ARTEN: We're not going to be specific about which city or cities, except to say that cities like Tel Aviv and London are just as likely targets as New York and Los Angeles. All these places and many others should be taking precautions against the biggest threat to civilization in the coming century, nuclear terrorism, which will be sanctioned by certain governments, especially Iran.

GARY: Wait a minute. You just implied that there could be more than one city hit.

ARTEN: When you asked us the question before, you're the one who asked if a major city would be hit. We answered yes, which was accurate. Also, remember that we weren't willing to give you details. What we *were* willing to do near the end of the conversation was give you the real purpose of the situation, which is the same for everything: forgiveness.

GARY: I remember. But you also predicted a Dow Jones Industrial average of 100,000 around the middle of the century. How can that happen at the same time you have this threat of nuclear terrorism hanging over everybody?

ARTEN: The key is in how the crisis is resolved, or at least how it appears to be resolved. You noticed that your stock market went down the tubes after 9/11, but it was temporary. After a while, people notice that these companies are still doing business, and they buy stock. After the resolution of the nuclear-terrorist threat, which will include the retaliatory nuclear destruction of the capital city of one of the countries involved in carrying out the terrorist action, people will breathe a sigh of relief, and business will eventually be bigger than ever. That won't happen overnight, but it will happen. There's going to be such an expansion of commerce that people will be falling over each other to buy stocks in the next 50 years. And in addition, when people feel relieved over a seemingly resolved situation, they really open up their wallets.

GARY: Yeah, I noticed last year on the planes there were still practically no children, and that was two-and-a-half, three years after 9/11. But now all of sudden, three-and-a-half years after 9/11, I'm starting to see a lot more children on the airplanes. Families are flying together again. That's a good indicator that people aren't as afraid of the hijacking threat as they used to be. And you seem to be saying that the real threat lies in other areas. Is that true?

ARTEN: I wouldn't use the word *real*. Remember, *none* of what you see is real. What you truly are is real, and nothing real can *be* threatened. Also, I'm not saying that every plane flight is guaranteed to be safe; I'm saying that there are bigger things coming up in the terrorist's handbook.

People are born with the ego intact. It then plays itself out.

GARY: Well, you also seem to be saying that Tehran is gonna get nuked by the allies in retaliation.

ARTEN: Just as with the targets in the West, I'm not going to be specific about which city is retaliated against.

GARY: It's sad. I mean, when you think about it, the world has made it through the last 60 years without using nuclear weapons. I was kind of hoping it would stay that way.

ARTEN: Has a weapon ever been made that wasn't used? If you don't want to use it, don't make it. Yes, since Hiroshima and Nagasaki, there has been a 60-year truce when it comes to the use of nuclear weapons, but for it to be permanent, you'd have to end conflict where it really is, which is in the mind.

PURSAH: I told you that the people of the world will never live in peace until the people of the world have inner peace. The problem must be solved on the level of cause, not the level of effect. Many famous teachers teach that people are born innocent, with a clean slate, and are then messed up by the world. *It's not true.* People are born with the ego intact. It then plays itself out. If the ego weren't already there, then they never would have come here in the first place! Still, every lifetime is an opportunity to undo the ego and break the cycle of birth and death. And in the meantime, if you want to have world peace, the only way to do it in a lasting and meaningful way is to bring about a condition of inner peace within the people who appear to be here. As J says in his *Course,* what you see is "the outside picture of an inward condition."[4]

Lately there's been a lot of talk about creating a "Department of Peace" in the U.S. government. That's a nice thought. But diplomacy has been tried forever. Sure, it was a good thought to have a League of Nations and a wonderful thought to have a United Nations, and it's a pretty thought to have a Department of Peace. There's nothing wrong with it. Just don't expect it to work. Any attempt to bring peace to the world *in* the world will have only a temporarily helpful impact at best, because you're trying to solve the problem where it isn't, instead of where it is.

Remember this poignant quotation from *A Course in Miracles* when it comes to trying to make peace in the world, because it's not about stopping wars, it's about stopping the cause of them: "Mistake not truce for peace, nor compromise for the escape from conflict. To be released from conflict means that it is over. The door is open; you have left the battleground. You have not lingered there in cowering hope that it will not return because the guns are stilled an instant, and the fear that haunts the place of death is not apparent. There *is* no safety in a battleground. You can look down on it in safety from above and not be touched. But from within it you can find no safety."[5]

So teach people to become invulnerable to anything the world appears to do, and the rest will take care of itself.

GARY: Cool. I'd be remiss if I didn't ask you more about what's gonna happen. For example, you said that hydrogen-powered cells are the energy of the future. Is that still the case?

ARTEN: Yes, but there will be a schism between Europe and America. The trend in America the next couple of decades will be toward hybrids. People will feel good driving cars that use less gasoline. In Europe, there will be a more concentrated effort to develop hydrogen power. As a result, in the long run, Europe will be ahead of America in that area. This brings up an issue that will play a role in the way the power of the world is distributed over the next century. America is not producing the number of engineers that it used to. The European Union and China recognize the importance of math and science and planning for the future. In America, all you recognize is the importance of money. That may work just fine when it comes to the short term, but it doesn't work in the long term.

Without a strong investment in the right kind of education and planning, America will start to slowly fall behind the European Union, which will be the economic powerhouse of the future. China will gain, also, but the lack of incentive that exists there for most of the people won't help them. And *there* you see a major advantage that's enjoyed by the European Union. There's enough capitalism in Europe for people to have incentive. There's also enough socialism for people to be taken care of in important areas like health care.

In America, the number one reason for bankruptcy is people being wiped out by medical bills. And now the people in your Congress have taken action to punish these people with health problems even more and make them hostage to the banks, hospitals, and credit-card companies that the people in the Congress work for. They'll also continue to sanction the trend of corporations cheating longtime employees out of their pensions.

In Europe, Canada, and other places with more sane policies, people don't have to worry about losing everything they have because of an illness. This gives them more incentive, not less. In America, the lack of intelligence, compassion, forward thinking, investment in math and science education, and just plain greed will within a few decades cause your country to fall behind the European Union as an economic leader. How ironic that the country that gained its freedom from England as a revolutionary force in a world of conservatism has become the conservative force that falls behind the times and begins to lose its edge to the very country it revolted against, and other countries that it considers to be allies.

GARY: Yet you still see the Dow going to 100,000?

ARTEN: Yes, this will be a worldwide economic boom. The first sign of changing times will be that Europe will benefit even more.

GARY: Could you tell me about some more trends of the future?

ARTEN: Quantum computers that would boggle your mind, space elevators that raise heavy cargo through the air and into orbit, tourist trips to the moon, teleportation—all of these things will happen in the not-too-distant future.

GARY: Teleportation? Do you mean like they did on *Star Trek?*

ARTEN: Many of the things that become science fact were science fiction not too long ago. You may recall in the original version of that series they used tools they called "communicators" to talk with each other. At the time it seemed like science fiction. Today, a high percentage of your population is using cell phones to talk with each other, and they look like the communicators that were used on that series.

GARY: Yeah. You know one of the good things about cell phones? I remember 15 or 20 years ago there used to be all these people walking around talking to themselves. Now they don't have to. They can walk around talking on their cell phones. Of course you know there are some of them walking around talking on their cell phones, and there's not really anybody on the other end.

ARTEN: The space travel of the future will not always be done on spacecraft. Trips to distant places will sometimes be accomplished by beaming people there. It takes days to fly to the moon, but you'll one day be able to beam someone there in three seconds. Indeed, as you look beyond the next century, that's the form of space travel that will become prevalent. Just as researchers have already successfully teleported beams of light across a laboratory bench, that technology will be implemented at the macroscopic biological level, and people will be beamed from one place to another. It has all kinds of advantages over other methods of space travel.

PURSAH: And that's it, buddy. We don't want to stretch that imagination of yours *too* much. You have a lot of work to do. Just remember what all of this is for. As you're walking through your dream movie, which you wrote and directed and then forgot about so it would seem real, forgive what you made and return to God. Demonstrate that you have true wisdom by seeing the innocence in everyone, and thus making it your own. And have a great couple of months.

ARTEN: Yes, and have fun!

GARY: Thanks, guys. And don't hesitate to drop in to one of the workshops if you're in the mood.

When they left, I sat there in quiet contemplation, thinking about all they had said, and I realized that given everything I had been taught, the only viable way of functioning in the world was to be prepared to forgive no matter what happened, and then it wouldn't *matter* what happened. I felt like an observer, watching the days go by with J, grateful to my friends for all they had taught me, slowly but steadily preparing to graduate to a higher form of life, and yet enjoying without guilt the pleasures that this one had to offer.

9

WHO'S ARTEN?

> The Voice of the Holy Spirit does not command,
> because it is incapable of arrogance. It does not demand,
> because it does not seek control. It does not overcome,
> because it does not attack. It merely reminds. It is
> compelling only because of what it reminds you *of*.[1]

The next couple of months were wild. I made a trip to Las Vegas for a big conference sponsored by my new publisher, Hay House. Vegas is the ultimate illusion. In fact, the hotel across the street was called "the Mirage." The legendary Louise Hay gave one of the keynote talks, and while I was sitting in the audience, she surprised me by saying in front of the huge crowd that I was one of her new "mentors," and that *The Disappearance of the Universe* was causing her to want to practice forgiveness all the time. I was very honored.

I also gave the keynote talk at the International *A Course in Miracles* Conference that was held in Salt Lake City, Utah. I spoke for two hours and received a standing ovation. I felt as if I were getting better at practicing forgiveness before I went out in front of the crowd. The coaching my teachers had given me was helping, and I realized more and more as I went along that true forgiveness, as opposed to the world's old-fashioned version of it, had very practical applications.

Being a dream of duality, the excitement of success also brought disappointments. For example, *Disappearance* sold enough copies to get to number four on the *New York Times* bestseller list, but then the paper decided not to include the book on its list because, according to them, too many of the sales had occurred online rather than in bookstores. It was a bitter pill to swallow, because it stopped the book from getting the exposure that would have gone along with the listing. It also prevented me from being presented as a *"New York Times* best-selling author." A high-ranking person in the publishing industry told me, "You got screwed." Even if I had wanted to play victim, I was too busy, and I decided to forgive and move on. Besides, I was still a "best-selling author" because of the book's presence on other lists.

Then there was an incident that occurred on a national radio program that's broadcast coast to coast and is heard by more than five million people. The experience was a difficult one, but the outcome was a miracle. I was being interviewed by the host of the show, a man who apparently wanted to talk only about the sensational aspects of the book rather than its spiritual message, when he suddenly started yelling at me! I was talking about our oneness, and he screamed, "If you use the word *oneness* one more time, I am going to go through the roof!" His disrespectful and attacking manner was very evident, and had to be noticed by the millions of people listening. I thought, *God, this guy's listeners are gonna hate me because he does.* Then, out of habit, I turned to J in my mind and asked, "What should I do?" Right away I heard the thought, *What do you think?*

With that, the answer was obvious. I forgave the host, and then I felt peaceful. I kept my cool and didn't respond in the same manner. I kept talking and answering his questions in a calm way, and eventually he calmed down, too, although he did kick me off the show after two hours instead of the three we were supposed to do. I figured I had taken a chance and lost. I did my best, but things just didn't work out. Being new at the national publicity game, I thought I had failed and was probably finished as an author.

I was wrong. Sales of the book underwent a big increase, and more important, I found myself being approached every week by people who would all say a very similar thing: "Hey, I heard you on that radio show, and it was *great!* Here you were talking about forgiveness and this guy was attacking you, and you actually did what you were talking about. I could see that you don't just talk about this stuff, you really live it!" Many people heard of me, *Disappearance,* and *A Course in Miracles* for the first time on that radio show, and it was a true-life example of applying forgiveness that had introduced them to the teachings. I realized that forgiveness could have many unforeseen fringe benefits, and I was very grateful for the unexpected happy outcome.

Spring had sprung, and it was time for another visit from my ascended sages. I had a question that had been bugging me for years, and I decided to ask it before I got caught up in discussing something else. It had been established that Pursah was Thomas 2,000 years ago, and she was Pursah in the future. I also knew that I was the reincarnation of Thomas in this lifetime and would be Pursah the next time around. It had been established that Arten was Thaddaeus 2,000 years ago, and he was Arten in the future. But I was never told, nor had I ever been able to figure out, who Arten is in this lifetime.

GARY: All right, guys. I have a question that's been nagging at me and has also been the subject of a great deal of speculation.

PURSAH: We know, but we'll let you ask it anyway.

GARY: Arten, do you mind me asking who you are in this lifetime?

ARTEN: I don't mind you asking, if you don't mind me not answering.

GARY: Oh, come on. I haven't been able to figure it out. When Pursah said I know you in this lifetime, too, I didn't get if she meant that I knew you really well or hardly at all, if I *already* knew you, or, since she speaks holographically sometimes, if I was still gonna meet you. At least give me a hint!

ARTEN: Okay, my friend, I'll narrow it down for you. In the lifetime that appears to occur in this thread of time, I'm a woman.

GARY: All right. That helps. So you're a babe, huh?

ARTEN: It stands to reason I'd be female. The percentages alone would suggest it. I was a man 2,000 years ago, and I'm a man again the second half of this century and into the next one for our final lifetime. Do you expect me to be a man *all* the time? I'm a woman right now as we speak, and I might add that I'm fetching.

GARY: My dog Nupey used to do a lot of fetching, too.

ARTEN: You know, we *could* make an exception to that nobody's-going-to-hell idea.

GARY: And you also said that our final lifetime takes place late in this century?

PURSAH: It's hard to get one past you, old buddy. Let's say that it starts in the early part of the second half of this century and continues into the next one, and that our biggest forgiveness lessons occur early in the next century.

ARTEN: Now, I'd like to help you out with discovering who I am in your present lifetime, but I'm sure you realize that since everything's already happened, it wouldn't be right for us to give you information that would cause you to seek out somebody before you were supposed to meet her.

GARY: Ah, I think you just gave something else away there. Are you saying I haven't met this woman . . . I mean, you, yet?

ARTEN: I'm not giving away anything I shouldn't. You can draw your own conclusions from what I've said, but I *have* narrowed it down for you. Now don't dwell on it. In fact, the best thing for you to do is forget about it. Just let things happen the way they're supposed to happen.

GARY: Well, I feel better knowing a little more, so I guess that's the way it's supposed to be for now. So I take it by fetching, you meant you're hot?

PURSAH: I think it's time to move on to other business.

ARTEN: Yes, and what we're about to say isn't meant to be anything but helpful. It's said with the understanding that everyone is completely innocent, and that they're doing their best to further whatever philosophy or method they sincerely believe in. That having been said, there are many spiritual teachers who are diluting the message of *A Course in Miracles* by teaching methods they claim are in agreement with the *Course* when they actually are not. This confuses the student by diverting attention from what the *Course* is teaching to something different, which the teachers of apparently don't even understand are different, or else they wouldn't be presenting them as though they're the same by quoting the *Course* out of context to support their teachings.

GARY: You said a mouthful there, but I know what you're talking about. I see it all the time. Instead of teaching the *Course,* there are students of it, some of whom are very famous, who make up their own thing and then quote from the *Course as if* it's saying the same thing when it's really not.

ARTEN: Exactly. One good example is the teaching that one should be *in the now.* Keep in mind that we're not saying there's anything *wrong* with the idea that there may be some good in focusing on the now rather than the past or the future. The quality of life would be improved. The problem is that doing so *cannot* remove the unconscious guilt over the original separation from God that's still hidden in the deep recesses of the mind. Because of that, it makes each experience of being in the now *temporary* by definition, because it fails to remove the blocks that prevent that experience from being permanent. All of which is to say that there's not just a minor difference

> **Until *all* unconscious guilt is removed from the mind, you cannot stay in the endless present on a permanent basis.**

between the approach of *The Power of Now* and the real power of *A Course in Miracles.* It's the difference between being temporarily in the now of an illusion, or being permanently in the *presence* of reality.

It's absolutely essential to remember that unless and until *all* unconscious guilt is removed from the mind, you cannot stay in the endless present on a permanent basis. It's impossible. Any attempt to remain in the now is doomed to failure without doing the work of true forgiveness. Until you've completely forgiven that which you made and projected outside of yourself, you are not forgiven in your own unconscious mind, and until you are, the cycle of birth and death cannot be broken. Being in the now does *not* heal your unconscious guilt and undo the ego. True forgiveness, on the other hand, removes the blocks to the awareness of love's presence that is your natural state of being, undoing the ego completely and making it possible to remain in the eternal "always" simply because that's all that's left. Here's some of what J says about this important issue in his Course:

"You are invulnerable because you are guiltless. You can hold on to the past only through guilt. For guilt establishes that you will be punished for what you have done, and thus depends on one-dimensional time, proceeding from past to future. No one who believes this can understand what 'always' means, and therefore guilt must deprive you of the appreciation of eternity. You are immortal because you are eternal, and 'always' must be now. Guilt, then, is a way of holding past and future in your mind to ensure the ego's continuity. For if what has been will be punished, the ego's continuity is guaranteed. Yet the guarantee of your continuity is God's, not the ego's. And immortality is the opposite of time, for time passes away, while immortality is constant."[2]

Before I continue, remember that any attempt at eternity is a nonstarter as long as there's any unconscious guilt in the mind, period. That guilt *must* be healed *before* you can permanently stay free of the past or future. And the way to undo it is not to ignore it, which is exactly what's going on when you shut off and deny the past or future. It's when you *forgive* the past and your concerns about the future that they are undone, and the endless present becomes truly available to you. That forgiveness always takes place now. Remember, we said that there's no difference between forgiving the original separation at the time it appeared to happen, and forgiving it right now, for they are one and the same. Now I'll continue with that quotation from J. By the way, Gary, for your benefit, the word in the *Course* I'm about to use, *expiation,* means "appeasement."

GARY: I knew that.

ARTEN: "Accepting the Atonement teaches you what immortality is, for by accepting your guiltlessness you learn that the past has never been, and so the future is needless and will not be. The future, in time, is always associated with expiation, and only guilt could induce a sense of a need for expiation. Accepting the guiltlessness of the Son of God as yours is therefore God's way of reminding you of His Son, and what he is in truth. For God has never condemned His Son, and being guiltless he is eternal."[3]

It's not about placating your ego by making friends with it and keeping it intact.

GARY: So there's no getting away from the fact that it's always about freeing ourselves from the unconscious guilt, which frees us from *everything*. And sooner or later, in order to do that, it always comes back to the forgiveness of relationships.

ARTEN: Superb. As the *Course* puts it: "The Holy Spirit teaches that you always meet yourself, and the encounter is holy because you are. The ego teaches that you always encounter your past, and because your dreams were not holy, the future cannot be, and the present is without meaning."[4]

The now is meaningless as long as guilt exists in the mind. But when you're free, you open up to the endless present and your oneness with God. And to add one point, with all due respect, you don't undo the separation from God by ignoring Him. How can you undo the sense of separation from your Source without acknowledging your Source? Whatever reason you make up for not doing so, the real reason is guilt and the resulting fear of Him.

GARY: I hear you. I don't ignore Him. If it weren't for God, I wouldn't have anybody to look up to.

ARTEN: Your joking aside, you get what I'm saying.

GARY: Yeah. It's about forgiveness. It's not about observing your thoughts and your judgments, which is not really forgiving them; it's not about placating your ego by making friends with it and keeping it intact, it's about undoing it and becoming whole again, which is what J was talking about all along, including in the Gospel of Thomas. I have a question, though: What about simple nonjudgment? Isn't nonjudgment the same as forgiveness?

PURSAH: That's an excellent question. It's true that the ego cannot survive without judgment, so *if* someone actually practiced complete nonjudgment, then it would eventually undo the ego, as Buddha did, except he had a little bit more to do, so even he came back one more time. The problem is that it takes longer to do it in the simple nonjudgment way, and it's actually harder to do. It's much better if you have the Holy Spirit's thought system to *replace* that which the ego has made. J not only practiced nonjudgment, he also employed a proactive form of forgiveness to change the way he looked at everything, thus greatly accelerating the process. That's why he emphasizes that the *Course* saves time. His background in both Jewish mysticism and Buddhism brought him to a faster version of salvation by not only undoing the ego, but actually replacing the ego thought system with the thought system of the Holy Spirit.

ARTEN: Which brings us to another topic, and once again, we mean this only to be helpful. We have nothing but respect for the person we're about to discuss. He's an early student of the *Course* who's a doctor, and because of that he has a tendency to put things in scientific terms. This can be very impressive to the uninitiated. One of the things he does is use kinesiology, which is muscle testing, to test the truthfulness of statements. Because of this doctor's research, some people mistakenly believe that he has perfected this method. However, because all he's really doing is using illusions to measure illusions, his tests are flawed by definition. He's using the body to test for the truth! As the *Course* clearly teaches, anything that can change or be changed is not real. How, then, can students of the *Course* put their faith in it?

GARY: Yeah, I know the doctor you're talking about. But my chiropractor was using kinesiology on me in the form of muscle testing 22 years ago. He was great, and most of the time he was right about his conclusions, but not always. Nothing's perfect. And besides, some people are better than others at doing that kind of thing, just like with any art.

ARTEN: Yes, and the doctor we're discussing now developed it into a method of testing the truthfulness of statements, making kind of a lie-detector test out of it. There's a bigger problem with that than just the fact that nothing on the level of form can ever be completely reliable, and things that are true can be mistakenly called untrue. The hidden ego hook is that now the student's attention is being put on the wrong place, focused on an illusory test of an illusory thing in an illusory world, instead of where the attention should be, which is the decision in the mind to forgive the world and leave the *entire* system behind. *That's* the focus of *A Course in Miracles*.

GARY: I know that this guy calibrates different teachings at various levels, from 1 to 1,000. People *love* it. But if he were an early student of the *Course,* it makes me wonder why he didn't pay more attention to what the *Course* was saying.

ARTEN: I think you mean teachings like the quotation we've used before: "Perception did not exist until the separation introduced degrees, aspects and intervals. Spirit has no levels, and all conflict arises from the concept of levels."[5]

GARY: Yeah. And the *Course* is trying to focus the student's attention on the fact that there are *really* only two things to choose from. And only *one* of them is real, which is spirit, and to make the choice for wholeness.

ARTEN: That's correct. Enlightenment *has* no levels; you're either whole or you're not. So not only do things like tests and calibrations distract the student from bringing illusions to the truth instead of giving truth to their illusions, but on top of it, testing in that manner can possibly steer a student away from something that may be helpful if the student tests something and comes up with the wrong result.

GARY: Yeah, like this doctor always seems to calibrate Republican as having integrity. He also calibrated Wal-Mart as being an enlightened company. I'm sorry, but this is a company that was just convicted in California of cheating their employees out of their lunchtimes. If that's the kind of conclusion that the doctor *himself* comes up with, what the hell are his students gonna come up with when you'd have to assume they're not as good at it as he is? And if he's letting his personal bias show, then how's anyone else going to avoid that?

> **Enlightenment *has* no levels; you're either whole or you're not.**

ARTEN: Just remember that the illusion wants to keep you stuck here. And in some cases, because of encouraging comparisons, categorizing teachings into numbers, and making it all real, the focus is now on the illusion, which is an *effect,* instead of on the mind, which is *cause.* Then before you know it, some people are testing other people's statements, calling people liars . . . in a nice, polite, enlightened way, of course, and all it really leads to is a lot of wasted time that could have been spent undoing the ego instead of unwittingly glorifying it.

GARY: Yeah, and it's not just the detailed scientific work done by some of the spiritual teachers that impresses people. In some cases, students are impressed by a certain teacher's voice, personality, or the way they look, which is actually nothing, but they mistake it for enlightenment. I mean, it's incredible how many teachers out there today seem to be either saying they're enlightened or at least not discouraging *other* people from saying they're enlightened. But are they really the same as J? Can they heal the sick and raise the dead? Can they have a nail driven through their wrist without feeling any pain because the guiltless mind cannot suffer? I haven't seen the level of J being attained by these people.

ARTEN: Another problem with calibrations is that if you make a simple, true metaphysical statement, such as "God is love," then it will calibrate near 1,000. It won't get anybody home, but it will calibrate near or at 1,000. If you *really* want to get people home much more quickly, then you have to talk about the ego and describe it, let people know what they're up against, and teach them to undo it. But just because you're talking about the ego, the teaching will calibrate lower!

GARY: So if you just talk about all sweetness and light, you'll calibrate near 1,000, and you'll stay stuck here for many, many more lifetimes than if you expose the ego, understand it, forgive it, and undo it. But obviously to do that, you have to learn about the ego, and whatever teacher is doing you the service of showing you what will actually get you home much faster will calibrate lower, and the more general teacher who won't get you home anywhere near as fast will calibrate higher.

ARTEN: I think you've got it. Add the lie-detector test to the mix and you have a lifetime's worth of distractions. Or instead, you can train the mind to go home.

GARY: Well, I guess doing a kinesiology test is easier than doing your forgiveness work, but I don't care. I want to go home.

ARTEN: And so you will, hotshot. Don't be discouraged by those who borrow from the *Course* instead of teaching it. There are even people who teach the *Course* exclusively who fail to understand it. They'll think that the *Course* is open to their interpretation. Yet if it were, it would be useless. What makes the *Course* unique is that what it says is *not* open to interpretation. It says there is no world and only God is real. The way to awaken from the dream of death is through total, uncompromising forgiveness of people because they haven't really done anything, which is how to forgive yourself. Any other interpretation is folly. Yet you have *Course* teachers who are right there, making the Holy Spirit out to be like a real person acting on your behalf out in a world that the *Course* says doesn't even exist, quickly taking the student's attention away from where it should be, on the cause instead of the effect, and delaying the student's progress. Then on top of that, it's a slippery slope from making the world real to eventually ending up like Pat Robertson and telling everybody exactly how they should behave in that illusory world, or else.

> **Don't compromise, don't sell out, and don't worry about what people think.**

Don't ever fall into that trap. Respect what the *Course* says. Honor the memory of Helen and Bill by telling people the truth about how it came and what it says. Don't compromise, don't sell out, and don't worry about what people think. If they were that smart, they wouldn't think they were here in the first place.

GARY: I'll consult my psychic about that. Just kidding. More illusions. The way out, according to the *Course,* is clear.

ARTEN: That's right, and we're *not* saying the *Course* is the only way. What we *are* saying is that if you're going to do the *Course,* then do it. Don't do something else and *call* it the *Course. A Course in Miracles* was given to save people time if they choose to. If they don't, then it doesn't matter, because time isn't real. But it's up to you how long you want to stay trapped in the cycle of birth and death.

PURSAH: And on that note, before we leave, I'd like to offer a quote from the *Course* that will continue to clarify things for you. When happenings get complicated, when your flight gets canceled, when someone is rude, when you're running late and there's a crowd waiting, when you feel like you don't want to forgive one more thing, and you *really* want a test to determine what is true and what is false, remember these words from J: "As God created you, you must remain unchangeable, with transitory states by definition false. And that includes all shifts in feeling, alterations in conditions of the body and the mind; in all awareness and in all response. This is the all-inclusiveness which sets the truth apart from falsehood, and the false kept separate from the truth, as what it is."[6]

As I sat there alone, I became more determined than ever to stay true to the teachings my friends had given me. I felt that it wouldn't be easy, but if I wanted everything to be easy, I probably wouldn't be on this particular spiritual path in the first place.

10

THE SHABBY TOYS OF EARTH

Here does the dream of separation start to fade and disappear. For here the gap that is not there begins to be perceived without the toys of terror that you made. No more than this is asked. Be glad indeed salvation asks so little, not so much. It asks for nothing in reality. And even in illusions it but asks forgiveness be the substitute for fear. Such is the only rule for happy dreams.[1]

It was a paradox to me that salvation was so simple yet so hard. Obviously the truth was simple, but not easy. Even though I understood it, there was a big difference between comprehending it and having the mental discipline to consistently apply it. I knew I was getting better at it. That was the result of practice. The more I practiced, the more natural forgiveness seemed, and the less natural the world seemed. This wasn't my home, but I could have a good time here when possible, and go home at the same time by seeing the world differently.

I found much encouragement while reading the *Course*. Everywhere I looked I saw that the things Arten and Pursah had said about it were true. Ideas were reinforced repeatedly, and the ego was being undone. For example, late in the Text, J says:

"Forgiving dreams have little need to last. They are not made to separate the mind from what it thinks. They do not seek to prove the dream is being dreamed by someone else."[2]

And shortly before that:

". . . You do but dream, and idols are the toys you dream you play with. Who has need of toys but children? They pretend they rule the world, and give their toys the power to move about, and talk and think and feel and speak for them. Yet everything their toys appear to do is in the minds of those who play with them. But they are eager to forget that they made up the dream in which their toys are real, nor recognize their wishes are their own.

"Nightmares are childish dreams. The toys have turned against the child who thought he made them real. Yet can a dream attack? Or can a toy grow large and dangerous and fierce and wild? This does the child believe, because he fears his thoughts and gives them to the toys instead. And their reality becomes his own, because they seem to save him from his thoughts. Yet do they keep his thoughts alive and real, but seen outside himself, where they can turn against him for his treachery to them. He thinks he needs them that he may escape his thoughts, because he thinks the thoughts are real. And so he makes of anything a toy, to make his world remain outside himself, and play that he is but a part of it.

"There is a time when childhood should be passed and gone forever. Seek not to retain the toys of children. Put them all away, for you have need of them no more."[3]

The beauty, the simplicity that branched out to intricacies and then circled back to simplicity again, made me enjoy the *Course* more and more as I progressed on my path with it. I didn't think of myself as being a "teacher" of the *Course,* just a student. I felt as though I had been in the right place at the right time, literally, and that I was lucky to be able to pass along my experiences. I didn't feel like a writer, either. My two writing speeds were slow and slower. When I got up in the morning, if I were to make a list of the ten things I'd most like to do that day, writing wouldn't even be on the list. Happily, I was only responsible for writing my narration and inserting my notes that shared some of my experiences and turned the books into my personal story. That was my contribution. The discussions with Arten and Pursah were handed to me on a silver platter. My part in them was fun, and all I had to do was transcribe them, although I was slow even at that.

In May, a couple weeks before my friends' next scheduled visit, I went to St. Louis for the first time to do a workshop. I had a lot of fun going up to the top of the famous St. Louis Arch, and also seeing a National League baseball game for the first time. I had a hidden agenda. This was the park where the Red Sox had won the World Series, and I wanted to see it before it was torn down and replaced by another stadium at the end of the season. It was a beautiful day, and the crowd was happy with the Cardinals' victory, during which they scored 11 runs in the first inning. It made me glad they didn't do that against the Red Sox.

A guy named Pierce, who was a friend of the people running the workshop and had also read *Disappearance,* volunteered to take me to Cahokia so I could see the place where I had lived as an Indian during the time of the Great Sun. Pierce became my guide and friend during the several days I spent in St. Louis, and a man named Carl came along with us to Cahokia. In being introduced to Carl, I felt a familiarity, like we were long-lost brothers. As we approached the parking lot, I had an eerie feeling. Then, when we pulled into the lot to park the car, I realized that everything that was happening was occurring *exactly* the same way it did the time Arten and Pursah had used their method of mind transport to show me my future visit here. It wasn't that it was similar; it was a carbon copy. Every little move of my body was exactly the same. The words that were spoken, the walk to the mound, and my climbing of it were identical to the first time. The experience was mind-blowing. This was very clearly happening *now,* yet it had already taken place *before.* The only difference was that this time Arten and Pursah were nowhere to be seen.

Even at the top of the mound, for just a few seconds, I had exactly the same vision of Cahokia a thousand years ago that I experienced during the mind-transport visit. And even during those few seconds of the vision, I looked in exactly the same direction, sensing that the Great Sun's house was there on the mound, yet not looking in its direction, and taking into my mind precisely the same images I had during that same several-second experience before.

The overwhelming feeling I had was that this was somehow "written" and *had* to happen the way that it did. There was nothing I could do about it. If I were meant to be somewhere, then that's where I'd be. I couldn't stop it if I wanted to. If I wasn't supposed to be somewhere, I couldn't get there no matter how hard I tried. It was preordained, a done deal before the fact. Every movement, every word, every friend, every foe . . . it was a script I had agreed to participate in, and here I was, appearing to be going through it for the first time, when in truth the movie was already filmed and I was an observer, appearing to walk through it as if I were playing a part in a universe-sized virtual reality game, and yet not really being there at all. And I realized that that's what my life had been, and there was never any reason to be concerned or upset about what I was seeing, because I was the one who made the whole thing up in the first place, and none of it was true.

Interestingly, there was no loss associated with this experience at all. In fact, I felt a sense of deep freedom, for now I could let things happen instead of trying to make them happen. I could forgive instead of judge, knowing that I was responsible for the world I was seeing, because I made it in order to see my thoughts as being outside of me instead of on the inside. I wanted them there because I was afraid of them, but the fear was based on false ideas. Now there was no need to fear them, but merely to forgive them and let them go, and free myself in the process. I surrendered to my own script, and saw the purpose of it differently. What had kept me a prisoner was now my ticket home. The rest of the visit to Cahokia and St. Louis went exactly the way it was supposed to, and my experience was that it could not have done otherwise.

In late June, I had just returned from a trip to Toronto when Arten and Pursah appeared before me for the tenth time in this series of visits.

PURSAH: So how'd you enjoy your second visit to Cahokia?

GARY: I think it had exactly the effect you knew it would, although I did miss you and that nice outfit of yours.

PURSAH: Nothing in this world's perfect, Gary.

ARTEN: Our last two visits will be brief, brother. We're here to sum up, encourage you, and answer any final questions you may have.

GARY: Final? I don't know if I like the sound of that.

ARTEN: In Heaven, there are no endings. Don't be concerned about beginnings and endings here, then. They'll disappear, and your reality will be all that's left. In the meantime, share the message with others. That's the best job you could hope for, and we know you realize how fortunate you are.

Don't be concerned about beginnings and endings here.

GARY: I sure do.

PURSAH: Hey, you haven't told us a joke for a while. Give us a quick one.

GARY: Okay. These three guys are in hell, right? They've been there for quite some time, burning away, and after a while one of them figures that since they're gonna be there for eternity, maybe they should introduce themselves. So the guy says, "Hi, my name's Arik, and I'm a rabbi. I'm here in hell because I cheated on my wife." So the second man says, "Hello, my name's John, and I'm a Catholic priest, and I'm here in hell because I *have* a wife." Then finally the third guy says, "Hi, my name's Alex, and I'm *A Course in Miracles* student, and I'm not here."

PURSAH: Cute. And remember, you're *not* here. You just thought you were. And you're lucky to have J to lead you out. As he reminds you in his *Course,* "When I said 'I am with you always,' I meant it literally. I am not absent to anyone in any situation. Because I am always with you, *you* are the way, the truth and the life."[4]

You're *not* here. You just thought you were.

He's also very clear about his method for bringing you home, if you're willing to do your part. "Life has no opposite, for it is God. Life and death seem to be opposites because you have decided death ends life. Forgive the world, and you will understand that everything that God created cannot have an end, and nothing He did not create is real. In this one sentence is our Course explained. In this one sentence is our practicing given its one direction. And in this one sentence is the Holy Spirit's whole curriculum specified exactly as it is."[5]

It's by forgiving the world that you will awaken, and realize that you never left Heaven, and have remained exactly as God created you, which is perfect spirit. As J puts it, reminding us again that his themes in the *Course* are simple and consistent, "You are as God created you. All else but this one thing is folly to believe. In this one thought is everyone set free. In this one truth are all illusions gone. In this one fact is sinlessness proclaimed to be forever part of everything, the central core of its existence and its guarantee of immortality."[6]

But always remember the forgiveness that leads to this experience must be done at the level of cause and not effect, as J points out very early in the Text, right in those first five chapters. "You must change your mind, not your behavior, and this *is* a matter of willingness. You do not need guidance except at the mind level. Correction belongs only at the level where change is possible. Change does not mean anything at the symptom level, where it cannot work."[7]

> **Always remember the forgiveness that leads to this experience must be done at the level of cause and not effect.**

GARY: Sharp as a laser beam, Pursah. And I want you to know that I feel very lucky to be able to participate in this whole thing.

ARTEN: Remember something about luck. If everything is already determined, as you've experienced so dramatically, then there's no such thing as luck. Yes, in the world there will be times when you *appear* to be lucky and unlucky, but that's just duality. That *doesn't* mean you don't do things and play your part. Remember everything we've talked about in regard to being normal and kind. And while you're doing it, the important thing is that your focus is now on the cause instead of the effect. That's a change that no one can see, but it's the biggest change in the universe, and the only one that matters.

PURSAH: And speaking of doing things and playing your part, I've noticed a high percentage of men coming to your workshops.

NOTE: In Toronto, the sponsor of the event told me they usually have about 85 percent women at their events, which has been normal in the spiritual community for many years. At my event, there were about 55 percent women and 45 percent men, and the sponsor said this *never* happens.

GARY: Yeah, I noticed that our book is speaking to men as much as women, which is really cool. I've also noticed younger people coming, both men and women in their 20s and 30s, which is different for the *Course,* as well as spiritual events in general. A lot of them are picking up the book at the big chain stores, and they don't even know what it's about, but the title and description speak to them. It's serving as their introduction to all this stuff. You guys really knew what you were doing, didn't you?

PURSAH: The Holy Spirit had an advantage when He decided to correct the ego's script, Gary. He was looking back from the end of time, so He couldn't miss.

GARY: I've also noticed in the public-opinion polls that most people are describing themselves as being spiritual rather than religious. That's an interesting development.

PURSAH: Yes, and one that will continue. The world is thirsty for this message. Keep putting it out there. People are ready for a lot more than traditional religion is willing to give them, and in your case, they're apparently also ready for a lot more than most forms of alternative spirituality are ready to give them!

ARTEN: We want you to continue to have fun, too. Enjoy your trips. You like to go to the top of things. As long as you forgive it and don't use it as a way to symbolically overthrow God, then why not enjoy it and give it as a *gift* to God?

GARY: I think I'll do that. Let me see, I may not get them all, but I've been to the top of Mt. Washington in New Hampshire; Mt. Mansfield in Vermont; both the Prudential Center and the Hancock Tower in Boston; the Empire State Building in New York City; the

St. Louis Arch; Monk's Mound in Cahokia; Mt. San Jacinto in Palm Springs; the Hyatt Regency on Sunset Strip, which has a great view of L.A.; the Berkeley Hills, with an awesome view of San Francisco, courtesy of my first publisher, D. Patrick Miller; the Seattle Space Needle; Diamond Head on Oahu; Mt. Haleakala on Maui; the CN Tower in Toronto; the Stratosphere hotel in Las Vegas; the observation tower at Kennedy Space Center; and the sixth floor of the Texas School Book Depository in Dallas, Texas (now a museum); and I'm sure some others.

ARTEN: And I happen to know you'll also go to the top of the London Eye when you're there this fall, which has a stellar view, and eventually the Sears Tower in Chicago.

GARY: Excellent. And I'd like to go to the top of that bridge in Sydney that they let you climb. I've flown over it and sailed under it to go to the Opera House, but it would be cool to go to the top. Sailing under bridges is cool, too. I sailed under the Golden Gate Bridge, and it was great. Okay, I see what you're doing. You want to make sure I don't ever feel guilty about having all these cool experiences, right? I mean, if none of it's true, then there's no need to feel guilty.

ARTEN: Exactly. Enjoy your success. We want you to be happy. Forgive whenever it feels appropriate and you'll be fine.

GARY: Thanks. Besides, I've already noticed that there's nothing at the top. Not just the top of high places, but at the top in regard to success. People spend their lives trying to get to the top, and then they get there and find that it's not all it's cracked up to be. It just has a whole new different set of headaches, and they feel kind of foolish, so they don't tell anybody and pretend it's very cool, when it's really just another problem.

ARTEN: Very observant, brother. Of course if you tell people that, they'll still want to find out for themselves! It's like telling people that money won't buy them happiness. They still want to get it and make sure. That is, until they're ready to leave the entire system behind.

GARY: I know money won't buy me happiness, but it will buy me a great big boat, and I can float right up next to it. I'm just kidding. Besides, after seeing what my parents went through, if I had a choice of the most practical and important gift in the illusion, it would be health, not money.

Remember that all that glitters in the dream is temporary.

PURSAH: Yes, and you've been very lucky when it comes to that. You enjoy excellent health and you look quite young, too. On that note, remember that all that glitters in the dream is temporary. No matter how much something attracts you, its transitory nature is woefully pale compared to the glorious permanence of Heaven. Go for the real deal instead of the counterfeit world, and you'll be making the wisest of decisions.

ARTEN: Helen Schucman wrote some beautiful poetry, which was eventually published by the Foundation for Inner Peace as a tribute to her after she made her transition. Helen said that this poetry was inspired, not channeled by J like the *Course*. Her book of poetry that the Foundation put out is called *The Gifts of God*. Remember this passage as you mentally review the script, and take heart as you realize that there's something much better in store for you; something wonderful, something permanent, and something that makes anything you've imagined in this lifetime seem like nothing, for such it is in comparison to reality:

> In my hands is everything you want and need and hoped
> to find among the shabby toys of earth.
> I take them all from you and they are gone.
> And shining in the place where once they stood there
> is a gateway to another world
> through which we enter in the Name of God."[8]

11

YOUR IMMORTAL REALITY

> Yet time has still one gift to give, in which
> true knowledge is reflected in a way so
> accurate its image shares its unseen holiness;
> its likeness shines with its immortal love.[1]

As I continued my travels, I was struck by the duality of the world, from the joy of doing a helicopter tour of Kauai to the sadness of visiting the Oklahoma City National Memorial. But the more I traveled across America, the more I was impressed by its diversity. Perhaps this was its real strength, and the ace in the hole that would keep our country great.

My discussions with Arten and Pursah had brought home to me the centrality of the body in all of my dreaming. Everything was connected to it. As the *Course* itself said: "As long as you perceive the body as your reality, so long will you perceive yourself as lonely and deprived. And so long will you also perceive yourself as a victim of sacrifice, justified in sacrificing others. For who could thrust Heaven and its Creator aside without a sense of sacrifice and loss? And who could suffer sacrifice and loss without attempting to restore himself? Yet how could you accomplish this yourself, when the basis of your attempts is the belief in the reality of the deprivation? Deprivation breeds attack, being the belief that attack is justified. And as long as you would retain the deprivation, attack becomes salvation and sacrifice becomes love."[2]

Yet the body was not my reality, and there was a way out. As the *Course* very clearly advised me: "Be willing to forgive the Son of God for what he did not do."[3]

The key was in the remembering. I was improving at remembering that when someone pushed my buttons, the purpose of it was to see the stupidity that I thought true of myself for throwing away everything, or Heaven, in exchange for nothing, or death, in that person instead of me. The quicker I stopped reacting and forgave my brother or sister for what they didn't really do, the quicker my suffering ceased. That alone would have made forgiveness worth doing, and I realized how important it was for me to continue practicing *remembering* the truth in any situation, no matter how quickly it came up, because I was the one whose life was transformed.

The times of inner peace and deep clarity became more frequent, and the knowledge that I was awakening in God became more real. I wanted to go home to reality and be there all the time. It didn't matter if I had to return first for one more lifetime or not. I knew that my practice of forgiveness was resulting in a happier dream for me. Sometimes I'd have to wipe a tear of gratitude from my eye as I was overwhelmed by the direction my life had taken since I embarked on this fascinating spiritual path some 13 years before.

I had mixed feelings about Arten and Pursah's next visit. I knew that it was the last of the series, and I didn't know if there would ever be *another* series. I had heard that good things come in threes, but at the same time I knew better than to take anything for granted, and my attitude was to make the most of now and not be concerned about the future.

Two months went by very fast, and my beloved Arten and Pursah were in my living room once again.

PURSAH: Hey, bro. I hear you're booked to do another workshop in Hawaii this winter. Congratulations!

GARY: Hey, I'd go there just for the chocolate-covered macadamia nuts. Those things are awesome! But yeah, I love that place. I'm gonna go there someday and never leave. They're gonna have to carry me out.

ARTEN: That won't be necessary, brother. When the time comes, you can just disappear.

GARY: Hey, I have a tough question, not from me, but from some other people.

ARTEN: The Holy Spirit's thought system doesn't leave you with unanswered questions. Ask away.

GARY: There are a couple of people who have suggested that the idea that God would let His child continue dreaming a nightmare is not very loving, and that He should wake His child up immediately. Also, the fact that He would let there be a "tiny, mad, idea" is not particularly loving either. What do you think?

ARTEN: The question overlooks what the *Course* is teaching and wants to make a statement that God knows about the tiny, mad idea and His child dreaming, which He doesn't. If He *did*, that would make it real. The whole point of the *Course* is that it's not real. So, to make it short and sweet, you fell asleep and starting dreaming, and when you're ready to wake up by listening to your memory of God, the Holy Spirit, instead of listening to the ego, then you'll wake up. It's *your* dream, so only *you* can wake yourself up. The Holy Spirit is actually your own Higher Self. But remember, God did not send the Holy Spirit. He was always with you, because even though you could deny the truth, you could never lose it. Once again, if the dream was created by God and He could wake you up from it, it would be real. It would be a reality that was done *to* you by an outside force. But it's not. God is still perfect love, and your job is to wake up and return your awareness to where you really are.

The Holy Spirit is actually your own Higher Self.

GARY: Makes sense to me, but I still get questions like how could there ever *be* a tiny, mad idea within perfection. Doesn't that make a flaw in perfection?

ARTEN: A dream of imperfection is not a real imperfection. A dream is a dream, *not* a defective part of reality. God did not create the dream; you made up yourself inside of your own dream. Then because it seems real to you, you ask, "Why did God make this dream real?" or "Why did God let me dream?" The answer is that He didn't do either, and it isn't really happening, so there's no point in asking how it could have come about, because it hasn't! It just isn't. When you awaken from a delusion, it simply vanishes, and you go on with your life, in this case your real life. As J puts it, "From the forgiven world the Son of God is lifted easily into his home. And there he knows he has always rested there in peace."[4]

> **When you awaken from a delusion, it simply vanishes.**

GARY: That helps. Thanks. I also want to thank you for something else. I did a weeklong workshop last month, and this guy was there who was a Vietnam veteran. He said that for 35 years he hasn't been able to forgive some of the things he saw in Vietnam, until he read our book. Now he says he's been able to forgive those experiences. He's also sharing the book with other Vietnam vets. So thanks a lot, man, it really means a great deal to some people.

ARTEN: Our pleasure. And by the way, if it weren't for you being out there sharing the message, a lot of people wouldn't know about it, so you're playing an important part. You don't *have* to, but as long as you enjoy it, keep it up.

PURSAH: As the *Course* says: "You have found your brother, and you will light each other's way. And from this light will the Great Rays extend back into darkness and forward unto God, to shine away the past and so make room for His eternal Presence, in which everything is radiant in the light."[5]

GARY: That's beautiful, Pursah. You know, I really want to ask you. . . . Am I gonna see you guys again after tonight?

PURSAH: You know what? We want *you* to decide that, with the Holy Spirit, of course. But don't do it now. Wait a while. You have a lot of work ahead of you. A year from now, think about whether or not the kind of life you're living is really what you want. Do you want to keep being an author? Do you want to keep up all that traveling? See how you feel about all this a year from now. If you really want us to come back, then we'll know. If you don't, then we won't show up.

GARY: Yeah, but you already know what's gonna happen! I don't.

ARTEN: Just the same, it's better that it be your decision. You've given up your privacy and been the object of a lot of projection. Take a fresh look at things next year, and ask the Holy Spirit what you should do. Then you'll know for sure.

In the meantime, keep on forgiving! J is well pleased with you. As he says, keep giving him the little gifts he asks, "and then no dark cloud will remain between you and the remembrance of your Father, for you will remember His guiltless Son, who did not die because he is immortal."[6]

PURSAH: When your forgiveness lessons are complete, then not one trace of guilt will remain in your unconscious mind. At that point, you will break the cycle of birth and death, and never dream of going into a body again. That is the end of reincarnation. In your case, you know when that's going to happen, but it doesn't matter. You still have to forgive whatever comes up in front of your face. That's the work of salvation, and it's the most important thing that anyone can ever do for themselves.

> **Not one trace of guilt will remain in your unconscious mind. At that point, you will break the cycle of birth and death.**

Have fun with your ministry. And don't worry about fitting in with the other teachers or the mainstream spiritual types who think they're so progressive when they're actually very conservative. Remember J's shortest saying of all?

GARY: Yes! Be passersby.

PURSAH: All right, then. Be a passerby, Gary. People will ask you where you fit in to the spiritual community. Tell them the truth.

> **Be passersby.**

Given what you're teaching, you *don't* fit in. You're not saying the same thing as the others, so don't even try to fit in; just be yourself.

ARTEN: It's fun to know the truth and share it. Keep teaching people how to forgive, and thus will they live, "for what has life has immortality."[7]

PURSAH: We want you to join with us for a little while as spirit. You're going to love it. You'll return to your body after a few minutes, but it will take hours for the awe to fade. Come and be love with us.

Suddenly I felt weightless as my body disappeared. There was nothing to see, only an experience of total awareness. The ecstasy of what I was experiencing was beyond words. It was the experience of revelation, and I had been within it before, but this time the awareness of my body wasn't returning, and I didn't know if I could stand the joy. In the wholeness of this experience, everyone was there whom I had ever loved—not as bodies, not as separate things, but in my awareness of perfect oneness. Nothing and no one was left out. My parents; every friend, relative, and lover; every animal I had ever cared for, were all there, for we were one. I loved Arten and Pursah, but I wouldn't miss them after this experience, for I completely understood that we can never be apart. Our love extended through eternity; it was totally unlimited, and the joy of being reality truly exceeded every expectation. In the all-encompassing wonder of God, there was no need to think, only to be love, only to be what I really am.

After this timeless experience, I was once again sitting in my chair, seemingly in a body. Then I heard the Voice of the Holy Spirit, full and whole, and I knew it was my voice, the voice of Arten and Pursah, the voice of J and Buddha, the Voice of All in One. As I listened to the message, I closed my eyes, not feeling any need to see the room around me. I wasn't tired, I just wasn't a body, and the words of Spirit were my own:

Each day that you forgive, the effects of all the world's mistakes are melted as snow into a burning fire. No more guilt, no more karma, no more fear of what may be. For you have met yourself and declared your innocence, and all that follows is as natural as God.

No more birth, nor old death; these were just ideas. If you should come again to help a few more to find the way, so be it; but you are not a body, you are love, and it matters not where love appears to be. For being love, it cannot be wrong.

The day will come when pain is impossible, love is everywhere, and truth is all there is. You've longed for this forever, often silently and without knowing it. The knowledge of what you are is more certain now, and love has forgotten no one.

The day will come when the world will sing the song of spirit instead of weeping tones that hide the Voice for truth. The day will come when there is nothing left to forgive, and celebration with your sisters and your brothers is in order.

And then the day will come when there is no more need for days. And you will live as one forever in the holiness of your immortal reality.

✦✧✦

INDEX OF REFERENCES

In the following Index, the first numeral listed is the footnote number for the given chapter, followed by the standard designation of the *page* number of a quoted reference from *A Course in Miracles*. *Course* references are signified as follows:

T: Text
W: Workbook for Students
M: Manual for Teachers
CL: Clarification of Terms

All page numbers are for the second edition of the *Course,* printed 1992 and after.

Frontispiece / 1. Arten and Pursah! 1. T59. 2. T115. 3. M53. 4. CL77. 5. W1. 6. W8. 7. CL77. 8. T586. 9. T376. 10. T182. 11. M31. 12. W324. 13. T4.

2. Real Power. 1. T231. 2. W115. 3. T142. 4. W115. 5. W298. 6. W252. 7. T463. 8. T14. 9. T42. 10. Introduction. 11. M49. 12. T19. 13. T515. 14. T373. 15. T84. 16. W294. 17. T445. 18. Ibid. 19. T400. 20. T552. 21. T668. 22. T373. 23. Ibid. 24. T454. 25. T660.

3. Life of Gary. 1. T68. 2. T176. 3. T131. 4. T666. 5. W48. 6. Introduction. 7. Ibid. 8. Ibid. 9. T515. 10. T514. 11. T667. 12. W1. 13. M40. 14. Introduction. 15. T28. 16. W270. 17. T417. 18. T616.

4. Murders Without Corpses. 1. T495. 2. T13. 3. T617. 4. W243. 5. Ibid. 6. Ibid. 7. Ibid. 8. M60. 9. T25. 10. Ibid. 11. T562. 12. W243. 13. Ibid. 14. M7. 15. T42. 16. T496. 17. T3. 18. T496. 19. M32. 20. T638. 21. T587. 22. CL85. 23. T13. 24. W401. 25. T589.

5. The "Hero" of the Dream. 1. T581. 2. T95. 3. T84. 4. T347. 5. T414. 6. T415. 7. T346. 8. W443. 9. M62. 10. T7. 11. T585-586. 12. T588. 13. M32. 14. T634. 15. W318. 16. Ibid. 17. W319. 18. Ibid. 19. Ibid. 20. T418. 21. M66. 22. Ibid. 23. M67. 24. M66. 25. Ibid. 26. W244.

6. It's This Lifetime, Stupid. 1. T54. 2. T429. 3. T176. 4. T493. 5. Preface xii. 6. W26. 7. T352. 8. T114. 9. T115. 10. T414.

7. Pursah's Gospel of Thomas. 1. T54. 2. W324. 3. T68. 4. CL77. 5. T79.

8. Looking into the Future, Part II. 1. T54. 2. W252. 3. W2. 4. T445. 5. T496.

9. Who's Arten? 1. T76. 2. T238–239. 3. T239. 4. T246. 5. T42. 6. W281.

10. The Shabby Toys of Earth. 1. T635. 2. T623. 3. T622–623. 4. T116. 5. M52. 6. W363. 7. T29. 8. *The Gifts of God,* by Helen Schucman, page 119.

11. Your Immortal Reality. 1. W299. 2. T328. 3. T354. 4. T354. 5. T380. 6. T241. 7. W473.

ABOUT *A COURSE IN MIRACLES*

Aside from being sold in many stores, the authentic three-in-one volume of *A Course in Miracles,* comprising the Text, Workbook for Students, and Manual for Teachers, is available in hardcover, tradepaper, and paperback English editions, as well as 14 translations, from the Foundation for Inner Peace (FIP), the original publisher. Write or call:

Foundation for Inner Peace
P.O. Box 598
Mill Valley, CA 94942-0598
(415) 388-2060
www.acim.org

ABOUT THE AUTHOR

Gary Renard, the best-selling author of *The Disappearance of the Universe*, was born on the historic North Shore of Massachusetts. He became a successful professional guitar player, but during the harmonic convergence of 1987, he heard a Calling and began to take his life in a different direction. At the beginning of the 1990s, he moved to Maine, where he underwent a powerful spiritual awakening. As instructed, he slowly and carefully wrote *The Disappearance of the Universe* (now referred to by many readers as "D.U.") over a period of nine years.

In the fall of 2003, after much personal encouragement from other speakers and students, Gary began to present talks and workshops in public. His speaking career took off remarkably fast, and today he lectures internationally as well as serving on the faculty of Omega Institute, considered by many to be the world's premier spiritual teaching organization. Combining a disarming sense of humor with radical, cutting-edge metaphysical information and experiential exercises, Gary has been described as one of the most interesting and courageous spiritual speakers in the world. In 2004 and 2005, Gary taught *A Course in Miracles* in 35 states, Canada, Australia, England, and Costa Rica; and he was the keynote speaker at the International *A Course in Miracles* Conference in Salt Lake City in 2005. His touring continues at a similar pace.

Website: **www.GaryRenard.com**

We hope you enjoyed this Hay House book. If you'd like to receive a free catalog featuring additional Hay House books and products, or if you'd like information about the Hay Foundation, please contact:

Hay House, Inc.
P.O. Box 5100
Carlsbad, CA 92018-5100

(760) 431-7695 or **(800) 654-5126**
(760) 431-6948 (fax) or **(800) 650-5115 (fax)**
www.hayhouse.com® • **www.hayfoundation.org**

Published and distributed in Australia by: Hay House Australia Pty. Ltd.
18/36 Ralph St. • Alexandria NSW 2015 • *Phone:* 612-9669-4299
Fax: 612-9669-4144 • www.hayhouse.com.au

Published and distributed in the United Kingdom by: Hay House UK, Ltd.,
292B Kensal Rd., London W10 5BE • *Phone:* 44-20-8962-1230
Fax: 44-20-8962-1239 • www.hayhouse.co.uk

Published and distributed in the Republic of South Africa by:
Hay House SA (Pty), Ltd., P.O. Box 990, Witkoppen 2068
Phone/Fax: 27-11-706-6612 • orders@psdprom.co.za

Published in India by: Hay House Publications (India) Pvt. Ltd.
www.hayhouseindia.co.in

Distributed in India by: Media Star, 7 Vaswani Mansion, 120 Dinshaw
Vachha Rd., Churchgate, Mumbai 400020 • *Phone:* 91 (22) 22815538-39-40
Fax: 91 (22) 22839619 • booksdivision@mediastar.co.in

Distributed in Canada by: Raincoast • 9050 Shaughnessy St., Vancouver, B.C.
V6P 6E5 • *Phone:* (604) 323-7100 • *Fax:* (604) 323-2600

Tune in to **HayHouseRadio.com®** for the best in inspirational
talk radio featuring top Hay House authors! And, sign up via the Hay House
USA Website to receive the Hay House online newsletter and stay informed
about what's going on with your favorite authors. You'll receive bimonthly
announcements about: Discounts and Offers, Special Events, Product
Highlights, Free Excerpts, Giveaways, and more!
www.hayhouse.com®